Joseph C. McGinn holds a J.D. from Boston University Law School and is a practicing attorney in Massachusetts. Before he established his own law practice, Joseph McGinn was an associate with Hartwell, Driscoll, Reardon & Keenan in Worcester, Massachusetts. He is the author of *Lawyers: A Client's Manual*, Prentice-Hall, 1979.

PRENTICE-HALL INTERNATIONAL, INC., *London*
PRENTICE-HALL OF AUSTRALIA PTY. LIMITED, *Sydney*
PRENTICE-HALL OF CANADA, LTD., *Toronto*
PRENTICE-HALL OF INDIA PRIVATE LIMITED, *New Delhi*
PRENTICE-HALL OF JAPAN, INC., *Tokyo*
PRENTICE-HALL OF SOUTHEAST ASIA PTE. LTD., *Singapore*
WHITEHALL BOOKS LIMITED, *Wellington, New Zealand*

Personal Law

The Most Common Legal Problems and How to Solve Them

JOSEPH C. McGINN, Attorney at Law

A SPECTRUM BOOK

PRENTICE-HALL, INC., Englewood Cliffs, New Jersey 07632

Library of Congress Cataloging in Publication Data

McGINN, JOSEPH C.
Personal Law.

"A Spectrum Book."
Includes index.
1. Attorney and client—United States. 2. Law—United States. I. Title.
KF311.M34 349.73 81-22727
ISBN 0-13-658138-2 347.3 AACR2
ISBN 0-13-658120-X(pbk.)

To Bob, Greg, and Pete—my brothers

A SPECTRUM BOOK. Printed in the United States of America.

10 9 8 7 6 5 4 3 2 1

ISBN 0-13-658138-2

ISBN 0-13-658120-X {PBK.}

Editorial/production supervision and interior design by Carol Smith
Cover design by Jeannette Jacobs
Manufacturing buyer: Barbara A. Frick

This Spectrum Book is available to businesses and organizations
at a special discount when ordered in large quantities.
For information, contact Prentice-Hall, Inc., General Publishing Division,
Special Sales, Englewood Cliffs, N.J. 07632.

Contents

Preface

My first book, *Lawyers: A Client's Manual*, explains what readers need to know about lawyers generally. This book, a complement to the first, examines common matters on which people consult lawyers and explains what readers need to know in order to deal effectively with lawyers on each of these particular subjects. Using both books, readers will find candid information, practical advice, and revealing insights into lawyers and the law and how you, as an informed client, can protect your interests, keep tabs on your lawyer, save money on lawyers' fees, and ensure that your case is handled competently.

There are important legal matters that should only be handled by a lawyer to ensure that they are handled in the proper manner and that people receive competent, experienced, up-to-date, and personalized legal assistance, tailored to their particular case, circumstances, and concerns. Yet, my years in private practice have made me keenly aware that people are often uncomfortable about dealing with a lawyer, because they don't know what to expect, how to approach the attorney, or why they would need an attorney at all. They are, in a word, uninformed. To meliorate this situation, both of my books are designed to provide readers with the basic knowledge and practical insights needed to successfully handle lawyers. As stated in the Preface to *Lawyers: A Client's Manual*, "Clients who have the information and techniques they need to give them confidence in their dealings with lawyers will be better clients. Lawyers who know they have such people as clients will be better lawyers because of it."

ACKNOWLEDGMENTS Special thanks go to Ann E. St. Onge for reviewing the original text of this book. I would also like to thank Attorney Robert P. Lombardi and Attorney Bradford Mauro for reviewing major portions of the text and offering their comments and corrections. Muriel L. Campbell deserves many thanks for her typing, proofing, and related assistance. I would also like to express my appreciation for the support of Michael Hunter, President, General Publishing Division at Prentice-Hall, Inc., and for the diligent and highly competent work of Carol Smith, production editor, and William S. Green, copyeditor.

1
Dealing with Lawyers

This chapter provides useful information, money-saving tips, and practical advice on how to deal effectively and successfully with lawyers. After reading this chapter, the reader can turn to the following 15 chapters and learn about the particular legal matters that concern him or her. The information and insights presented in this chapter will equip you to select a good lawyer, work well with that lawyer, supervise and scrutinize the lawyer's work, and learn about the law so that you can make well-informed decisions.

SELECTING A LAWYER

Shop around for an experienced attorney. Ask about the attorney's qualifications, training, and experience. If appropriate, find out about government agencies or private groups that provide free legal information and assistance.

Lawyers vary. They differ in the types of cases they handle, amount of experience and expertise in given areas of law, and in competence, conscientiousness, and talent. And price.

Because lawyers differ so much in background, ability, and price, you should shop around for an attorney who has the proper qualifications to handle your case. Contact three, four, or more lawyers. Ask each how many cases he or she has handled in the area of law with which you are concerned. How many cases like yours has he or she handled and how recently?

The more complicated or contested your case, the more careful you should be to hire a lawyer with proven experience and qualifications. For example, if you seek a lawyer to represent you on a divorce that is uncontested and uncomplicated, it may be appropriate to hire a younger lawyer who has had some but not a great deal of experience in divorce work and who charges a lower fee than older lawyers who specialize in complicated divorce cases. If your divorce is uncontested and uncomplicated, an attorney with a minimum of experience should be able to handle it properly. By contrast, if your divorce is bitterly contested and will radically affect your property, income, taxes, and other important and complex matters, it would be unwise to hire an attorney who has little or no experience in handling difficult divorces of that nature.

The same is true of other cases. If you received minor injuries in a motor vehicle accident and the other party is clearly at fault, it should be safe to hire an attorney who handles motor vehicle cases only occasionally and who charges less than a motor vehicle personal injury specialist. However, if you received major injuries, the other party denies any fault or liability, and it looks like you will have a tough legal battle against the other party and his or her insurance company, hire an attorney who handles cases of that nature on a regular basis and has proven himself or herself to be competent and successful on such complicated and difficult cases.

If your case will go to trial or a hearing before an administrative agency, be sure to ask each attorney you contact how much experience he or she has at such trials or administrative hearings. For instance, if you want to contest the validity of your uncle's will because some of your relatives deviously tricked your uncle into signing a will that left them everything and you nothing, that type of case is likely to result in a protracted and difficult trial. Hire an attorney who has noted trial experience, preferably an attorney who has tried cases like that before. Similarly, if your Workers' Compensation case will be heard by an administrative hearing officer or a panel of hearing officers, ask each attorney you contact how many times he or she has appeared before a Workers' Compensation tribunal on cases like yours.

All attorneys are licensed to do trial work and to appear before administrative tribunals. That does not, however, mean that all attorneys are equally proficient at trial work and administrative hearings. Many trials and administrative cases have been lost because the lawyer was inexperienced or incompetent, not because the client had a bad case. Make sure the lawyer you hire has proven ability and credentials.

To get the names of lawyers to contact, ask members of your family, friends, co-workers, and other associates or acquaintances about lawyers they have hired and whose work they respect. Even better, if you know someone who has or has had a case similar to yours, ask that person about their lawyer's ability, professionalism, and conscientiousness. In many communities the local bar association operates a lawyer referral service. If you call the local bar association (listed in the Yellow Pages) and explain your case, they may provide the names, addresses, and telephone numbers of lawyers who handle that type of case. Also check newspapers and other media for lawyers who advertise.

Other methods of obtaining the names of lawyers to contact include contacting the court or administrative agency that will hear your case. Go to the court or administrative agency when they are conducting trials or hearings and talk with lawyers there. For example, if you want a lawyer for a divorce, go to the local divorce court. Ask people there about their lawyers. That can be an excellent way to get the names of lawyers to consider—and the names of other lawyers to avoid. Similarly, if you have a Workers' Compensation case that will be heard by a hearing officer or panel or if you have an unlawful discrimination case that will be heard by a state or federal administrative agency, contact the appropriate administrative agency, find out where and when they hold hearings, then go to those hearings and scrutinize the lawyers there. One or more of those lawyers may impress you as someone to consider hiring. Sometimes the clerk of court will provide the names of lawyers whose work he or she respects. For instance, if you have a landlord-tenant dispute that will be heard in the local housing court or local trial court, the clerk of that court may help you find a good lawyer. Similarly, if your case will be heard in probate court or divorce court, the clerk of the court might recommend several experienced, reputable lawyers.

Before hiring a private attorney who will charge a fee, find out if there are government agencies or private groups and organizations that provide free legal information and assistance. For example, if you have a consumer rights case, there may be a state or federal consumer affairs agency that will provide information and assistance at no charge. If you have an unlawful discrimination case, there may be a state or federal antidiscrimination agency or a private antidiscrimination group (such as the American Civil Liberties Union, the NAACP, or the National Organization for Women) that will assist you in many ways and, in some cases, handle your case for free. Similarly, there are tenants' associations that provide legal and other assistance to tenants whose rights have been violated.

By contacting government agencies and private groups and organizations, you may get important information and some assistance at no charge. You may also get names of reputable lawyers to contact if you have to hire an attorney.

Also shop around and negotiate for a reasonable price. Ask about the attorney's fee and available fee payment arrangements.

Because lawyers differ in ability, experience, background, and conscientiousness—and fee aggressiveness—they also differ in price. Naturally, a lawyer who rents an expensive office must pass on that higher overhead to clients in the form of higher fees. Some lawyers charge more than others because they have more expertise or because they have fewer clients to charge or because they feel higher fees reflect their higher standing in the legal community. Higher profits and greed also enter into the picture. Other lawyers charge less because they have lower overhead, or have less experience, or are more efficient or less greedy.

By contacting three, four, or more lawyers, you will probably find considerable differences in the fees different lawyers would charge to handle your case. Do not blindly hire the lawyer who charges the lowest fee. He or she may be inexperienced or even incompetent. Ask each lawyer, as noted above, about his or her qualifications, training, and experience. Then hire the best combination of lawyer and price.

When the subject of the fee comes up, ask the lawyer if there is any procedure by which you can have another party pay or reimburse you for part or all of your attorney's fee. There are many cases in which this can be done. For example, in divorce, legal separation, and annulment cases, the judge may have authority to order your spouse to pay for or reimburse you for part or all of your attorney's fee if you have limited financial means. If you are the executor or administrator of a deceased person's estate, the lawyer's fee should come out of the assets in that estate—not out of your pocket. If you serve as someone's guardian or conservator, the attorney's fee should be paid out of that person's assets, not your own. In some Workers' Compensation cases your employer or your employer's insurance company can be ordered to reimburse you for part or all of your attorney's fee. On debt collection cases the judge may have authority to order the debtor to pay part or all of your attorney's fee as well as other costs related to bringing the debtor to court. Likewise, many consumer protection laws and antidiscrimination laws authorize the judge or administrative hearing officer to order the party who violated your rights to reimburse you for part or all of your attorney's fee if you win your case.

To effectively assert and protect your rights and interests when discussing legal fees with an attorney, you should understand the following important points about the different types of lawyers' fees.

Flat Fee A flat fee is a specific amount of money for which the attorney expressly or implicitly agrees to perform the necessary and customary work required to properly handle your case. If there will be a trial or administrative hearing, the flat fee normally covers the attorney's work through that trial or hearing. An appeal, however, or a rehearing is a separate matter not covered by the initial flat fee. Also, a flat fee is based on the attorney's understanding, at the outset, of what your case will require on his or her part. If complications develop which require additional work, that will require an additional fee. Ask the attorney to explain in detail what services the flat fee covers and what complications or developments would require an additional fee.

To illustrate some important points about flat fees by way of examples, suppose you go to a lawyer for a divorce that you believe will not be contested by your spouse. The lawyer quotes a flat fee. A month later, your spouse informs you that he or she is no longer agreeable to certain informal understandings you had made earlier and wants to contest such matters as child custody, alimony, and the division of property. When you inform your lawyer that the divorce is no longer an uncontested one, the lawyer will inform you that the additional work required on his or her part to handle the divorce under these new circumstances will warrant a substantial additional fee.

Suppose you were injured at work but your employer's Workers' Compensation insurance company argues that you are now able to go back to work. They cut off your Workers' Compensation benefits. Your doctor says you are not ready to return to work. You hire a lawyer to have your case heard before a Workers' Compensation hearing officer. The lawyer sets a flat fee to prepare for and represent you at that hearing. The hearing officer agrees with the insurance company and rules against you. Your only recourse now is to appeal that decision to a higher administrative tribunal or a court. That, however, is not covered by the initial flat fee. A separate fee must be worked out if the attorney is to handle an appeal.

Hourly Fee An hourly fee is a set rate the attorney charges for each hour he or she puts into your case. You may be shocked by the hourly rates attorneys charge. In rural and smaller communities lawyers may charge $40, $50, even $75 an hour. In large metropolitan areas, private attorneys charge $50, $75, even $85 or $90 per hour. The most expensive attorneys at prestigious urban law firms charge $100 an hour, $150 an hour, and more!

Before agreeing to an hourly fee, have the lawyer estimate how many hours your case may take. That is the only way you can calculate how much the total fee may be.

Although it may seem logical, do not simply hire the attorney who charges the lowest hourly rate. At least do not do so until you have inquired about that lawyer's experience and ability. An attorney who quotes a low hourly rate may do so because his or her office overhead and other expenses are lower than his or her colleagues and he or she can pass some of the savings on to you while still providing competent services. On the other hand, some attorneys, particularly younger attorneys, charge low hourly rates because they are not as experienced as many of their colleagues. On cases that do not require considerable experience, it may be safe to hire an attorney who charges a low hourly rate. On cases that involve difficult or complicated legal matters, particularly trial work, however, it may be a serious mistake to blindly hire the attorney who quotes the lowest hourly rate. If the lawyer with the low hourly rate is inexperienced, he or she may have to put a considerable number of hours into your case and his or her total fee could be substantial. By contrast, another attorney who charges a higher hourly rate but who is more experienced may not have to put as many hours into your case and his or her total fee might be lower than that of the less experienced attorney with the deceptively low rate. For example, suppose you have been unlawfully discriminated against and hire an attorney who charges $40 an hour but who is inexperienced in handling discrimination cases. He puts 40 hours into your case. That adds up to $1,600. Suppose, on the other hand, you hired an attorney who specializes in discrimination cases but who charges $60 an hour. That attorney could have handled your case in only 20 hours. That adds up to $1,200. By hiring the second attorney, you could save $400 on the total fee even though the second attorney charges more per hour than the first. Also, the second attorney would have brought more experience and ability to your case.

If you agree to an hourly fee, make sure the lawyer notifies you periodically, perhaps once each month, of how many hours he or she has put into your case and how much the fee is amounting to.

Make sure you understand what rate the attorney will charge for the time he or she puts into your case and what rates you will be charged for work done by other persons on your attorney's staff. It is not uncommon, although it is unethical and illegal, for an attorney to charge a client the attorney's hourly rate of, say, $60 per hour for work done by a junior associate whom the lawyer pays $10 an hour or by a law student or paralegal whom the attorney pays $6 per hour. To avoid that chicanery, make sure the lawyer explains who will do what work on your case and sets appropriate hourly rates for each of those persons.

If a lawyer quotes an hourly rate of $50 or $75 an hour, you should realize that typically, 50 percent or more of that money goes to pay the attorney's overhead and professional expenses. Fifty percent or less is actual profit before tax (personal income) to the lawyer.

Percentage Fee A percentage fee is based on some value involved in the case. For example, on real estate transfers (buying or selling your house), attorneys may charge a fee of 1 percent (or some other percentage) of the sales price of the house. To draft a trust document, the attorney may charge a fee based on a given percentage of the value of the assets in the trust. Because percentage fees are unique to the particular legal matter, little can be said generally. Percentage fees are sometimes charged when buying or selling a house (see Chapter 2), drafting a Will (see Chapter 6), drafting a trust (see Chapter 7), or handling the estate of a deceased person (see Chapter 8).

Contingent Percentage Fee This fee is based on a percentage of an amount of money involved in the case but the attorney charges a fee only if he or she is successful in recovering money. For example, many attorneys take motor vehicle personal injury cases on a contingent fee basis. They will take, as their fee, one-third (or some other percentage) of the money recovered but only if money is recovered. If no money is obtained, the attorney will not charge for his or her services. Recovering money is the "contingency" which determines whether or not the attorney collects a fee. Contingent percentage fees are also unique to the particular type of case. They are charged by lawyers on inheritance cases (see Chapter 8), employment-related injury, illness, or disability cases (see Chapter 13), and collecting money from a debtor (see Chapter 12).

As discussed earlier, by contacting three, four, or more lawyers, you can shop around for a qualified lawyer who charges a relatively low fee and save considerable money. You can also save money by negotiating with the lawyer over the fee. Far too many clients simply acquiesce when a lawyer quotes a fee. Do not agree to pay a fee you feel is too high or is inappropriate for some reason. Tell the lawyer you believe the fee is too high and why you think so. Tell the lawyer you simply won't agree to that fee and start negotiating by quoting what you feel is a more reasonable fee. The following points will make you a more effective and successful negotiator.

- Most lawyers would rather have your case for a fee that is lower than they would like than have no case and no fee.

Lawyers make their living by selling legal services. Naturally, this creates a conflict between the lawyer's desire to make as much money as possible and your desire to save as much money as possible. One of the most effective negotiating points you can bring to bear on your behalf is to point out to the lawyer that it is *your* case and *your* money you and the lawyer are negotiating over. It's what *you* think is a reasonable fee that matters most to you. If the lawyer argues that you don't understand the overhead he or she must pay, the cost of law school, and other professional expenses, you should reply that the lawyer doesn't understand your overhead, your background, or your personal and family expenses.

If you were a lawyer, would you let a potential client walk out the door because you insist on charging $500 but the client will not agree to pay more than $350? If you were a lawyer, would you let a client who is willing to pay up to $2,000 walk out the door because you want no less than $2,500 for the case?

- If your case is routine, uncomplicated, or uncontested, emphasize those points.

If your case does not present any substantial difficulties—if it is uncomplicated and uncontested—a "routine" matter, point that out. For example, if you hire a lawyer on an uncontested divorce or an uncontested adoption, drafting the necessary papers is a simple matter of putting information in the right places on the right forms. The court hearing on an uncontested divorce or uncontested adoption will be a perfunctory one that will only take a few minutes. Surely, easy work for the lawyer of that nature does not warrant the high fee a lawyer would charge when handling a difficult, complex, or contested case. On routine cases, if the attorney tries to justify what you feel is a high fee by saying, "But this case will require filling out several forms and appearing in court," you should respond, "Yes, but given the uncomplicated nature of my case, it will be easy for you to fill out those forms and the court appearance will be only a brief, perfunctory matter." On wills, trusts and real estate transfers (buying or selling a house) emphasize that your case involves no court appearance at all.

After talking with you for 15 or 30 minutes, the lawyer will usually be able to gauge how difficult or easy your case will be. If the lawyer quotes a fee that seems unreasonably high, ask him or her to explain why your case should cost so much when it is a routine matter. Keep reiterating that the work the lawyer must do is easy. It may take time for the lawyer to do that work, perhaps a few or several hours, but simple, routine work does not deserve a high fee.

- Ask the lawyer how much—or how little—time your case will take.

If you pay an hourly fee, you will know how many hours your attorney put into your case (unless the attorney falsifies the number of hours charged). If you pay a flat fee, a percentage fee, or a contingent percentage fee, the attorney may never inform you how much—or how little—time he or she put into your case. In many cases, clients would be shocked by the fee charged when compared to the time put in by the lawyer. For example, it is not uncommon for attorneys to charge a flat fee of $500 to $750 for a "routine" uncontested, uncomplicated divorce even though the attorney knows the case will not take more than 3 or 4 hours (in client consultations, document preparation, waiting for the case to be called at court and presenting the case in a 5- or 10-minute ceremony at court). On an hour-for-hour basis, these attorneys are making $125 to $250 per hour or more! Likewise, many attorneys charge flat fees of several hundred dollars for routine house sales, adoptions, guardianships, tenant evictions, and other standard cases that do not require more than 3, 4, or 5 hours of the attorney's time. It is commonplace for attorneys to "earn" fees of $100, $200, and $300 an hour and more in this deceptive manner. Some attorneys have their secretary or a law student or paralegal do most of the work but charge the attorney's exorbitant fee nonetheless.

Worse abuses are perpetrated by lawyers by means of percentage fees. If your motor vehicle personal injury case is settled out of court for $5,000 and the attorney charges a one-third contingent percentage fee, the attorney will collect a fee of $1,666.66. Suppose the attorney put 10 hours into your case (consulting with you and the witnesses, examining the scene of the accident, preparing pleadings, etc.). The attorney is, in reality, making $166.66 per hour for your case. Some windfall profits reaped by means of percentage fees are almost unbelievably exorbitant. An attorney settled a motor vehicle personal injury case out of court (without even filing a lawsuit in court) for $21,000. That attorney put no more than 10 hours into the case. The attorney took a one-third contingent fee of $7,000.

That figures out to $700 per hour! Of course, the attorney never informed the client how few hours he put into that case.

An effective tactic for successfully negotiating a lower fee is to insist that the lawyer explain how many hours he or she expects to put into your case. If you hire a lawyer to handle the legal aspects of a routine, uncontested adoption and that lawyer quotes a flat fee of $600, insist that the lawyer explain, in detail, how much time your case will take. If the lawyer has any honesty at all, he or she would have to acknowledge that most uncontested, routine adoptions take no more than 5 hours. If you divide 5 hours into the $600 flat fee, you will realize that the attorney is hiding a $120 per hour fee behind the facade of a $600 flat fee. Point that out and insist on less money for only 5 hours of "routine" work.

Most attorneys will be very reluctant to tell you how much time they anticipate putting into your case if your case is routine and they know it can be handled in just a few hours. Any hesitancy on your lawyer's part to tell you how many hours your case will take—if your case is routine—is a telltale indication that the lawyer is probably hiding an exorbitant hourly rate behind a deceptive flat fee or percentage fee.

- Don't pay the same fee whether or not your case goes to trial or is settled out of court.

Most attorneys on motor vehicle personal injury cases, unlawful discrimination cases, debt collection cases, and inheritance and other cases will try to get you to agree to pay one fee—regardless of whether the case goes to trial or is settled out of court. It is simple common sense that an attorney should not make the same amount of money for a case that is settled out of court as he or she should make for a case that requires the difficult and demanding additional work involved in a trial. To illustrate, suppose your attorney quotes a one-third contingent percentage fee to handle your motor vehicle personal injury case. Nothing more is said. Suppose further that your case goes to trial and a $10,000 judgment in your favor is awarded. The attorney spent 10 hours preparing for trial. The attorney charges a fee of $3,333.33. In addition to the 10 hours spent preparing for trial and the 10 hours spent on trial, the attorney put 10 hours into investigating the scene of the accident, reviewing police and other reports of the accident, interviewing witnesses, and so on. The attorney put a total of 30 hours into your case. Dividing those 30 hours into the $3,333.33 fee, the attorney is receiving $111.11 per hour. Suppose, on the other hand, the attorney settled your case out of court for $10,000. The attorney didn't have to put 10 hours into preparing your case for trial not an additional 10 hours on trial. Nonetheless, the attorney receives the same $3,333.33 fee, but for only 10 hours of work—that means $333.33 per hour!

A simple way to avoid the exorbitant fees attorneys garner by charging one fee regardless of whether the case goes to trial or is settled out of court is to insist that the lawyer charge a substantially lower fee if the case is settled out of court. Less work deserves less pay.

- If you cannot afford the fee, say so and ask for a lower fee.

Most attorneys will take your ability to pay into consideration when setting the fee. If you cannot afford the fee quoted by the lawyer, say so and explain your financial limitations or difficulties. Let the attorney know you cannot legitimately pay the fee quoted. The attorney may offer to extend the period of time in which the fee can be paid. Or he or she may tell you to take out a loan, if necessary, to pay the fee. Do not do so if you honestly cannot pay the fee quoted without getting into serious financial difficulty.

- Let the attorney know you will go to other lawyers rather than pay a fee you feel is unreasonable.

Lawyers tremble at the thought of clients who are smart enough to shop around. They tremble because they know shopping around is the best tactic a client can use to find a good lawyer at a decent price and avoid incompetent lawyers and exorbitant prices. There is considerable pressure among lawyers to charge the same or similar prices. They do so, of course, to minimize price competition and collusively maintain high fees. Nonetheless, you may be surprised by the results of contacting a second lawyer and a third before deciding which one to hire and at what price. Remember, all you need is to find one good lawyer who will handle your case for a fee you feel is reasonable. Although you need a lawyer, you needn't hire the first attorney you contact. Do some comparison shopping, as you would when purchasing a car or an insurance policy.

After a fee is agreed upon, determine how and when the fee is to be paid. If you agree to a contingent percentage fee, no fee will be due the lawyer until an amount of money is recovered from the other party.

If you agree to an hourly fee, the lawyer should be willing to accept a monthly or other periodic billing plan. If the bill for one or more months is too much for you to pay, ask the lawyer to stretch out the payments over a longer period of time. After all, if businesses are willing to extend you credit, your lawyer should. In fact, more and more lawyers accept payment by credit card.

You may encounter difficulties with some lawyers when they charge a flat fee or a percentage fee that is not contingent. Some lawyers will insist that the entire fee be paid "up front" (at the outset) or that half or more of the fee be paid up front and the rest within a very short period of time. Do not agree to those harsh terms. Insist on an installment payment schedule you can afford. For example, suppose a lawyer quotes a fee of $500 to handle your uncontested divorce, then adds, "I must have that fee, in full, within one week or I cannot do business with you." Don't succumb to that cheap pressure tactic. Tell the lawyer, "That's not the way I do business. I'll pay you $100 per month [or some other affordable monthly amount]." As another illustration, suppose you hire an attorney to purchase a $55,000 house. The attorney quotes a 1 percent fee—$550. He or she declares, "I want half that amount within 2 days and the other half no later than 10 days before the sale goes through." Don't agree to those terms. Your position should be, "I'll send in $100 within 2 days, another $200 before the sale goes through, and the remaining $250 after the sale goes through."

Insist on an installment payment schedule. The advantages are numerous and important. First, an installment payment schedule is more affordable. You won't have to withdraw large sums out of your savings or take out expensive short-term loans. Second, an installment payment schedule gives the lawyer a clear incentive to work diligently on your case. If the lawyer knows he or she has a large portion of the fee due *after* the house sale goes through, he or she has an incentive to make sure the sale goes through smoothly and properly. Third, an installment payment schedule gives you leverage over the attorney you can use if the attorney neglects your case, doesn't follow your instructions or otherwise mishandles your case or mistreats you. For example, suppose you did agree to pay the fee, in full, at the outset for your divorce case. Weeks go by. Months go by. Your attorney is neglecting your case. What control do you have over him or her? If you were paying on an installment schedule, you could withhold further installments until he or she earns them to your satisfaction. As another example, suppose you pay an attorney $1,500 up front to represent you in suing a business that sold you a defective product. Many months later, your case receives a trial date. The day before trial, your attorney calls and tells you he is going to postpone your case for several more months because he has other matters occupying his time. What can you do? If you had paid the attorney only $500 at the outset and were to pay the remaining

$1,000 the day you go to court, you would still have that $1,000 balance and you could either use it as leverage to get your attorney to handle your case tomorrow—and postpone those other matters—or agree to the postponement (if there is a legitimate reason for it) but remind the lawyer that he or she won't get any of the $1,000 balance until your case gets another trial date and the lawyer appears in court.

Realistically, you may fail to get an attorney to accept most or many of the money-saving points discussed in this section. Nonetheless, even one or two of these techniques will save you considerable money. In addition, an installment payment schedule will protect your rights and interests. Just as importantly, if you try to use the techniques discussed in this section, the attorney will realize you are a client who knows something about how lawyers operate and how to counter their unfair fee practices.

Ask about other fees, costs, and expenses for which you will be responsible.

Your case may involve a number of expenses in addition to the lawyer's fee. Generally, you will be responsible for those cost items, although in some situations you may be able to have the other party reimburse you for some or all of your expenses if you win your case. This can occur in divorce, legal separation, annulment, debt collection, consumer rights, and unlawful discrimination cases. Ask your lawyer to pursue such reimbursement procedures where they are available.

If you file a lawsuit, there will be court filing fees and fees due a sheriff or constable for serving official papers on the other party or parties to the lawsuit. If you hire a stenographer to record testimony under oath, you will be responsible for the stenographer's fee. Similarly, if consultants, experts, or investigators are hired, you must pay their fees. In addition, there may be fees for certified copies of official records, for medical records or reports, or for subpoenaing documents. Your lawyer will bill you for printing, photocopying, telephone calls, postage, photographs, and travel expenses if they amount to more than a few dollars.

At the outset of your case, ask your lawyer for an estimate of the expenses that will be incurred, how much they may amount to, and when and how they must be paid. Although in many routine cases these cost items do not amount to more than $25 to $100, in complicated cases, particularly lawsuits in which experts and private investigators are hired, these expenses could add up to hundreds, even thousands of dollars.

Have the services to be rendered by the attorney, the fee, and the fee payment arrangement put in writing. Insist on written, detailed bills.

Insist that the lawyer draft a written contract or agreement, in language you understand, that explains in detail what services the lawyer will provide, the amount of the fee, and how the fee is to be paid. Harmful disagreements and hostilities can develop between lawyer and client because of misunderstandings by the lawyer, the client, or both as to what was agreed to with respect to the lawyer's services, the fee, and the manner of payment. Disagreements and hostilities of that nature can be easily avoided if the lawyer takes 10 minutes to write out the terms agreed upon. Keep in mind, when you hire an attorney you are entering into a contract. The attorney agrees to provide specific services and you agree to pay a given price. As any attorney would agree, it is a serious mistake not to put the basic terms of a contract in writing. Whatever excuse the lawyer advances for not putting the services, fee, and payment schedule in writing, insist on it.

You should be aware that if a dispute develops over what the lawyer was supposed to do on your case or the amount of the fee, the lawyer may be successful at having that dispute heard by the local or state bar association—a panel of lawyers—or by a judge—another lawyer. If you don't have a written contract signed by the lawyer, whose side do you expect those other lawyers to take if it comes down to your word against the lawyer's?

Your lawyer should be more than willing to put the services, fee, and fee payment arrangement in writing. If for any reason the lawyer fails to do so, write out your own understanding of those terms and mail a copy to the lawyer. Make sure the contract your lawyer drafts or the letter you draft accurately reflects the agreement you and your lawyer came to.

Do not pay the lawyer's fee, in part or in full, unless the lawyer drafts a written bill. Ask for a copy for your records. The bill should explain, in detail, what services were provided, the fee, how the fee was calculated, who performed the various services, what payment is due, and what balance, if any, remains. Many bitter disputes—and lawsuits—have developed between lawyers and clients because the fee was paid in cash with no written bill or receipt to prove payment—or nonpayment. Insist on a detailed, written bill. Make a copy. When you pay the bill, have someone at the lawyer's office mark "Paid" on your copy or provide you a receipt. Pay the bill with a check, bank draft, money order, or credit card. Do not pay with cash if possible; if you do, insist on a receipt signed by the lawyer or an authorized member of his or her staff. If someone other than the lawyer works on your case—for example, if the lawyer uses a junior associate, law student, or paralegal—make sure that is pointed out on the bill and that the fee charged for work done by the junior associate, law student, or paralegal is disclosed.

WORKING WITH THE LAWYER

Ask what you can do.

There may be many important tasks you can perform on your case. By doing these things yourself, you can make sure they are done promptly and you won't have to pay your attorney to do them for you. There may be information, documents, records, or evidence you can obtain. For instance, you can gather most of the information the attorney needs on your real estate sale. You may be able to obtain the original or a copy of the will about which you have questions and bring it with you to the attorney's office. You can get certified copies of the birth certificate or death certificate or other documents pertaining to an adoption, a probate case, or other matters. You can take the attorney to the scene of the motor vehicle accident or the scene of your workplace injury and explain what happened. Perhaps you can contact other people—especially persons who may prove to be valuable witnesses—and find out whether they would be willing to testify on your behalf and what they would say. It is often very helpful if you take photographs to help your attorney—and the judge and jury—understand your case. For example, photographs of your injuries from a motor vehicle accident or workplace accident will be very effective in conveying to the judge and jury the nature and extent of those injuries and the course of your recovery. If you have a consumer complaint about repair work, decorative or construction work, or other work or products that have visible manifestations, photographs can be the key to winning your case.

Write out a chronology of the events involved in your case or legal matter and bring that chronology with you to the attorney's office. If you write a chronology of your marital problems, that will make it easier for the attorney to understand your situation and concerns. Similarly, a chronology of your dealings with a debtor who won't pay or a tenant you want to evict will make it easier for the lawyer to understand what has happened. Also, writing out these matters will reduce the chances that you will inadvertently overlook important points when you tell the lawyer about your situation.

In some circumstances it may be worthwhile for you to talk to the other party or person involved in the case or legal matter in an attempt to settle the dispute, come to some agreement, or at least listen to each other's views and positions. For example, in a divorce, the spouses should make every effort to reconcile their differences. If divorce is decided upon, the spouses should try to work out agreements wherever possible. Similarly, if you are buying a house, there may be many details you can work out by talking things over with the sellers. In other situations, however, it may be advisable that you avoid dealing with the other party or person. Let your lawyer represent you instead. For instance, if someone owes you money and considerable ill will has developed between you and that debtor, let the lawyer deal with the debtor. Similarly, if your employer has discriminated against you and it is difficult for you to talk about the matter with your employer, let your lawyer do the talking. You should deal directly with the other party or person if something constructive can come of those talks. But if the situation is fraught with tension, ill will, or potential belligerence, let your lawyer deal with that person as your legal representative.

Keep in touch regularly.

Do not let weeks or months go by without communicating with your lawyer and reviewing the status of your case. When you become aware of new information or developments that affect your case or how you want your lawyer to handle it, notify your lawyer promptly. Conversely, your lawyer may have become aware of new information and developments since your last consultation and he or she will need to know how you view the new situation.

Make sure your lawyer can reach you, preferably by phone, when you are at home or at work, while you are away or on vacation, and at other times.

If your lawyer doesn't respond to your phone calls or letters, notify him or her that you will not tolerate that. If your communications are ignored or your case neglected in a serious manner, file a complaint with the local bar association, the state bar association, and your state's lawyer review board (if your state has one). You have the right to fire your lawyer if he or she ignores your communications or neglects your case. You can then take your case to a more conscientious attorney.

Get timetables and investigate delays.

Have your lawyer break your case down into specific steps or stages and estimate when each step will be taken and when each stage should be completed. Keep those timetables in mind. If important dates are missed or serious delays occur, contact the lawyer and find out why. Determine what, if anything, can be done. If your lawyer is to blame for neglecting your case, causing undue delays or procrastinating excessively, you have the right to dismiss him or her and bring your case to a more diligent lawyer.

Review alternative courses of action.

Although you may be determined to pursue a given course of action, explain to the lawyer what has happened and who is involved, then ask what alternatives are available. There may be a number of options you can choose. Discuss with your lawyer the advantages and disadvantages of each and ask for his or her advice and recommendations. You will then be in a better position to decide which course or courses to take. In some situations, you may be able to pursue two or more courses of action at the same time and thereby increase your chances of accomplishing your objectives.

If circumstances change or new developments occur, review your case with your lawyer and take appropriate steps to keep your case on the track most likely to achieve your goals.

Keep a diary and file. Review all documents and correspondence prepared or received by your attorney.

To effectively keep tabs on your lawyer and your case and to preserve your own account of your case, maintain a diary that records the details of your consultations with your lawyer, what he or she is to do or has done and what you are to do or have done, timetables, and other important matters.

Have your lawyer provide copies of all documents and correspondence he or she prepares or receives on your case. Keep these copies and all other material related to your case in a file folder. If you have any questions about any documents or correspondence, have your lawyer answer those questions. It is very important to review with your lawyer papers such as deeds, purchase and sale agreements, divorce agreements, lawsuit documents, wills, trusts, leases, and other important documents. Go over those documents word by word with your lawyer and make sure you understand what they mean, why they are necessary, what they accomplish, and how they affect your rights and interests.

Before testifying, review your case and testimony with your lawyer.

Before appearing in court or before an administrative tribunal or elsewhere to give testimony, review your case with your lawyer. Make sure you understand the nature and purpose of the proceeding and what you can reasonably expect to accomplish. Review the questions you will be asked and the answers you should be prepared to give. This will ensure that you—and your lawyer—are prepared for the trial, hearing, or meeting.

Ask your lawyer about confidentiality.

There are two confidentiality obligations an attorney must observe with regard to a client's case. First, there is an attorney-client privilege. That is a rule of evidence which means your lawyer cannot be compelled to take the witness stand or otherwise testify to or divulge secret or private information which you imparted to your lawyer in confidence. For example, if you tell your lawyer in private about actions on your part which could be used against you in your case, the other party cannot compel your lawyer to take the witness stand or otherwise disclose that confidential information.

Your lawyer also has a professional ethical obligation to handle secret, private, or personal information which you disclose to him or her in a discreet and confidential manner. For example, it is improper for your lawyer to gossip with outsiders about you, your case, or your conduct. Also, a lawyer cannot use confidential information received from a client to take advantage of the client. For example, if you disclose to your attorney information about property or assets that can be purchased at bargain prices, the attorney cannot use that information to purchase the property or assets and thereby deprive you of the bargain.

Your lawyer's employees, assistants, and agents are also bound by the lawyer's professional ethical obligation of confidentiality. However, they may not be within the protection of the attorney-client privilege rule of law. To be safe, disclose secret, private, or personal information directly to your lawyer and out of the presence of all other people—unless your lawyer assures you that the presence of another person or persons will not impair the attorney-client privilege.

Given these privacy protections, you should feel free to disclose to your attorney any and all sensitive information that has a bearing on your case. In cases involving personal and family matters, such as divorce, wills, trusts, adoptions, guardianships, and probating an estate, do not hesitate to provide your attorney with a complete picture of the matters that concern you even if that means disclosing personally embarrassing or even incriminating matters. In adoption cases, be sure to ask your lawyer about protecting the confidentiality of the identity of the adopted child's natural parents. The laws in this area have changed considerably in many states in recent years. If you wish to change public and other records pertaining to the identities of the child's natural parents and the child's birth name, ask your lawyer to investigate the procedures for doing so.

LEARN ABOUT THE LAW

You will be better equipped to make informed decisions and intelligently scrutinize the work done by your lawyer or legal advisor if you learn about the laws and procedures that govern your case.

Your primary source of knowledge should be your lawyer. Ask as many questions as necessary to understand the legal aspects of your case, what the law allows or requires, what the law prohibits, and what procedures must be followed. If you encounter a lawyer who is reluctant to answer questions or who discourages you from asking questions, dismiss that lawyer. Insist on being fully informed and advised about the law. If you have serious doubts about something the lawyer tells you or advises, get a second opinion from another lawyer.

Don't expect your lawyer to know everything. The law is often complex and always changing. If your lawyer must do some research or contact other people before answering a question, that is usually an indication that the lawyer is conscientious and wants to be sure he or she provides accurate answers.

You may find useful books or other helpful written material about your type of case at the local law library (many county courthouses have law libraries open to the public), at a law school library (only some are open to the public), or at a public library or bookstore. There may be government agencies or private groups or organizations that provide legal information about your type of case. For example, consumer rights agencies and groups, antidiscrimination agencies and groups, and tenants' associations provide free legal information. If you obtain information from printed material, government officials or employees, or private persons or groups, review that information with your lawyer to make sure it is accurate and appropriate for your case.

You may encounter books or pamphlets of the "do-it-yourself" or "be-your-own-lawyer" variety. These materials may appear to be very useful. They may tempt you with the promise that you can save hundreds, even thousands of dollars on attorneys' fees by handling your case yourself. In reality, however, it is extremely dangerous to try to handle an important legal matter with only the aid of a do-it-yourself chapter or book. If you carefully examine these do-it-yourself books, you will find that many are out of date, many are incomplete or inaccurate, many do not adequately cover the particular laws of your state, and all are misleading—encouraging you to be your own lawyer is like encouraging you to be your own doctor. The sensible course is to hire an attorney. Only a lawyer can provide accurate, up-to-date, comprehensive, and personalized legal assistance tailored to your case, circumstances, and objectives.

Keep in mind that if you try to handle an important legal matter yourself and you make a mistake that costs you money or forfeits your rights, you have only yourself to blame. In contrast, by hiring a lawyer you will reduce the chances of a mistake being made. Moreover, if the lawyer does make a mistake that damages your case or your rights or interests, you can sue that lawyer for malpractice and receive compensation for your losses. Thus, by hiring a lawyer you reduce the chances of a mistake being made and you gain the protection of malpractice coverage.

Having read this chapter, you should now turn to the chapter or chapters which review the legal matter or matters about which you are concerned. If you have other questions about lawyers or the practice of law or want additional information on how to deal effectively with lawyers, consult my previous book *Lawyers: A Client's Manual*, also published by Prentice-Hall.

2
Buying or Selling a House and Real Estate

WHAT IS INVOLVED IN BUYING OR SELLING A HOUSE AND REAL ESTATE?

When you are considering buying or selling a house and real estate, keep in mind that two entities are involved: (1) a house, its contents, and related structures; and (2) the plot of land on which the house stands. Both the house and the plot of land have physical characteristics that will affect the sale—especially the purchase price. Just as important, if not more important, there are legal aspects involved in selling or buying a house and there are distinct legal aspects involved in selling or buying a plot of land.

Beginning with the house, naturally, the house is a physical structure which the seller and buyer can view and inspect. Physical aspects of the house that are not readily subject to visual inspection (the insulation, the plumbing and electrical systems, insect infestation, etc.) can be tested or examined by the appropriate professionals. The physical aspects of the house, once determined, are largely matters of personal value and taste. Whether one likes the "style" of the house, the number of rooms, the type of heating or insulation, the location and neighborhood, or other features are largely issues of personal preference and valuation reflected in the sales price.

There are, as well, legal aspects to selling or buying a house. The present owners have a deed to the land on which the house stands (which gives them legal ownership of what is on the land—the house), but there may be legal encumbrances on the house of which the seller and buyer should both be aware so that they can properly deal with such matters. For example, the seller may have a mortgage on the house and perhaps a sizable personal loan for which the house serves as collateral (that is, a second mortgage was put on the house as security for repayment of that personal loan). The sellers may have fallen behind on a debt obligation or one of the sellers may be a defendant in a lawsuit—in either case, the creditor of the debt or the plaintiff in the lawsuit may have obtained an attachment on the seller's house. An *attachment* is a legal process by which a court makes the seller's ownership of the house subject to the proven or alleged obligation of the seller to another person (here, the creditor of the debt or the plaintiff in the lawsuit). The seller, in effect, cannot sell the house without making arrangements to have the attachment removed (by paying the money owed, by showing that the attachment is groundless, or otherwise).

The point is that there are physical aspects to the house which the seller and buyer must be aware of and come to certain agreements on and there are legal aspects to the house which the seller and buyer must also investigate and deal with.

Similarly, the land on which the house stands has physical and legal aspects which must be investigated. The physical aspects of the land include its size, location, layout, uses, whether anyone else has the right to cross over or use the land, and so forth. Most of the physical aspects of the land can be determined by a simple visual inspection.

The legal aspects of the land, however, involve the ownership rights and obligations of the present owners and possibly others. The most important consideration is the "title" to the land—who owns the land and, just as importantly, whether the owner's use of the land is restricted in any way and whether any other persons have a right to use the land in any way.

Although the house you are selling or buying may be only a few years or a few decades old, the land on which the house stands may have passed through many different owners in the previous decades and centuries. Official records are kept in each county and state to record title to land and other interests, documents and legal actions which may affect title to a given plot of land. These records must be carefully checked to determine whether the seller has good title to the land and what restrictions or limitations, if any, there may be on the title.

To reiterate, the seller and the buyer should keep in mind that two entities are involved in the sale and the purchase of a house and real estate—the house and the land. Each has physical and legal aspects which must be investigated and dealt with before a proper and successful sale and purchase can be completed.

In addition to the physical and legal aspects of the house and the land, there are also matters of timing and financing which must be considered and worked out. The seller and purchaser must come to some agreement as to when title will be transferred, when the purchase money will be paid, and when the sellers will vacate the house so that the buyers can move in. In a typical situation, all three elements—the transfer of title, payment of purchase money, and occupancy by the purchaser—occur on the same day. However, it is not unusual for one or more of those elements to occur on different days, necessitating agreements as to how that is to be done and at whose expense or inconvenience.

Moreover, numerous matters pertaining to the physical and legal aspects of the house and the land must be worked out. Agreement must be reached as to what removable items in the house are included in the sale—for example, are the refrigerator and other appliances staying or will the sellers be taking them? Also, who will pay for the various services and costs involved in the sale—for example, will the seller or the buyer pay to have the title to the land checked? These and many other related matters must be worked out so that each party knows what his or her obligations and rights are and under what conditions.

Selling or buying a house also involves major financial considerations. Typically, the house and real estate you are about to sell or purchase comprise one of the largest and most important single investments you will ever make. The financial arrangements regarding the sale and purchase must be understood by both seller and buyer and there must be agreement as to who has what rights and obligations. Usually, the purchaser finances a large part of the purchase with mortgage money from an institutional lender (most commonly a bank or a government mortgage lending program). The terms and conditions of that financing often have great bearing on the sale. For example, the buyer's mortgage institution may require that a certain type of deed be used, or that the sellers sign papers which warrant or guarantee certain conditions pertaining to the property and their use of it. Moreover, several financial adjustments are necessary so that outstanding real estate taxes, water and sewer bills, fuel allotments, and other expenses on the house and land are properly apportioned between seller and buyer.

Given all these aspects to selling or buying a house and real estate, it should be apparent that the seller and the buyer should each have legal counsel to represent and protect their rights and interests in such a major transaction.

We are talking about the home you and your family live in or will be living in. We are also talking about one of the most important physical and financial investments you will ever make. Given that, there is little to be gained by trying to save a few hundred dollars on lawyer's fees by attempting to sell or purchase a house and real estate without the advice and assistance of a lawyer. Why risk an investment worth tens of thousands of dollars to save a few hundred dollars?

A lawyer is trained in the law of real estate and conveyancing (the transfer of title to land). The lawyer knows the rights and obligations of the seller and those of the buyer under current local, state, and federal law. In addition to his or her knowledge of the law, an experienced real estate lawyer knows what to look for and what to look out for regarding the physical, practical, and financial aspects of selling or buying a house and real estate. This may be the only time you will sell or buy a house and land for years to come. An experienced real estate lawyer, on the other hand, handles numerous real estate transfers every year. Because of this experience, the lawyer is familiar with the customary practices in your area pertaining to the sale and purchase of a house and real estate. Many aspects of such a sale are not specifically covered by law. Many matters must be worked out between the seller and the buyer by negotiation—usually by reference to customary practices. An experienced real estate lawyer will be familiar with the negotiation process as well as customary and accepted practices.

Often, an experienced real estate attorney can provide you with time-saving and money-saving information and advice.

More importantly, the attorney's advice and assistance will be tailored to your needs and aimed at protecting and asserting your rights and interests. The attorney is there to serve you.

For a successful sale to occur, everything has to go right; if anything goes wrong, the sale may be delayed or even canceled. An experienced attorney can avoid many problems that might otherwise occur. If things do go wrong, the attorney can use his or her knowledge and experience to iron things out and correct the situation—with your rights and interests in mind.

On some occasions, the seller and buyer agree to hire the same lawyer to represent both of them. In some of these instances, there is an understanding that each will pay half the attorney's fee. Despite the fact that some attorneys regularly or occasionally participate in these arrangements, you should never agree to such an arrangement.

How can one lawyer represent both the seller and the buyer? If there is a disagreement over any matter, to whom does the lawyer owe first loyalty? If the seller or the buyer decides, for whatever reason, not to go through with the sale but the other party is depending on the sale going through, who does the "joint" lawyer represent then? Only a lawyer who represents you and only you (whether you are the seller or the buyer) can do the job that must be done and do it keeping your interests paramount.

The lawyer you hire works for you. The lawyer is there to answer your questions and represent you in all the necessary and customary aspects of selling or buying a house and real estate. If you are the seller, you may hear various things from the buyer, the buyer's attorney, the buyer's real estate broker, the buyer's mortgage institution, and others. Only your attorney, however, represents you and no one but you. If you are the buyer, you may hear various things from the seller, the seller's attorney, the seller's real estate broker, and others; again, only your lawyer represents you and no one but you.

If your lawyer fails to render proper and competent legal advice and services, you can sue the lawyer for malpractice. You should ask the lawyer, before hiring, whether he or she carries malpractice insurance. By hiring a lawyer who carries malpractice insurance, you are, literally, buying insurance against many of the losses that might be caused by the lawyer's mistakes or misconduct. If you were to sell or buy the house without the aid of a lawyer and you made a mistake or overlooked something, you would have only yourself to blame and nowhere to go to compensate yourself for your losses.

HOW TO THINK ABOUT LEGAL AND RELATED ASPECTS

Given the physical, legal, practical, and financial aspects to buying or selling a house and real estate, you should do some thinking and organizing as soon as you decide to sell or buy. The following sections discuss important areas with which you should be concerned.

Consult a lawyer when you decide to put your house up for sale or when you decide to look for a house to buy.

The best way to be prepared for the physical, legal, practical, and financial aspects to selling or buying a house is to consult a lawyer early on. Inform the lawyer about the house you want to sell or buy, then review with the lawyer the questions and subjects in the following sections. The sooner you become informed as to what to look for and what to look out for, the better equipped you will be and the better your chances will be for a successful transaction.

Find out about the law, procedures, customs, and timetables.

Have the attorney explain the laws and procedures involved in selling or buying a house and real estate. What legal papers and documents are involved? What significance do they have and what function do they serve? Who usually prepares them? What do they cost and who pays the cost? The nature and names for the various legal papers and documents involved in the sale and purchase of a house and real estate vary greatly from state to state. Your attorney can explain what the typical legal documents and procedures are in your area (more specifically, the locale where the house and real estate are located). Also, the attorney can make sure that the real estate transfer complies with all applicable federal and state laws such as the federal Real Estate Settlement Procedures Act (RESPA).

Also, ask the attorney about the customary practices of which you should be aware. Although customs are not enforceable in court the way a law is, many problems and misunderstandings are easily avoided if both the seller and the buyer agree to follow the customary practices. Who is responsible for the title search? Who draws up the deed? Where does the "closing" (the exchange of the deed for the money) take place? These and many other matters must be ironed out sooner or later. It will be very helpful if you are aware of the customary practices from the outset. Even if the seller and buyer agree to handle a particular matter in a manner different from the customary practice, the important thing is to know what matters are dictated by law and what matters are left to custom and negotiation between seller and buyer.

Also, ask the attorney about typical or expected timetables involved in selling or buying a house and real estate. It is important for both seller and buyer to have a realistic understanding of how long the various steps will take. How much time should the buyer have to get confirmed financing? How long should the title search take? What tests or inspections must be done on the house or property and how long will they take? How long may the seller stay in the house and when does the buyer plan to move in? All these factors involve timing and planning.

Find out about the role and responsibility of the real estate broker.

Many sales of a house and real estate involve a real estate broker. In the majority of cases, the broker is hired by the seller. The broker's job is to find a buyer and successfully negotiate the sales price, a tentative closing date, and other matters. In some instances, it is the buyer who hires the real estate broker. In that situation, the broker's job is to find an acceptable house at an acceptable price. Whichever the case may be, have your lawyer explain the role and responsibilities of a real estate broker. Be sure the lawyer does that if you hired the broker.

Each state has specific laws governing the obligations of the person who hired the broker. An important question is under what circumstances will the broker be entitled to his or her commission. In some states, the broker is entitled to a commission—even though the sale does not take place—if the sale is obstructed or prevented through no fault of the broker. In other states, however, the broker is entitled to a commission only if the sale is completed. Your lawyer can advise you as to the law that applies in your state.

Find out about the seller's rights and obligations.

Laws differ from state to state regarding what a seller may or may not do or say when selling a house and real estate. In some states, the sale can be rescinded (the seller must take back the property and the buyer gets his or her money back) if the seller fails to disclose major defects in the house or property or serious violations of health or safety codes. In other states, however, the seller can be held liable only if he or she actually makes a statement (as opposed to simply remaining silent) that is later shown to be a misrepresentation of fact (and not simply a matter of taste or opinion).

It is important to understand under what conditions, if any, the seller will have the right not to go through with the sale. This should be discussed with your attorney so that appropriate legal measures are taken and so that you understand the remedies that will be available if the sale does not go through because of the actions or omissions of the seller.

The legal papers and documents you sign govern many of the seller's rights and obligations (as well as the buyer's rights and obligations); be sure the lawyer explains those papers and documents to you in terms you understand.

Find out about the buyer's rights and obligations.

Whether you are the seller or buyer, find out about the rights and obligations of the buyer. Under what conditions, if any, will the buyer have the right not to go through with the purchase? For example, the sale of the house and real estate may be conditioned on the buyer obtaining a mortgage for a certain amount by a certain date. If the buyer makes reasonable efforts to obtain the mortgage but no lending institution approves a mortgage, the buyer normally has the right to call off the sale and have any deposit money returned. Any other conditions which would give the buyer the right to avoid the sale should be discussed with your attorney.

If you are the buyer, review your financing—especially your mortgage (type, amount, when available, terms and conditions, etc.).

It is important for the buyer to determine how he or she is going to finance the purchase of the house and real estate. In the majority of cases, the buyer uses a mortgage to pay most or all of the sales price. Mortgages, however, come in many varieties and are issued by many different types of institutions (public and private). Review with your lawyer the types of mortgages you can apply for, how much money you will be requesting, the available interest rates, how long it will take to process the mortgage application, when the funds will be available, the amount of the monthly payments, what are the credits for early payments and the penalties for late payments, and so on.

It is important to discuss your financing picture with your attorney at the outset so that the attorney can protect your interests in the legal papers and documents pertaining to the sale.

Work out the necessary moving arrangements tentatively (for the seller, arrange move into new abode; for buyer, arrange termination of present abode).

It is essential to successfully coordinate the timetable by which the seller is to be out of the house so that the buyer can move in. Few problems are as costly or as exasperating as a mistake or intentional breach of an agreement regarding when the house is to be vacated by the seller and occupied by the buyer.

The seller must coordinate his or her move out of the house with a move into a new abode. The buyer must coordinate his or her move into the house with a move out of the present abode. Where timing presents the problem, planning is invariably the solution.

It is often helpful for the seller to have the same attorney handle both the sale of the present house and the purchase or rental of the seller's new abode. In this way, one attorney can coordinate both transactions. Likewise, the buyer would be wise to have the attorney who is handling the purchase of the new house also handle the sale of the buyer's present house or the termination of the buyer's present lease.

Clarify as many details as possible as early as possible.

The sale and purchase of a house and real estate involve many details which can cause headaches and costly delays and problems unless they are worked out by mutual agreement. It can happen that, with so many people involved in the sale (buyer, buyer's attorney, seller, seller's attorney, and perhaps one or two real estate brokers), confusion and misunderstandings may arise. Every effort should be made to clarify the following:

Sales Price What is the final sales price agreed upon by the seller and buyer?

Length of Offer How much time does the buyer have to arrange financing and be ready to buy? How much time does the seller have to get the property and the title ready for sale?

Deposit How much of a deposit should the buyer advance? Who will hold the deposit and under what conditions will the deposit be returned to the buyer or forfeited to the seller?

Closing Date What date should be set as the closing date—when the deed is exchanged for the purchase money? Is that date tentative or is it binding? Is there some leeway or will the sale be off automatically if either party is not able to fulfill his or her obligations at that time? Who shall pay what penalties or forfeit what to whom if one party or the other is unable to proceed at the closing date?

Contents of House What removable contents of the house are included in the sale (appliances, rugs, furniture, etc.)? Will there be a separate sales agreement for each item or are they included in the total sales price?

Title Search Who will do the title search and who will pay for it?

Buyer's Financing How will the buyer pay the sales price? (How much in his or her own money? How much in mortgage money?)

Type of Deed and Title Have your lawyer explain the different types of deeds and the consequences of the particular type of deed to be used in this transfer. Is it a warranty deed, a quitclaim deed, a release deed, a fiduciary's deed or some other type of deed? If you are the buyer, make sure your lawyer explains exactly what legal rights and protections you are getting as a result of the type of deed being used.

If you are the buyer and you are purchasing the property along with someone else, have your lawyer explain the type of title you and that other person will have to the property. What happens if, later on, one of you wants to sell his or her share but the other doesn't? Who gets the other person's share if he or she dies? Who gets your share if you die?

Is the Sale Dependent Upon Certain Conditions? Is the sale conditioned upon the seller altering or fixing the house or property? Is the sale dependent upon the buyer doing something?

Inspections, Tests, Permits, Zoning Matters Is the sale conditioned upon certain inspections (of the insulation, the electrical or plumbing systems, etc.)? Is the sale conditioned upon certain tests (water quality tests, land use tests, lead-based paint tests, etc.)? Is the sale conditioned upon the seller or buyer obtaining certain permits, licenses, or zoning changes (to operate a retail outlet on the premises, to rent part of the premises, etc.)?

Insurance Is the house presently insured? For how much? Does the buyer have an insurance binder or other agreement with an insurance company to have the house insured as of the closing date?

Tenants and Rents Are there rental units in the house or other buildings on the premises? Are the tenants to remain or vacate before the closing? What are the rental rates and terms?

Apportionments for Outstanding Real Estate and Other Taxes, Water and Sewer Bills, Fuel, Rents, and So On Have the seller and buyer agreed to apportion these and other costs and charges related to the house and property as of the closing date or another date?

Have the details and agreements put in writing and signed by the buyer and seller. (Consult your lawyer *before* signing.)

Have resolutions of all the above matters and any others put in writing and have the papers signed by the seller and buyer. The time and effort that goes into working out agreements can be wasted if those agreements are not put in writing and signed by the parties. Attorneys often use standard forms with numerous blank spaces in which to insert these details and agreements.

Make sure you review the papers and agreements with your attorney before you sign. Too often sellers or buyers come to an attorney *after* they have signed agreements which forfeit or jeopardize their rights or which obligate them in a manner which would have been avoided if they had sought a lawyer's advice before signing.

Make sure your lawyer explains the various terms and conditions and the various documents you are called upon to sign. It is easy for an attorney to tell the client that the legal terms and phrases are too complicated to explain or that the client should simply trust the lawyer and not ask questions. Nonetheless, insist that the lawyer read every clause in every document and explain any words or clauses you do not understand. It would hardly be appropriate for your lawyer to ask you to sign a document without first making sure you understand that document—after all, you are paying the attorney for that advice and assistance.

DEALING WITH LAWYERS

In addition to the general points about lawyers in Chapter 1, keep in mind the following advice about dealing with lawyers on a real estate transfer.

A good method of getting the names of lawyers with experience in real estate work is to call a local title company (listed in the Yellow Pages) and ask for the names of lawyers whose work they respect.

With regard to fees, in many areas of the country lawyers charge percentage fees on real estate transfers. That is, the fee is a percentage of the sales price of the house being sold. The specific percentages vary with the prevailing rates for residential property. For example, for houses that sell for between $20,000 and $100,000 some lawyers charge 1 percent of the sales price. In the case of houses that sell for over $100,000, some lawyers charge three-quarters or one-half of 1 percent of the sales price.

If the lawyer you contact informs you that he or she charges a certain percentage of the sales price as the fee, take a moment to compute how much that is in actual cash terms. If you are selling or buying a $40,000 house and the lawyer quotes a fee of 1 percent of the sales price, that comes out to $400. If you are selling or buying a $125,00 house and the lawyer quotes a fee of one-half of 1 percent of the sales price, that works out to $625. Convert the percentage fee into actual cash terms so that you know how much money—in actual dollars—you will pay the lawyer if you hire him or her.

Some lawyers charge a flat fee, that is, a specific amount of money. Even flat fees, however, vary according to the sales price of the house. For example, an attorney might quote you a flat fee of $500 to handle the sale or purchase of a $60,000 house. That same attorney might quote a flat fee of $1,000 to handle a $130,000 house.

Before agreeing to pay a flat fee, have the lawyer explain what services the flat fee covers. Normally, a flat fee means that the lawyer agrees to render the necessary and customary services provided by a lawyer on a real estate transfer. That, however, usually assumes that the real estate transfer is a more or less routine one. If unexpected complications arise which require additional time and work by your attorney, he or she will charge an additional fee for that additional work. For example, if the purchase and sale agreement breaks down and you must initiate a lawsuit or the other party sues you, a considerable amount of additional time and effort will be required by the lawyer. A lawsuit is not covered by the original flat fee; the fee for that lawsuit must be worked out through separate negotiations and agreement.

Some lawyers charge an hourly fee. (See Chapter 1 for a detailed discussion of hourly fees.)

Ask each lawyer you contact about fee payment arrangements. Some lawyers insist on being paid in full at the outset. Do not agree to that. Other lawyers may want half the fee up front and the other half at some point before the closing. Other attorneys allow other payment schedules. Compare the fee payment schedules which various attorneys would require or allow. You can save a lot of money by comparing the fees which different lawyers would charge. You can also spare yourself some financial burdens by working out an affordable installment payment schedule.

Furthermore, you can save yourself considerable money by negotiating with the lawyer for a lower fee. A lawyer may tell you that his or her fee for a $50,000 house is 1 percent of the sales price—which works out to $500. Nevertheless, that lawyer may be surprisingly reluctant to pass up your case if you reply that you would like to hire the attorney but only if he or she agrees to a fee of $400. The same can be true when the lawyer quotes a flat fee or an hourly fee.

During the negotiations over the fee, stress how routine and uncomplicated your real estate transfer is (if, of course, it is a routine matter and not an unusual or complicated one). Also emphasize that the lawyer's work on a real estate transfer is largely paperwork—there is no trial or court appearance required and, normally, the entire process is fairly amicable.

Whether you are the seller or buyer, in a typical real estate transfer you will be responsible for various fees, costs, and expenses that are not included in the lawyer's fee. For example, the seller or buyer will pay for a title search—which could cost $100 or $200 or even more. Also, there may be state revenue taxes which must be paid upon the sale of the house—those can also amount to $100 or

$200 or more. In addition, there are fees charged for recording documents such as deeds, mortgages, discharges, liens, and other papers. Your lawyer should be able to give you an estimate of what your share of those fees, costs, and expenses will be. Ask the lawyer about them early on. You could find yourself in a difficult financial situation if you found out about significant costs at the last minute without having set aside enough money to pay them.

3
Divorce

WHAT IS INVOLVED IN A DIVORCE?

Divorce terminates the legal bond of marriage. When a court issues a judgment or decree of divorce, the spouses become single persons. In some instances, this means that all the rights and obligations which the law imposes on married persons come to an end. However, if there are minor children of the marriage, the care, custody, and support of the children must be determined. Marital property must be divided or otherwise apportioned between the spouses. If one spouse has been economically dependent upon the other or for some other reason cannot establish economic independence, the other spouse may be required to provide alimony.

The termination of the interspousal rights and obligations of marriage, child custody, care and support, the division or apportionment of personal and marital property, and alimony are all aspects of divorce that are infused with emotional, moral, social, financial, and many other elements. Doubtlessly, divorce has varied and enduring effects on the spouses and other family members. Although the complex of marital rights and obligations which exist between husband and wife are terminated, postdivorce obligations may be agreed upon or imposed by law through the courts. For example, where there are minor children, custody must be decided. Along with custody, the visitation rights of the noncustodial parent must be worked out as well as other decisions regarding how the children are to be supported by each spouse financially. Children may become more vocal and assertive in decisions which affect them during and after a divorce. Or they may withdraw into or vacillate between states of depression, guilt, hostility, and awareness, and growth. Like their lives, they may become more difficult to deal with.

In addition to child custody, support, and related matters, one of the spouses may call upon the other to provide spousal support—alimony—for a limited or indefinite period of time. Strains on financial resources and problems in resolving the amount and manner of child and spousal support lay bare the difficulty and complexity of dissolving a marriage and, what is more, breaking up a family.

Personal and marital property must be divided or apportioned. Each spouse may have his or her own views as to what principles should prevail regarding the division of property. As with child custody and child and spousal support decisions, the division of personal and marital property is infused with emotional, social, moral, and financial elements. All of these must be resolved—by agreement between the spouses or by imposition of a court order—within the framework of legal standards and procedures for divorce.

In addition to the actions and reactions of the spouses in ending their marital relationship, there are many problem areas encountered by each spouse in trying to build a new life as a single person—often as a single parent. Other problems are faced by the spouse who undergoes a divorce with the intention of remarrying.

For the ex-spouse who remains single, important steps must be taken to establish one's own economic, social, and legal identity. Ownership of property once held jointly must be clarified. Credit, bank accounts, all forms of insurance (health, life, medical, disability, etc.) and other matters must be adjusted to fit the new status of single person or single parent. Each ex-spouse should also make appropriate changes in his or her will and estate plan (see Chapter 6).

Many persons, while going through a divorce or sometime after the divorce, must call upon various government or private agencies, for information, counseling, financial assistance, protection from physical assault or abuse, employment assistance, child care and counseling, and numerous other services. Difficulties may arise in not knowing where to go or, worse, not being able to identify and acknowledge the need for assistance and help.

Unfortunately, during and shortly after a divorce, many people fail to deal with long-term considerations and future developments which should be dealt with and resolved, wholly or partially, at the time of the divorce. Spouses are sometimes preoccupied with the immediate needs of the children—and overlook working out agreements or arrangements for the children's future needs. In regard to financial and property matters, many spouses are unrealistic about their own or, more likely, their spouse's anticipated future needs and capabilities. Some spouses, emotionally or mentally distraught, capitulate to the demands and concerns of the present only to encounter problems in the future which could have been avoided or minimized by appropriate planning during the divorce.

Most people undergoing a divorce are not aware of the role and reach of the law and the courts even into the future—well after the divorce becomes "final." What if problems develop a year after the divorce? Ten years after the divorce? Many people do not think in those terms during the divorce—only to find themselves in difficult circumstances later on and not knowing how to deal with their problems or how to seek legal action.

Both spouses have their own attitudes and viewpoints on how these and other matters should be handled. On the other hand, the trauma, strain, and duration of divorce may diminish or destroy one or both spouses' ability to understand and accommodate in a realistic manner. One or both spouses may be in such emotional or mental dismay that their perceptions and feelings become distorted and their capacity for mature judgment impaired. Some divorces are amicable. Some, although difficult, are eventually resolved in a reasonable though begrudging manner. Other divorces are from the outset grueling contests between equally embittered people. Still other divorces are marred by the insidious, even cruel dominance of one spouse over the other.

In contrast to the charged interpersonal relations of the spouses is the official neutrality of the judge. The rights and obligations of the spouses, the custody and care of the children, child support, spousal support, the division of personal and marital property, and almost all other matters involved in a divorce are subject to the jurisdiction of the courts—during and after the divorce. In handling divorce cases, judges are granted wide discretionary powers to review, revise, and even act contrary to the actions and decisions of the spouses. Legally, a divorce is a decree from a court declaring that a marriage has been terminated for proper legal grounds and on terms acceptable to the court. Needless to say, a judge's role is difficult, complex, and demanding. The judge's authority is considerable. The judge must determine the genuineness and seriousness of the request for a divorce. The judge must review all agreements and arrangements to safeguard against those situations in which one spouse or the children are treated inadequately or unfairly. Not uncommonly, ignorance, intimidation, or even carelessness enables one spouse to take undue advantage of the other or disregard the needs and best interests of the children. The courts are primarily concerned with the fairness of the divorce terms and especially with the welfare and interests of any minor children. Even well-meaning spouses sometimes fail to properly provide for the children. Spouses sometimes make decisions affecting the children for personal convenience or on the basis of an uncritical assumption that one or both parents unerringly know what is best for "their" children. In every divorce case, the judge must measure the actions and decisions of the spouses—especially those which effect minor children—in light of more dispassionate standards that draw upon the requirements and reasoning of the law and the detachment, experience, and authority of the judge as representative of society.

As can be seen, virtually every issue involved in a divorce has legal aspects and ramifications. Even in what are referred to as "routine" or "uncontested" divorces there are many important legal and related issues which all too many spouses ignore or overlook—to their detriment.

Whether contested or uncontested, whether routine or complicated, each spouse should consult an experienced divorce lawyer.

WHY DO YOU NEED TO CONSULT A LAWYER?

Because divorce affects so many aspects of a person's life and so many legal rights and obligations, every person who is contemplating or undergoing a divorce should consult a lawyer. How else can you fully protect and assert your rights and interests regarding the grounds for divorce and how the divorce proceedings are conducted? How else can you make sure your needs and interests are protected and asserted in such vital areas as child custody, care and support, spousal support, and the division of property? How else can you make sure that the legal aspects of your life and status as a single person—perhaps a single parent—will be dealt with properly and effectively?

Many people do not realize the significance of such matters as what grounds for divorce are alleged and proven or how the proceedings are conducted in and out of court. Failure to investigate such matters can lead to problems that may not be correctable at a later date. During divorce proceedings each spouse must make any objections or arguments in a particular manner and at a specific time or forever lose his or her right to make objections, present arguments, and be heard. Adverse decisions have been incurred on many occasions by spouses who chose not to be represented by a lawyer and who did not know how to protect their rights and interests.

Some spouses feel that their divorce case is amicable enough and uncomplicated enough to warrant not hiring a lawyer. Some spouses feel that hiring a lawyer would be an indication of distrust of the other spouse and agreements made between them or that hiring a lawyer might be seen as an attempt to take advantage of the other spouse—who has said that he or she will not hire a lawyer. Despite all the purported reasons for not hiring a lawyer, there is one overriding reason for hiring a lawyer: by hiring a lawyer you will have a trained and experienced advisor who will look out for your rights and interests in light of your objectives and do so in a legally proper, effective manner.

Sometimes a spouse tries to argue his or her own case in (or out of) court. Usually, inarticulateness, confusion, anxiety or nervousness, ignorance of the required rules and procedures, or any of a number of other factors make such efforts ineffective and often counterproductive. Just as importantly, most people do not know what to look for and what to look out for in divorce proceedings. Only a few minutes of consultation with an experienced divorce lawyer would convince most of these people that they have overlooked a number of important matters and were unwittingly forfeiting or jeopardizing their rights and interests in other areas. Quite simply, most spouses contemplating or undergoing a divorce do not know what their legal rights and obligations are, nor do they have the practical knowledge or negotiating ability an experienced divorce lawyer can provide.

In addition, a lawyer is needed by every person who is contemplating or undergoing a divorce so that that person can properly establish himself or herself as a single person—perhaps as a single parent. As noted earlier, many legal, economic, and social considerations must be resolved when one's legal status changes from that of a married person and parent to that of a single person or single parent. An experienced divorce lawyer will identify those areas of concern and help you deal with them.

A lawyer can also explain what your future rights and obligations are. Many people mistakenly feel that if the divorce is fairly amicable or uncontested, there is nothing else to worry about or be concerned with. Unfortunately, many of these people encounter problems later on with child custody, care, or support, spousal support, or property or financial affairs which stem from the original divorce agreement or decree. Circumstances may change dramatically for one or both spouses within months or years of the divorce. The agreements and arrangements made at the time of the divorce, of course, were based on the circumstances and attitudes of the spouses at that time. If times and circumstances change, especially if they change drastically, one spouse may have considerably greater financial ability to provide child support or spousal support. Or the spouse who was awarded custody of the children may not be living up to proper standards of child care. Or the noncustodial parent may be having problems with visitation rights that jeopardize his or her relationship with the children. The point is that numerous problems can and do develop within months or years after the divorce is granted. If each spouse had consulted an attorney at the time of the divorce, some of those problems might have been anticipated and contingent plans and arrangements drawn up. Even if the problems caused by changed circumstances were not anticipated, by having your own lawyer at the time of the divorce you can find out how to handle future problems should they arise. An ex-spouse can go back into court to seek changes in the original divorce agreement or decree that will properly reflect changed circumstances and behavior since the divorce. Far too many divorced persons suffer needlessly when their or their children's circumstances change for the worse some time after the divorce. Ironically, although relief may be available, many ex-spouses are not aware that they have the right to renegotiate the original divorce agreements or, if that fails, to go back into court and request that the court make appropriate changes to reflect changed circumstances and abilities. Whether an ex-spouse seeks to have the court change the original arrangement—by changing custody, or altering visitation rights, or lowering or raising child support or spousal support, or making other modifications—those changes can only be made if that spouse follows the appropriate legal procedures.

Similarly, if either spouse is not abiding by the original agreements or court decree, and the other spouse or the children are detrimentally effected, the harmed spouse can go back into court to seek judicial enforcement against the wrongdoing spouse.

Few legal matters present so many real and potential legal concerns and problems as a divorce. Because of this, every person who is undergoing or who has undergone a divorce should consult an experienced divorce lawyer to make sure that his or her rights and interests and those of the children are protected and asserted fully.

HOW TO THINK ABOUT LEGAL AND RELATED ASPECTS

The following sections discuss important areas which any person going through a divorce should think about seriously.

Consult a lawyer if you or your spouse is contemplating a divorce or has decided to seek a divorce.

You will have many questions only a lawyer can answer. There will be problems on which you will need legal advice. In all likelihood, there will be many matters you would overlook or not deal with properly without good legal counsel. Many myths, misconceptions, and worries can be dispelled, dismissed, or alleviated by consulting a lawyer. Few events in your life will affect you—and your family—in as many ways as a divorce. A lawyer's advice is necessary no matter how uncomplicated the situation, no matter how uncontested it may be. Of course, if the divorce is complicated or contested, you will need legal advice and assistance all the more.

Find out about the grounds for divorce and the legal procedures and timetables involved.

Each state recognizes various "grounds" for divorce. One (or more) of these must be accepted by the court before a divorce decree will be issued. Grounds for divorce differ from state to state. Moreover, new laws may change or add to the available grounds. Also, judges often vary considerably in their interpretations of what constitutes proof of a particular ground for divorce. By explaining your marital situation to a lawyer you can determine what grounds for divorce are available and the advantages of each. It is important to determine the available grounds for divorce. For example, many states recognize "cruel and abusive treatment" as one ground for divorce and also recognize "irretrievable breakdown of the marriage" (popularly called no-fault divorce) as another ground for divorce. Both of those grounds are available in many divorce cases. Yet each has its advantages and disadvantages. One ground for divorce may require more extensive evidence and proof than another ground. One ground may require a considerably longer period of time before you go to court or before the divorce becomes final than would another ground. One ground may require that the spouses resolve custody, support, property, and other matters before they file for divorce on that ground, while with another ground no prior agreements are required. In these and many other ways there are important differences—advantages and disadvantages—to the particular grounds on which the divorce is filed. Your lawyer can explain these matters. You can then determine which ground or grounds are suitable given your situation and objectives. (Both spouses can file for divorce. Also, each can allege one or more different grounds for divorce.)

The various grounds for divorce are reviewed briefly below.

Your state may accept some but not all of the following grounds. Also, these general definitions may vary significantly from how a particular ground is defined by the laws of your state. Consult a lawyer for accurate, up-to-date information appropriate to your situation.

No-Fault or Incompatibility or Irretrievable Breakdown Most states now recognize what is popularly referred to as a "no-fault" divorce. More accurately, a no-fault divorce means that one or both spouses are alleging that there has been a breakdown in the marriage that is not attributable to any of the traditional "fault" grounds (such as cruelty, desertion, adultery, etc.). Depending on the laws of the state, a no-fault divorce usually requires a showing that the spouses are "incompatible" or that there has been an "irretrievable breakdown" in the marriage or that an irreconcilable difficulty has developed.

Cruelty or Cruel and Abusive Treatment Most states will grant a divorce if one spouse shows that the other spouse engaged in acts of physical or mental cruelty. Contrary to what many people mistakenly believe, most states will grant a divorce even if the cruelty is only threatened—as long as the spouse to whom the threats are directed fears that the threats will be carried out; that is, a spouse does not have to wait for serious physical abuse or harm to occur. Also, mental anguish and emotional anguish are often included in the legal definition of cruelty or cruel and abusive treatment and would establish grounds for divorce.

Adultery Adultery is sexual intercourse between one spouse and any person other than the other spouse. Proving adultery is not as difficult in some states as many people suppose. For example, in some states all that need be shown is that the other spouse was involved in circumstances which give rise to a reasonable suspicion that adultery took place. In other states, by contrast, more compelling and explicit evidence must be presented.

Abandonment or Desertion If one spouse leaves, leaves with the intent of not returning, and leaves against the wishes of the other spouse, the spouse who has been abandoned or deserted may file for divorce.

Habitual Intoxication by Drugs or Alcohol If one spouse is habitually intoxicated by the voluntary use of drugs or alcohol, the other spouse may seek a divorce. The habitual intoxication must be such that it prevents or ruins a normal marital relationship.

Nonsupport Traditionally, nonsupport, as ground for divorce, was interpreted to cover only the situation where a husband failed utterly to provide for the support and well-being of his wife. The wife had to show that the husband severely neglected his obligation to provide food, clothing, and shelter for her. In recent times, nonsupport is used only rarely as a ground for divorce.

Imprisonment In most states if one spouse is sentenced to prison for a period of years, that constitutes grounds for divorce. The number of years required varies from state to state. Typically, a sentence of five years or more constitutes grounds for divorce.

Impotence, Insanity, Other Grounds The seven grounds for divorce defined in the preceding paragraphs are the most common. Some states also accept impotence and insanity as grounds for divorce as well as other, rarely encountered grounds.

The best approach, if you have doubts or questions, is to explain your marital situation thoroughly to your lawyer so that he or she can determine whether your circumstances give rise to more than one ground for divorce. If you qualify for more than one ground for divorce, the lawyer can explain the differences—the advantages and disadvantages of each—regarding evidence, procedure, time, and cost. Also, what ground you allege may affect your spouse's reactions and conduct. Be sure you have thoroughly discussed with your lawyer the pros and cons of each available ground for divorce.

Also, have your lawyer explain the legal procedures, courtroom format, and timetables. Ask about the steps involved in filing for divorce, having papers served on your spouse, and when you will be assigned a court date. Be sure your lawyer explains what the court hearing or trial will be like and prepares you for the questions you will be asked. Finally, get some idea of how long it will be before the divorce becomes final.

Find out about rights and obligations regarding minor children.

The most important decision regarding the children is custody. In some states (or with some judges) separate custody is the norm and only rarely do courts (judges) approve of joint custody in which both parents retain equal custodial rights to the minor children. Your lawyer can explain the accepted legal standards in your jurisdiction given the facts of your situation. Also, ask about visitation rights for the noncustodial parent. How limited or extensive should they be? How specific or open-ended?

The financial needs of the children must also be determined and provided for. To what extent and in what manner shall each spouse contribute to the support of the children? Child support involves not only food, clothing, and payment of medical and dental insurance and bills but also school fees and expenses, babysitting expenses, hygiene, recreation, and many other expenses. Again, your lawyer can advise you about your rights and obligations in these areas. Just as importantly, your lawyer can assist you in working out these matters by agreement with your spouse, if that is possible. Those matters that cannot be resolved in a reasonable and fair manner between the spouses will be resolved (or imposed) by the court. In court, your lawyer can assert and protect your rights and interests in the legally required or appropriate manner.

Unfortunately, in some cases, one spouse seeks not only a divorce from the other spouse but, in a real sense, seeks a divorce from the entire family—that is, from the children as well as from the other spouse. Once that spouse moves out of the house or otherwise separates from the other spouse, that spouse may have little or no contact with the children. Despite whatever legally enforceable financial obligations may exist, the role of parent remains unfulfilled and ultimately becomes extinct.

On the other hand, there are many cases where one or both spouses want a divorce and both are capable, caring, and effective parents. In these situations it is particularly difficult for the spouses or anyone else to determine who shall be the custodial parent and who shall be the noncustodial parent. Although, as noted, many judges disfavor joint custody of children, such arrangements are sometimes allowed. More often, the spouses agree between themselves to maintain a near-joint custody arrangement with or without the court's knowledge or approval.

Often, particularly with adolescent children, the question arises whether to ask the children which parent they would prefer to live with given the inevitability of the divorce and separation of the parents. In these and many related areas, your lawyer may be of assistance or he or she may be able to recommend marriage or family counseling services.

In determining how to advise and assist you in custody, visitation, child support, and other child-related matters, your lawyer must be fully and candidly informed about your relationships and your spouse's relationships with the children—throughout the marriage. If evidence or testimony must be introduced in court on these matters, your lawyer will need to know how to prove your side of the case—for example, who would speak as a witness in your behalf, whether school records or medical records would substantiate certain claims, and so forth.

An experienced divorce lawyer can advise you of the laws regarding your rights and obligations toward your minor children. Also, the lawyer can give you practical advice about the attitudes and standards of the judge who will hear your case and the generally accepted practices that are followed in situations like yours.

Find out about your rights and obligations regarding your spouse.

Depending on the circumstances of your divorce, ask your lawyer the following: What are your rights and obligations regarding the marital home? Which spouse should vacate the home? Or which spouse can be ordered by the court to vacate the marital home? Given the financial ability and needs of each spouse, does one owe the other financial support? How much and for how long? How do child custody and child support affect spousal support? Also, inquire whether one spouse should or can be required to maintain medical, health, and other insurance coverage for the other spouse and the children. If physical or emotional abuse has occurred or may occur, how can one spouse go about protecting himself or herself? Where appropriate, how can immediate measures be taken in court to prevent one spouse from squandering or sequestering property, money, or assets? How is the personal and marital property to be divided? Some or all of these questions may be resolved by agreements worked out by the spouses, either directly or through their attorneys. Where out-of-court agreements cannot be reached, your attorney may have to go to court. If that happens, ask the attorney what orders the court can issue. How long will it take to get to court? What does your attorney need to prove your side of the case? What will you be called upon to say in court? How will the decision of the court be enforced—against your spouse? Against you?

It is sometimes difficult for an attorney to work with his or her client on a divorce case. The attorney may have a good idea of what a fair and workable arrangement would be on various issues. However, one or even both spouses may be unwilling or unable to make decisions that are objectively sensible or practical. One spouse may be so fearful of or intimidated by the other spouse that he or she capitulates to the other spouse. One spouse may be so committed to salvaging the marriage that he or she may refuse even to talk about divorce. Needless to say, agreements cannot be reached when one spouse refuses to agree to anything. Numerous other situations can develop which obstruct or prevent the spouses and their attorneys from working out agreements. Court then becomes the only resort.

In regard to both out-of-court and in-court matters, it is important for you to be completely candid with your attorney. The attorney may know the law very well. The attorney may know the attitudes and quirks of the judge very well. But the attorney must also know you and your spouse. At various points in the proceedings your lawyer will talk with your spouse's attorney or with your spouse directly. Your lawyer must have a realistic understanding of the kind of spouse and person you are and have been and the kind of spouse and person your spouse is and has been. These areas also involve you and your spouse's relationships with the children. Many decisions depend not only on facts such as how much income you and your spouse make but also on your conduct and behavior, past and present, and your spouse's conduct and behavior. Your lawyer must have an accurate and complete picture, particularly where there are major contested areas, such as custody, child support, spousal support, or division of major property interests. Because of this, the attorney will want to know a lot about you and your spouse. Although many persons involved in a divorce want to talk only about their spouse, you must be prepared to talk about yourself so that your attorney can understand you and represent your interests and objectives effectively.

There is, to protect you, an attorney-client privilege. Also, there is a requirement of confidentiality on the attorney's part which protects you from unwarranted disclosures by your attorney (or his or her associates or employees) of matters which you related to the attorney in a confidential manner. These protections are intended to encourage the client to be candid with his or her attorney without fear of having the attorney called to the witness stand or otherwise required to disclose to others personal or secret information imparted to the attorney in a confidential manner.

Review all property and financial matters—including tax matters and your estate plan.

Make sure you provide your attorney with a complete and accurate list of all personal and marital property and financial resources. This means listing your income, employment benefits, real estate, bank accounts, credit, motor vehicles, and insurance policies. It also means an itemization of the contents of the marital home—if there is disagreement as to how the contents are to be divided. It means deciding how the family unit is to manage with one spouse living outside the family abode. The income or incomes which once supported one family in one abode must be apportioned between one spouse and the rest of the family living in one abode while the noncustodial spouse lives apart in a second abode. It means reviewing property and financial matters so that arrangements can be made to change, where necessary, the names on deeds, bank accounts, motor vehicle registrations, titles, and so on.

You should also talk to your lawyer about the tax aspects of the arrangements regarding property and financial matters. If a house must be sold or stock liquidated, there may be capital gains taxes. What about the tax deductibility of child support payments? Who should claim the children for income tax deduction purposes? Also ask about converting from joint income tax returns to individual or head-of-household returns.

Another area you should discuss with your lawyer is what changes to make in your estate plan—primarily your will—in light of the divorce. Upon your death, what property will you own or have the power to dispose of? To whom do you want that property to go and under what terms and conditions? When there are children, especially very young children, this becomes all the more important. If you were to die after the divorce becomes final, your ex-spouse will inherit nothing (except in the unlikely event that you provide otherwise in your will). However, your property may go directly to your children—unless you provide in your will that your property go to someone else, perhaps into a trust for the benefit and upbringing of the children. Or if you remarry, your property may go partly to your children and partly to your new spouse in proportions and in a manner you may not like. This will happen *unless* you provide otherwise in your will. These eventualities can cause needless and costly problems. On the other hand, your lawyer can take the necessary measures to protect the persons whom you want to protect and provide for the persons whom you want to provide for upon your death. Normally, this can be accomplished quite easily by a properly drafted will and, where appropriate, the use of a trust.

Thus, it is important to review all property and financial matters with your lawyer so that the lawyer can bring his or her knowledge of the law and practical experience into operation for your protection and benefit.

Review the legal and related aspects of becoming a single person or single parent.

As noted earlier, many people who go through a divorce think only of their immediate, divorce-related concerns. They concentrate on working out present problems and issues related to the other spouse and the children. In doing so, however, they frequently fail to think about the many legal, economic, and social aspects of becoming a single person or single parent and what the future will bring. By talking about these matters with your lawyer, you can gain valuable legal knowledge and practical insight and make preparations for your post-divorce status. Important changes may have to be made in title to property, your tax situation, your will and estate plan, and many other areas. You can avoid many problems—and save considerable money—by discussing these matters with your attorney during and after the divorce.

Find out how to deal with future changes and problems regarding the terms of the divorce agreement or decree (particularly how to change those terms and how to enforce them).

Many people who go through a divorce do not understand or anticipate the changes and problems which may occur at any point in the future or how to deal with them. What if your financial situation changes for the worse? What if the children need more child support? What if you or your ex-spouse needs more spousal support? What if your financial situation changes significantly for the better—will you be entitled to less child and spousal support? Or will you be obliged to pay more child and spousal support?

On the other hand, what if one of the spouses violates the divorce agreement or decree some time after the divorce becomes final? What if child support is not being paid? What if the custodial parent is not treating the children properly? What if visitation rights are interfered with? These and other violations of the divorce agreement or decree can occur at any time.

During your conversations and conferences with your attorney, find out what legal procedures are available to deal with these changes and violations should they occur. In many instances, changes that should be brought to the attention of the other spouse or the court are ignored because the spouse who could benefit from those changes is ignorant of his or her rights. Similarly, violations of the divorce agreement or court decree sometimes go unrectified because the innocent spouse does not know that remedies are available or how to put them into operation.

For these reasons, be sure to ask the attorney what rights you would have if—during or at any point after the divorce—your or your spouse's circumstances change significantly or if you or your spouse violates the divorce agreement or court decree.

DEALING WITH LAWYERS

In addition to the general points about lawyers in Chapter 1, keep in mind the following advice about dealing with lawyers on a divorce case.

If your divorce is complicated or contested, or if it involves considerable money or property, consider selecting a lawyer who specializes in divorce work. A lawyer who specializes in divorce may cost more than a lawyer who handles a wide variety of legal matters. Nonetheless, if your case is complicated or contested or involves large sums of money or considerable property, you will probably be better off with an attorney who has developed an expertise in divorce cases.

Many people, on the other hand, have routine or largely uncontested divorces. This is usually the case where there are no minor children or, if there are minor children, there is no dispute as to custody of the children, visitation rights, and child support. Also, if there is agreement between the spouses as to how personal and marital property and financial interests are to be divided, most lawyers would consider the case routine. Although many lawyers handle uncontested or routine divorces occasionally, it is usually better to hire an attorney who handles divorce cases on a regular basis. Divorce laws and procedures are continually changing in many states. Moreover, much of divorce practice centers on the attitudes, standards, and quirks of the judge who hears your case at court. A lawyer who handles divorce cases infrequently may not have a complete and up-to-date knowledge of divorce law and procedures and probably would not have much insight into the judge. An attorney who handles divorce cases on a regular basis, on the other hand, is likely to be more knowledgeable of the requirements and idiosyncracies of the judge and more likely to have a thorough grasp of the laws and procedures applicable to your divorce case.

If your divorce is complicated or contested or if it involves large amounts of money and property, you can still save yourself considerable money by contacting three or four or more lawyers and comparing the fees quoted. In a difficult divorce case you may think you will save money by hiring the least expensive lawyer, but if in doing so you hire an inexperienced or poor-quality lawyer, you will be doing yourself a disservice.

Many lawyers charge a flat fee for a divorce case. The flat fee is most common where the divorce is uncomplicated. Before agreeing to a flat fee, have the lawyer explain what services that fee covers and what developments would lead to an additional fee. If the lawyer sets a flat fee because you believe your case will be uncontested and later on your spouse contests several critical areas, the lawyer will have to put additional time and effort into your case and that will require an additional fee. Also, if the lawyer must go to court more than once, each additional appearance will normally cost an additional fee. Find out exactly what you are getting for the flat fee quoted and what additional work would necessitate an additional fee.

Some attorneys, particularly on contested or complicated cases, charge an hourly fee. (See Chapter 1 for a detailed discussion of hourly fees.)

Discuss with the attorney what fee payment arrangements he or she would require or accept. In most jurisdictions, it takes a few or many months to get into court on a divorce; you can use that fact to work out an affordable installment payment schedule.

In negotiating with the lawyer for a lower fee, if your divorce is a routine, uncontested, uncomplicated one, stress those points emphatically. Many divorces involve nothing more than some paperwork on the attorney's part and a brief, perfunctory appearance in court. Such routine work does not justify a high fee. Also, if you would have difficulty paying the fee which the lawyer quotes initially, point that out and ask for a more affordable fee.

Finally, ask the lawyer about the likelihood of having your spouse pay your attorney's fee (or a portion of it). Every state has laws or court rules which authorize the judge to order one spouse to pay part or all of the other spouse's attorney's fee in certain situations. The most common situation in which this is done is where one spouse (usually the wife) has no independent income and does not have access to the family finances. In this situation, the judge may order the other spouse (usually the husband) to pay the first spouse's attorney's fee. If you cannot afford an attorney because you have little or no income of your own and little or no financial reserves, but your spouse does have income or savings, have your lawyer pursue efforts to have your spouse pay your attorney's fee. Sometimes agreements of this nature are worked out between the spouses (more likely between their attorneys), thus avoiding the necessity of having a judge order one spouse to pay the other spouse's attorney's fee.

4
Legal Separation of Spouses

WHAT IS INVOLVED IN A LEGAL SEPARATION OF SPOUSES?

A *legal separation* occurs when a court declares that one spouse has the right to live separate and apart from the other spouse. Many spouses, during marital difficulties, decide to live apart on a more or less voluntary or agreed-to basis. The spouses work out informal arrangements regarding custody of the children, visitation, child support, spousal support, and use or division of property and financial interests. A legal separation, on the other hand, means a hearing in court at which a judge determines whether, under state law, one spouse has the legal right to live separate and apart from the other and what arrangements shall be made or imposed (by the court) regarding custody, visitation, support, and the use or division of property and financial interests.

Two important differences between a legal separation and a divorce should be kept in mind. First, a divorce terminates the marriage. When a divorce becomes final and absolute, the parties are no longer husband and wife; they are single persons (or single parents) with no legal obligations to one another other than those set forth in the divorce settlement or divorce decree. By contrast, a legal separation does not terminate the marriage. The husband and wife continue to be husband and wife despite the fact that a court has declared that one has the right to live separate and apart from the other. After a divorce becomes final and absolute, either ex-spouse can remarry.

Also, after a divorce becomes final and absolute, if either ex-spouse were to die, the surviving ex-spouse would inherit nothing (unless the deceased spouse provided otherwise in his or her will). By contrast, when a court enters a decree establishing a legal separation, the spouses remain married and neither can remarry (without committing bigamy). Also, if either spouse were to die during the legal separation, the surviving spouse would have all normal rights of inheritance.

A second major difference between a divorce and a legal separation involves the reasons why a spouse would seek a divorce instead of a legal separation. Usually, a spouse seeks a divorce because the marriage has deteriorated to a point where that spouse believes it would be best to terminate the marriage. On the other hand, a spouse who seeks a legal separation instead of a divorce often does so only to establish the right to live apart from the other spouse and have certain ground rules (regarding custody, support, etc.) established. The court-recognized right to live apart and the court-approved ground rules serve as a *temporary* (although indefinite) measure; the spouse continues to be married but is relieved of the intolerable situation which exists when the spouses live together.

Again, divorce terminates the marriage, whereas a legal separation is a temporary living-apart arrangement. As an illustration, a spouse who is being abused may feel that the situation cannot be corrected and that only a divorce—a termination of the marriage—would be appropriate. In other instances, however, the abused spouse may feel that a temporary separation would free him or her from the abusive acts of the other spouse and, hopefully, provide some time and opportunities in which to work out their marital problems—without terminating the marriage.

Under the law, one spouse does not normally have the right to live apart from the other. For example, an abused wife may want her husband to leave the house for an indefinite period until he corrects his untoward behavior. The husband, however, is under no legal obligation to do so unless a court orders him to leave. Similarly, if a husband feels that an intolerable situation has developed and wants to leave the home and set up living quarters alone, the wife, in most instances, has the right to continue to live with him, unless a court orders her to live apart from him. In both examples, the spouse who seeks a legal separation does so to receive court approval (and enforcement) of his or her right to live apart. There is usually an expectation or hope that a separation may lead the miscreant spouse to mend his or her ways so that, at some point in the future, both spouses can live together again in harmony.

Many spouses, because of religious or other beliefs, are inalterably opposed to divorce. When a situation develops which makes it intolerable for both spouses to live under the same roof, one spouse may seek a legal separation if acceptable arrangements cannot be worked out by voluntary agreement.

Despite the differences between divorce and legal separation, many of the issues and problems involved in a legal separation are the same as would be involved in a divorce. If there are children, the custody of the children must be determined. Likewise, the visitation of the noncustodial parent must be worked out. Also, child support and spousal support must be determined as well as the use or division of property and financial interests.

It should be pointed out that a high percentage of legal separations end up in divorce. After the legal separation has been established, one or even both spouses may conclude that a reconciliation is impossible or undesirable. One or both may subsequently file for divorce. On the other hand, if, during the legal separation, both spouses believe they have worked out their difficulties, they can move back together and request that the court dissolve the legal separation decree.

WHY DO YOU NEED TO CONSULT A LAWYER?

A court will grant a legal separation if the requesting spouse proves that certain conditions or "grounds" exist which, under the law of that state, permit the judge to enter a decree of legal separation. A lawyer can explain what grounds for legal separation are recognized by the laws of your state. In addition, many people who are thinking about a legal separation don't understand the differences between a legal separation and a divorce. A lawyer can explain those matters as well.

A lawyer's advice is also needed on important and difficult questions such as child custody, visitation, child support, spousal support, use or division of marital property and financial interests, and many other areas. As with a divorce, a legal separation involves rearranging many basic family patterns and circumstances. An experienced lawyer will be able to guide you through most of these problem areas with sound legal and practical advice.

It is also important to consult a lawyer to determine what legal recourse and protection you may have to seek in addition to the legal separation. In many situations physical harm or abuse is present or threatened. A lawyer can advise you as to what legal measures you can take to protect yourself and, if necessary, the children.

An attorney may be needed to contact your spouse or your spouse's attorney to work out as many aspects of the separation as possible by mutual agreement or compromise. Since many people who seek a legal separation (instead of a divorce) do so to save the marriage, it can be very helpful to have your lawyer act as a conciliator. Moreover, in many states, although the judge can decide such matters as child custody and child and spousal support, the judge cannot divide real estate or personal property. That is because the spouses remain married during a legal separation; their real estate and personal property remain joint property. A lawyer can be helpful in working with your spouse or your spouse's attorney to arrive at a voluntary—but legally binding—agreement regarding real estate, personal property, and financial matters.

Another reason for having a lawyer handle your legal separation is that most legal separations involve a developing, changing situation. What you want to do may change over time or in light of the reactions of your spouse and the effect the legal separation has on you, your spouse, the children, and others. At various points you may want or need additional legal assistance. If your spouse will not vacate the marital home peaceably, you may have to go to court to get a court order against him or her. If your spouse does not pay the required amount of spousal support or child support or otherwise violates the terms of the separation agreement or decree, you may have to resort to further legal recourse. In these and other situations, you will need a lawyer's advice and assistance.

HOW TO THINK ABOUT LEGAL AND RELATED ASPECTS

The following sections discuss a number of important legal and related matters you should think about and questions you should ask your attorney.

Consult a lawyer when you or your spouse decides to seek a legal separation.

It is important to consult a lawyer soon after you determine that a separation is necessary or your spouse has decided to do so. In some circumstances, an informal separation may be worked out. In other circumstances, only a court-ordered separation is possible. In either case, a lawyer can explain the legal and practical aspects of a separation. An experienced lawyer can provide insight into the pros and cons of an informal separation as opposed to a formal, court-ordered separation in light of your circumstances, needs, and objectives.

Find out about the grounds for a legal separation, the procedures and timetables.

Your lawyer can explain what a legal separation will involve given your situation. There are various grounds for a legal separation, one of which must be proven before a judge can grant a legal separation. For example, despite the fact that most states recognize "no-fault" (or irretrievable breakdown) as grounds for a divorce, no-fault is not recognized as a ground for a legal separation. The lawyer can explain what grounds would apply to your circumstances and what must be shown to establish those grounds. The lawyer can also explain what papers must be filed in court, what the court hearing will be like, how long these procedures will take, and related matters.

A brief review of the gounds for legal separation recognized by most states follows:

Cruelty or Cruel and Abusive Treatment Most states will grant a legal separation if one spouse shows that the other spouse engaged in acts of physical or mental cruelty. In many states, the court will grant a legal separation even if there has been no actual harm or abuse but only threats of harm or abuse—as long as the spouse to whom the threats are directed is in real fear that the threats will be carried out. Also, the cruelty or cruel and abusive treatment does not have to be physical, nor does it have to be manifested by bruises, scars, and so on. Mental or emotional anguish or mistreatment are recognized by many states as justifying a legal separation.

Abandonment or Desertion If one spouse leaves, leaves with the intent of not returning, and leaves against the wishes of the other spouse, the other spouse may seek a legal separation. Although the court cannot order the absent spouse to return, the court can determine the absent spouse's monetary and other obligations to the abandoned or deserted spouse and children.

Adultery Adultery is sexual intercourse between a spouse and any person other than the other spouse.

Habitual Intoxication by Drugs or Alcohol If one spouse is habitually intoxicated by the voluntary use of drugs or alcohol, the other spouse may seek a legal separation.

Insanity, Nonsupport, Imprisonment, Others Several states will grant a legal separation to a spouse who demonstrates that the other spouse is insane, that the husband has utterly failed to provide food, clothing, and shelter for the wife, or that the other spouse has been sentenced to prison for a period of years. Other grounds may also be available in your state.

It is important to determine whether there are more than one ground on which you may file for a legal separation. The evidence, procedures, time, and costs may vary. Have your lawyer review the pros and cons of each ground for which you qualify.

Explain your situation fully to the lawyer. This is especially necessary if physical harm or abuse is present or threatened. In addition to filing for a legal separation, the lawyer may have to seek a court order protecting you and the rest of the family from assault or abuse from your spouse. In some cases, immediate measures must be taken in court to prevent a spouse from squandering or sequestering property or financial assets.

Also discuss with the lawyer the present posture of your marriage and what your objectives are. The lawyer will want to know what efforts you are willing to make and what measures you want the lawyer to take to minimize the discordant aspects of the separation and maximize the opportunities for reconciliation and reunification. In this area, an experienced lawyer may be able to advise you regarding marriage, family, and other counseling services.

Find out about your rights and obligations regarding minor children.

If the parents are going to separate, either voluntarily or as a result of a court order, the custody of the children must be determined.

The visitation rights of the noncustodial parent must also be resolved, and the amount and nature of child support must be worked out. Depending on the ages of the children, their views and desires should be elicited. An experienced lawyer can advise you of your rights and obligations regarding the minor children given the circumstances of your legal separation.

Where there are minor children, it is particularly important to make it clear to the attorney what you hope to accomplish by a legal separation. If you are seeking a legal separation mainly to remove yourself—and the children—from a difficult or dangerous situation but with the hope and expectation of working things out and returning to connubial life with your spouse, make this clear to the attorney. If, on the other hand, you are seeking a legal separation because you do not want to live with your spouse ever again but you don't believe in divorce, make that clear to the lawyer. How temporary or permanent the separation is to be will have a great effect on the children and will determine how final and far-reaching the decisions regarding the children should be.

Find out about your rights and obligations regarding your spouse.

If there is going to be a separation, it must be determined which spouse will vacate the marital home. If one spouse is financially dependent on the other, spousal support must be worked out. There will also be many questions and issues regarding personal property and financial matters. As noted, if physical abuse or harm has occurred, you must take steps to protect yourself and the rest of your family. Some of these matters may be worked out between the spouses in a mutually acceptable manner. Those issues or problems that cannot be worked out may have to be presented to a judge. In either case, it is important to maintain the right perspective during the negotiations or court hearing. If the separation is to be temporary and is intended to ease or avoid a difficult but resolvable problem in the marriage, that should be kept in mind. On the other hand, if the separation is to be permanent or if there is little hope for a reconciliation, it is important for you to be completely candid with your attorney. The attorney can learn about the family property, family income, which spouse wants what items of personal property, and other matters. But the attorney also needs to know what your expectations and objectives are. What is it you want to accomplish? Given the widely divergent reasons why people seek a legal separation, it is important to make your expectations and objectives clear to the attorney and to inform the attorney of changes in your expectations or objectives as time passes and you reassess your situation and needs. It may be necessary for you to disclose to your attorney many matters regarding your marriage, your relationship with your spouse and the children, and your spouse's relationship with the children. The attorney will need to know about those matters so that he or she can effectively represent your interests and effectively deal with your spouse and your spouse's attorney.

Find out how to deal with future changes and problems regarding the terms of the separation agreement or decree (particularly how to change those terms and how to enforce them).

Needless to say, a separation of spouses involves a developing, changing interpersonal relationship. Problems that were serious at one point may be resolved; later, other problems may arise. Terms or agreements made in light of one set of circumstances may become ineffective or inappropriate if circumstances change significantly. Also, one or both spouses may violate those terms and agreements. Because of these possibilities, it is important to find out how to deal with future developments. Can you renegotiate certain terms or conditions of the separation if circumstances change? If your spouse does not agree to the changes you want to make, can you go back into court and ask the judge to make those changes? If you or your spouse violates the terms and conditions of the separation, what can you do? What can be done to you? Have your attorney explain these procedures so that you will know what your rights and liabilities are and so that you will know how to handle problems or changes that may occur in the future. Of course, if you expect the separation to be of long duration, it is all the more important to anticipate future changes in circumstances or problems and deal with them, to the extent possible, in the separation agreement or decree. If that is impossible or impractical, have the lawyer explain how you can renegotiate the separation agreement or how you can go back into court later to have the separation decree modified.

DEALING WITH LAWYERS

In addition to the general points about lawyers in Chapter 1, keep in mind the following advice about dealing with lawyers on a legal separation case.

Legal separations are much rarer than divorces. For this reason, you should try to select an attorney who has had experience with legal separations. Contact a number of attorneys and ask each how many legal separation cases he or she has handled and how recently. If you cannot find an attorney with notable experience in legal separations, find an attorney with experience in divorce cases—but make it clear that you want a legal separation and not a divorce. Some attorneys try to talk clients out of a legal separation and into a divorce. This can happen when the client isn't sure which route to follow. If you are unsure, have the attorney explain the pros and cons of a legal separation as opposed to a divorce, then take some time to make up your mind.

In talking with the lawyer, try to anticipate how complicated or contested your legal separation will be. If your spouse is agreeable to a separation and the two of you can work out such matters as custody, spousal support, property, and money matters, yours will be a much easier case for the attorney than if you anticipate a bitter and protracted contest from your spouse on several major areas. The more complicated or contested your legal separation will be, the more careful you should be to hire an attorney with experience, particularly trial experience.

Whether your legal separation case is a simple, uncontested one or a complicated, contested matter, you will probably find a wide disparity in the fees quoted by the attorneys you contact. Often it is difficult for an attorney to gauge what will be involved in a legal separation—unless it is an uncomplicated and uncontested one. For example, some legal separations require one court appearance to have a spouse ordered out of the marital home or to obtain an order protecting one spouse from abuse by the other and a second court hearing on the grounds for the separation and other matters. Needless to say, the more court appearances your case involves, the more expensive the attorney's fee.

Generally speaking, if your legal separation is uncomplicated and uncontested, you will usually be safe in hiring a less expensive lawyer—as long as the lawyer you hire has ample experience.

If, on the other hand, your legal separation involves major contested areas, you can still save a great deal of money by contacting a number of lawyers and then hiring the lawyer who offers the best combination of experience and price.

Attorneys, on legal separation cases, may charge a flat fee or an hourly fee. (See Chapter 1 for a detailed discussion of those types of fees.)

If your case is uncontested and uncomplicated, you should not pay a lawyer a lot of money to simply put the basic terms on paper, file the papers in court, and then appear with you in court for a brief, perfunctory hearing. If the fee initially quoted by the lawyer strikes you as being a lot of money, emphasize how uncontested and uncomplicated your case is, and counter with a lower fee. In addition, if you would have difficulty paying the fee quoted initially by the lawyer, point that out and ask for a lower fee.

If you do not have income of your own and do not have financial reserves, have your attorney investigate the procedures for having your spouse pay part or all of your attorney's fee. In most states there are statutes or court rules which authorize a judge to order one spouse to pay the other spouse's attorney's fee.

5
Annulment of Marriage

WHAT IS AN ANNULMENT?

An *annulment* is a declaration by a court that, due to some disability or defect at the time of the marriage ceremony, a valid marriage did not occur and a valid marriage relationship does not exist between the man and woman.

By contrast, a divorce requires that a valid marriage took place. Similarly, a legal separation requires that a valid marriage took place. A divorce decree terminates a valid marriage. During a legal separation, the spouses continue to be married; the legal separation provides court approval and protection of the right of one spouse to live separate and apart from the other spouse.

The purpose of an annulment, on the other hand, is to legally establish that no valid marriage took place and that therefore no valid marital relationship exists. If that be so, the man and woman have no marital rights or obligations toward one another. A divorce is not needed to sever their marital relationship since they were not legally married in the first place.

It should be pointed out that many religious organizations and groups grant an annulment of a marriage if specific conditions are met. This chapter, however, deals only with legal annulments obtained through a court. A court can only declare the civil aspect of the marriage to be void and invalid. This chapter does not discuss annulments granted by religious organizations or groups regarding the religious aspects of a marriage.

Several conditions must be met for a valid marriage to occur in the eyes of the law. If one or more of those conditions are not met, one or both of the parties to the marriage may seek an annulment. The most common grounds for annulment are discussed below.

WHY DO YOU NEED TO CONSULT A LAWYER?

The validity of a marriage is a legal question. If one person wants to officially terminate what is thought to be an invalid marriage, a lawyer's advice is usually necessary to determine whether grounds for an annulment exist and how to go about having the marriage declared invalid. (Of course, if the marriage is a valid one, a divorce would be the appropriate proceeding to terminate the marriage.) It is also important to seek a lawyer's advice if you aren't sure whether an annulment or a divorce would be the correct legal proceeding in your situation.

There are many popular misconceptions regarding annulment. Generally, the fact that a husband and wife never sexually consummated the marriage is not, in and of itself, grounds for an annulment. Many people mistakenly believe it is. Also, many people confuse the requirements for a religious annulment with the requirements for a civil (or legal) annulment. A lawyer can explain the procedures and consequences involved in a civil or legal annulment. The lawyer may also be able to find out how you can obtain an annulment from the proper authorities of the religious organization to which you belong.

A lawyer's advice will also be needed to resolve important matters such as the legitimacy of children born to the couple, the division of property and financial interests, and other areas that may present difficult legal and practical problems. If there are children born to the couple, there may be complex legal questions as to the rights and obligations of the father toward those children. An annulment is granted if it is shown that the marriage was invalid. An invalid marriage, however, may mean that the children are illegitimate. Illegitimacy is the condition of being born out of lawful wedlock. In many states, however, special statutes have been enacted which declare that the children of an annulled marriage shall not be considered illegitimate.

Another important area that must be resolved involves the rights of the man and woman and their obligations to each other. If the man and woman lived together for a considerable length of time, there may be questions and problems regarding what financial obligations one may have toward the other. Similar questions and problems may arise regarding how the property and financial interests which were shared by the man and woman are to be divided.

An experienced lawyer will be familiar with the legal principles which apply to those matters. Just as importantly, an experienced lawyer will know what customary and accepted practices are used to resolve problems.

HOW TO THINK ABOUT LEGAL AND RELATED ASPECTS

The following sections discuss important aspects of obtaining an annulment and dealing with lawyers.

Consult a lawyer to determine whether you qualify for an annulment.

Doubts about the validity of your marriage can cause serious problems and anxieties. A lawyer can review and investigate the facts and circumstances of your marriage and determine, if you wish to terminate the relationship, whether an annulment would be appropriate—and what the consequences of an annulment would be—or whether a divorce would be the appropriate procedure for terminating the marriage.

An annulment is not a commonplace proceeding. On the other hand, misconceptions and misunderstandings about annulment are commonplace. The best way to handle the situation is to consult an experienced lawyer.

Find out about the grounds for annulment and the procedures and timetables involved.

The laws governing the grounds for annulment vary from state to state. Therefore, you must consult an attorney who is familiar with the laws of your state.

Generally, a valid marriage requires that both parties to the marriage consent to the marriage freely and voluntarily, that each party have attained a specific age, that neither party be still married to someone else, and that certain physical and mental disabilities not be present. If any of these preconditions to a valid marriage is absent, an annulment of the marriage may be obtained.

The following paragraphs review the most common grounds for annulment.

One Party Still Married to Someone Else at the Time of the Wedding Ceremony If either the man or the woman is legally married to another person at the time of the marriage ceremony, that marriage can be annulled. Normally, the annulment will be granted even if both people knew that one of them was already married at the time of their wedding. In some states, it is not necessary to go to court to have a marriage annulled if, at the time of the marriage ceremony, one of the parties was still legally married to another person. In those states, the second marriage is considered void and no court proceeding is necessary. Nonetheless, a lawyer's advice should be sought in that situation.

It is not uncommon that one person seeks a divorce from one spouse and then marries a second spouse before the divorce from the first spouse has become final. Most states have waiting periods of six months, one year, or longer after the divorce hearing in court before the divorce becomes final and absolute. If a person marries before the waiting period expires and the divorce becomes final, he or she has entered into a voidable marriage. However, if the parties continue to live as husband and wife after the divorce becomes final and absolute, their marriage will generally be regarded as valid from that time on and not annullable.

Marriage Entered Into without the Intent that It Be Binding—Mock Marriage, Jest Marriage Most states will grant an annulment of a marriage if either or both parties show that one or both of them did not seriously intend that the marriage be valid and binding. Mock marriage ceremonies do occur. Or one or both parties may go through the marriage ceremony out of levity or in jest. This does not mean that courts will grant an annulment if either or both parties pretend or fabricate that they were not serious about getting married at the wedding ceremony. Before the court will grant an annulment, the judge must be convinced that either or both of the parties did not regard the marriage ceremony as binding.

One or Both Partites Under Age at the Time of the Marriage Ceremony Each state has laws which set minimum ages at which a man and a woman may enter into a valid marriage. Actually, most states have two sets of minimum ages—one age at which the man or woman does not need parental consent and another (lower) age at which the man or woman must have parental consent. If either or both of the parties are under the minimum legal age for marriage at the time of the marriage ceremony, that marriage can be annulled. However, if the parties remain as husband and wife after they have attained the minimum age for marriage, the court may refuse to grant an annulment.

Marriage Involving an Incestuous Relationship A man and woman who are related by blood and who are first cousins or closer are prohibited from marrying one another by the laws of almost every state. Generally, brothers and sisters cannot marry. Nor can father and daughter, mother and son, uncle and niece, aunt and nephew, or first cousin and first cousin. A marriage between such close blood relatives can be annulled.

Marriage Induced by Fraud or Deceit If a person enters into a marriage having relied on what turns out to be a serious fraud or deception and that fraud or deception pertains to a vital or essential aspect of the marriage, an annulment of such a marriage may be granted. For an annulment to be granted, however, the fraudulent or deceitful act or representation must be serious. The fraud or deceit must have induced one of the parties to enter the marriage. Also, the fraud or deceit must have occurred at or before the marriage ceremony—not after it. Some courts will refuse to grant an annulment for fraud or deceit where the party subjected to the fraud or deceit could have learned the truth by taking reasonable steps or making reasonable inquiries.

Typical examples of the kinds of fraud or deceit or concealment which may justify an annulment are those which relate to important matters that affect the health or well-being of the parties or their offspring. For instance, in some states, if you marry a person who conceals the fact that he or she has a congenital or hereditary infirmity or illness of a serious nature, you may be entitled to an annulment.

Another instance in which courts will grant annulments is where one party fails to participate in a separate religious marriage ceremony as promised or where one party fails to convert to a particular religion as promised.

Many states have granted annulments where it was shown that one party failed to disclose an intention not to have children. The same is true where one party failed to disclose an intention never to have sexual intercourse with his or her spouse.

On the other hand, many courts have denied annulments where the alleged fraud or deceit related only to birth status, family, or reputation.

Also, in some states an annulment may not be granted despite the fact that fraud or deceit occurred at the time the marriage was entered into if the marriage has been sexually consummated and the parties have assumed the rights and obligations of married persons.

Marriage Induced by Duress A valid marriage is one that is entered into freely and voluntarily. If a marriage was entered into as a result of duress or coercion, the marriage can be annuled. However, if the party subjected to the duress or coercion fails to end the marriage by means of annulment within a reasonable time after the duress or coercion has been removed, an annulment may be denied.

The duress or coercion must have induced the marriage and it must have so overcome the person's free will that he or she would not have entered into the marriage were it not for the duress or coercion.

Typically, such duress or coercion takes the form of threats of physical violence or abuse if the person does not go through with the marriage.

Mental Incapacity For a marriage to be valid, both parties must have sufficient mental capacity to understand the purpose and meaning of marriage and sufficient mental capacity to consent to marriage. If either party lacks such mental capacity, the marriage may be annulled.

Physical Incapacity, Defect, or Infirmity A physical incapacity or disease which prevents sexual consummation of the marriage may be grounds for an annulment. For example, impotency is a ground for annulment (but not sterility or barrenness). Whether other physical incapacities, defects, or infirmities are grounds for annulment depends on each state's statutes and court decisions. Concealment of a serious physical incapacity or infirmity (such as venereal disease) may constitute grounds for annulment on the basis of fraud or deceit.

A Note on Ratification, Waiver, and Antenuptial Knowledge An annulment may be denied for a number of reasons. One such reason is called *ratification*. If the defect in the marriage is cured or removed and the parties remain as husband and wife, they are said to have ratified the marriage, thereby making it valid. For example, if a marriage takes place before the husband's divorce from his first wife is final, the marriage is annullable. However, if the husband and the second wife continue to live as married persons after the husband's divorce from his first wife becomes final, the second marriage may no longer be annullable.

Another reason for denying an annulment is called *waiver*. As an example, if a marriage was induced by fraud or deceit but the parties continue to live as husband and wife after the defrauded or deceived party learns the truth, he or she may be deemed to have waived that ground for annulment.

A third reason for denying an annulment is called *antenuptial knowledge*. If a person enters into a marriage with knowledge of a defect or disability that would make the marriage invalid, he or she may be prevented from raising that defect or disability in an annulment proceeding. For example, if a man marries a woman whom he knows has not attained the legal age for marriage, he may be prevented from later trying to annul the marriage on that ground because he had antenuptial (before-marriage) knowledge of that fact. That is, he was aware of it before the marriage but went ahead anyway.

A Note on Legal Procedures and Timetables Once you and your attorney have identified the specific ground on which you will ask the court for an annulment, find out from the attorney what legal procedures are involved. What proof or documentation or testimony will be needed to establish your case? What will the hearing at court be like? If the court does grant the annulment, what must be done to straighten out such matters as the legitimacy of the children, support for the children, the division of property and financial interests?

Also find out about the timetables involved. How long will it take to get into court? Will the annulment become effective the day you go to court or is there an interim period before the annulment becomes effective?

Find out about your rights and obligations regarding children.

Children born of parents whose marriage is annulled may be considered illegitimate, although most states have statutes which protect the legitimacy of children born of an annulled marriage. Naturally, it is important to determine how to handle that aspect of the annulment. The possible effects of an annulment on the legitimacy of the children are so controversial and upsetting that many persons who were invalidly married seek a divorce rather than an annulment. By seeking a divorce you are not questioning the validity of the marriage—even though you may suspect or know that the marriage was not valid. A divorce assumes that the marriage was valid and therefore that the children are legitimate. An annulment means that the marriage was invalid and therefore the children were not born of lawful wedlock. Be sure to have your lawyer investigate the legitimacy of children born of an annulled marriage under your state's current laws.

Many other important matters concerning the children must also be worked out. There may be financial obligations imposed on one parent to support the children. In these and related matters, the advice and assistance of an experienced attorney will be needed.

Find out about your rights and obligations regarding the other party to the marriage.

Although an annulment means that the man and woman were never legally husband and wife, certain rights and obligations may arise simply because they (or at least one of them) thought they were validly married. This is especially true if the man and woman lived together as husband and wife for a length of time before the annulment. For example, some unmarried couples who lived together and then separated are involved in lawsuits to determine whether one party owes the other party financial support. This is analogous to an annulment. If one party was economically dependent on the other party while they lived together as husband and wife, the court may find an enforceable obligation on the part of the party who has income to support the other party until he or she regains economic independence.

Review all property and financial matters.

When an annulment is granted, it must be determined how the property of the man and woman is to be divided and how their financial interests should be separated. The manner in which these matters are resolved depends largely on the facts of the purported marriage. For example, if there are children, the court may favor granting the custodial parent as much property and financial security as possible for the benefit of the children. On the other hand, if there are no children and the man and woman lived together for only a short time, the court may order that each party retain whatever he or she brought into the relationship and split joint or mutual property on a fifty-fifty basis. Again, an experienced attorney can provide guidance and assistance in this area.

DEALING WITH LAWYERS

In addition to the general points about lawyers in Chapter 1, you should keep in mind the following advice about dealing with lawyers on an annulment case.

As pointed out earlier, annulments are considerably more uncommon than divorces or even legal separations. Because of this, it is important to make sure you hire an attorney who has experience with annulments or at least experience in the general area of marriage law. If you cannot find an attorney who has handled even one annulment recently, your best approach is to hire an attorney with experience in divorce, legal separation, and other matters which involve marriage law.

Since annulments are relatively uncommon, most attorneys do

not have a standard fee for an annulment case. The attorney would normally have to spend some time with you to determine what legal procedures have to be followed and how much work will be involved. After reviewing those matters, the attorney should be able to quote a flat fee or an hourly fee. (See Chapter 1 for a detailed discussion of those types of fees.)

If you have limited financial resources, ask the attorney to find out whether there is a procedure by which your purported spouse can be ordered to pay your attorney's fee. If you participated in the wedding ceremony and the marriage in good faith but your purported spouse engaged in deception, fraud, duress, or coercion, some courts will order your spouse to pay your attorney's fee. Have your attorney investigate those possibilities.

6
Wills and Estate Planning

WHAT IS A WILL?

A *will* is a written document containing your instructions as to what is to happen to your property and assets after you die. If you have minor children, your will should instruct who shall be guardians for your children. Also, you may want instructions placing some of your property or assets in a trust for the benefit of a particular person or persons rather than having the property or assets (or their cash value) go directly to those persons.

A will takes effect when a person dies. Until then, you can change any or all of the provisions in your will. Also, a will applies only to the property you own at the time of your death.

In sum, a will is a set of instructions which go into effect when you die; those instructions delineate how and to whom you want your property distributed after your death.

WHO NEEDS A WILL AND WHY?

Since a will directs what happens to a person's property after that person dies, anyone who owns property or has money should have a will. Also, because a will can be used by parents to name guardians for their minor children (should both parents die before all the children reach adulthood), every parent should have a will.

If a person dies without a will, that person is said to have died "intestate." (A person who dies with a will is said to have died "testate.") If you die without a will, what happens to your property will be dictated by state laws called laws of descent and distribution. In many states, those laws provide that one-third or one-half of a deceased person's property goes to his or her surviving spouse (if there is one) and the other one-half or two-thirds to his or her surviving children (if there are any). By contrast, most married couples want all the property of either of them to go to the surviving spouse. There is little sense in having a large portion of one spouse's assets or property go directly to the children, who may be very young at the time. Nonetheless, that is what the laws of descent and distribution provide in most states.

Where there is no surviving spouse and no surviving children, and you do not have a will, your property may go entirely to your surviving parents. Where there are no surviving parents, your property may be divided equally between your surviving brothers and sisters. If you have no surviving brothers or sisters, your property will probably go, in equal shares, to aunts and uncles or cousins or even more distant blood relatives.

The laws of descent and distribution follow blood lines (with the exception of the surviving spouse) and move from one level of blood relations to the next in a rigid, everyone-is-equal basis. Your favorite relatives, closest friends, special charities, and others may receive nothing if you die without a will that mentions them. That is because the laws of descent and distribution follow rigid, level-by-level categories based strictly on blood relationships. In addition, those laws treat persons who have the same blood relationship to you as equals. For example, suppose you have one son in his 30s who is successful in business. Your other son, however, may be a teenager with a handicap or other special problems. If you do not have a will that specifies how much of your property goes to each son and under what conditions, the laws of descent and distribution will treat your sons equally; the well-off son will inherit just as much as the needy son.

The only way to avoid having your property controlled by the laws of descent and distribution is to have a will. The contrast between having a will and not having one is immense. A will allows you to leave whatever you want to whomever you want under whatever conditions you want (with only a few limitations and exceptions). If you don't have a will, your property will go according to old laws that are likely to be quite contrary to your objectives and intentions regarding who you want to provide for and how.

You owe it to yourself and to the people you want your property to go to upon your death to have a will.

WHY DO YOU NEED A LAWYER TO DRAFT YOUR WILL?

Every state has laws which establish specific requirements and formalities which must be met for a will to be valid and effective. For example, most states require that the signature of the person making the will be witnessed by two other persons. The two witnesses serve as observers. (The witnesses need not know the contents of the will.) They bear witness that the signature on the will is that of the person making the will and that the maker of the will acknowledged the document to be his or her will. The witnesses can be called upon in the future to testify that the person who made the will was of sound mind at the time and not under duress or coercion in signing the will. Notably, a witness cannot receive anything under the will. Nor can a witness be married to someone who receives anything under the will. These and other requirements are intended to ensure that the witnesses are objective and do not have a self-serving interest in the will.

There are numerous other requirements and formalities regarding wills. These requirements and formalities differ from state to state. They may also be changed from time to time by the legislature or courts of a state. Because of this, it is necessary to consult a lawyer and have him or her draft a will for you to make sure it complies with all the legal requisites for a valid and effective will.

The money you pay a lawyer to draft your will for you, in almost every case, will be worth the expense and problems you and others will avoid regarding the disposition of your property by having a properly drafted will.

YOUR WILL AS A KEY TO ESTATE PLANNING

The word *estate* refers to your worldly possessions—your real property (land and buildings), personal property, money, investments, and so on. Interestingly, most people give considerable thought to producing income and acquiring property during their lifetime but devote relatively little thought to what should happen to their money and property after they die. The phrase *estate planning* is a term used to describe a thoughtful and thorough effort to make yourself aware of all the property you own or have an interest in—your estate—and to plan how that estate is to be managed while you are alive and distributed after you die.

A will is one part of your entire estate plan. A will, after all, only governs property you own exclusively at the time of your death. If, for instance, you own property jointly with another person, that jointly owned property may go automatically to the other person upon your death. A common example is a home owned jointly by a husband and wife. Upon the death of one, the property automatically becomes that of the survivor; the deceased spouse cannot direct otherwise in his or her will.

Also, your will only governs property you own at the time of your death. If you transfer property to another person before you die, that property will not be affected by your will. For example, a well-to-do person might give money or other assets to his adult children or others while he or she is still living to avoid estate taxes and so that the adult children or others can use the money or assets immediately.

Use the drafting of your will as an opportunity to review your entire estate. Plan how to manage your property during the rest of your lifetime. A properly drafted will can then ensure that your property will be distributed, after your death, the way you want it to be distributed.

A Note on Death Arrangements During the drafting of your will, it is useful to think about and make arrangements regarding various aspects of your death. For the sake of others as well as one's own peace of mind, you should make known your desires regarding those ceremonies and activities that necessarily accompany death.

Some people put in their will provisions regarding a wake, religious observations and ceremonies, funeral services, burial or cremation, and other related activities. It should be kept in mind, however, as a practical matter, that unexpected circumstances and the effects of bereavement may result in several days or even weeks passing before your will is located and filed in court so that an executor (the person who manages your estate after your death) can begin to follow the instructions in your will. For these and other reasons, you should make known the specifics you desire along those lines to those family members or others who will have charge of the immediate and subsequent arrangements relating to your death.

In addition to religious, ceremonial, and burial or cremation arrangements, you may want to donate usable organs or other bodily parts to medical or scientific authorities. These are often referred to as anatomical gifts. Plans in that regard should be made by having your lawyer contact the appropriate medical or other authorities and draft the necessary papers.

A Note on Taxes One of the most important goals of good estate planning is to manage your estate while you are alive and provide for the distribution of your estate after your death so as to preserve as much of your assets as possible. A crucial element in achieving that goal, particularly for well-to-do persons, is to be aware of and plan for the tax consequences of your death. Estate and inheritance taxes can be avoided in many cases and minimized in all cases by good estate planning.

Estate taxes are imposed by each state (except Nevada) and by the federal government on the property you own or have an interest in at the time of your death. Although some state estate tax schedules start as low as $20,000, usually a person must have an estate of $100,000 or $150,000 or more before the state estate taxes become considerable. Regarding federal estate taxes, from 1981 on the tax is zero unless the value of the estate is over $175,000, and in many cases a person can leave an estate of up to $250,000 without paying sizable federal estate taxes.

Inheritance taxes, which are distinct from estate taxes, are taxes on the value of the money or property received by the persons to whom your money and property goes after your death. Many people direct in their will that inheritance taxes due on the money and property that passes under the will are to be paid out of the general assets in the estate so that the persons who receive that money and property receive them with the inheritance taxes already paid by the estate. You should also be aware that inheritance tax rates are based not only on the value of the property or money bequeathed but also on the relationship to you of the person who receives that property or money. In those states that have inheritance taxes, the tax rate is higher on property or money you bequeath to a friend or a distant relative than on property or money bequeathed to your child or a brother or sister.

By consulting a lawyer, you can learn how estate taxes and inheritance taxes will affect your estate and the people to whom you want to leave your property. Additional advice may be needed from a tax specialist. Many lawyers who draft wills are not as qualified to give tax advice as they are to give advice regarding the legal formalities and requirements of wills and estate plans. If you have a large estate, tax planning will be an important part of your total estate plan. It will be worthwhile to consult a tax expert as well as a lawyer.

A Note on Debts Many people mistakenly believe that death wipes out a person's debts. You may hear that creditors cannot be paid out of the money or assets in a person's estate after that person dies. That is not true.

In fact, debts owed by the deceased person (to those creditors who file proper claims against the estate) are given a priority. Other priority items are taxes owed by the estate, funeral expenses, and the costs of administering the deceased person's estate (which include the attorney's fee). Priority items must be paid even if doing so would diminish the amount of money or property that is supposed to go to the persons named in the will.

Also, suppose you own property which is subject to a debt. In your will you leave that property to a particular person but without providing that the debt is to be paid out of the other assets in your estate. The person who inherits that property also inherits that debt. For example, if you leave your house to your son and daughter but say nothing about paying off the mortgage with other assets in your estate, your son and daughter will inherit the house subject to the mortgage. They may have to pay off the mortgage or, at least, assume the payments or refinance the house.

HOW TO THINK ABOUT LEGAL AND RELATED ASPECTS

Every will requires careful thought and planning.

No matter how much or how little property or money you may have, it is all you have. The time and thought you put into your will has a direct bearing on how well and how wisely you provide for the persons you want your property and money to go to after your death.

Name guardians for your minor children.

If you have minor children, decide who should be the legal guardians of your children in the event you and your spouse die before some or all of the children reach adulthood. If you do not name guardians for your children in your will, there may be confusion and even conflict if you and your spouse die without making it known who should take care of and have custody of your children. Also, you may want to specify in the will that the guardians will have the right to use some or most of your property for the benefit of your children until the children reach a certain age, at which time the property (or its cash value) will go directly to them.

Of course, you should talk to the person or persons you want to name as guardians. Make sure they would be willing to serve as guardians and understand what that responsibility entails. (See Chapter 10.)

List all the property you own or have an ownership interest in.

To develop a thorough estate plan, you must be aware of what is in your estate; your estate includes everything you own or have an ownership interest in. Make a detailed list of each asset or property under your ownership or control. Bring the list to the lawyer's office. Doing so will make it easier for the lawyer to help you plan your estate intelligently.

Although the following list may seem imposing, keep in mind that the more thoroughly you account for your property and assets, the better your estate plan will be. Include on your list the following:

- real estate—where located, owned individually or with others, original cost, present market value
- buildings—where located, owned individually or with others, what type of building, original cost, present market value, any rental income, any debts thereon
- motor vehicles—include automobiles, trucks, trailers, campers, etc.; make, model and year; owned individually or with others, present market value; any debt thereon
- other personal property—contents of home or apartment, etc.; especially items of unique or unusual value such as collections, antiques, jewelry, furs, art work, etc.; estimate present market value; list any amounts owed on the personal property
- your job income—name of employer, type of work, wage or salary, bonuses, commissions, etc.
- job-related assets—pension plan, annuity plan, profit-sharing plan, stock bonus plan, deferred compensation plan, etc.
- savings and other bank accounts—name of bank, present balance in each account, in whose names
- other investments and money owed to you—stocks, bonds, other securities, personal notes or debts owed to you
- any other income or benefits—veterans benefits, Social Security payments, income from any source other than your regular employment
- insurance—type, company and agent, amounts, who are beneficiaries
- business interests—if you own a business or if you have a share in a business or partnership
- outstanding debts and liabilities or other obligations—mortgage, loans, list any property used as security or collateral.

Make arrangements regarding property not controlled by your will.

Some property is not subject to the instructions in your will. For example, your life insurance is a contract between you and the insurance company which provides that upon your death the insurance company will pay a certain amount to a certain person or persons. The insurance policy (the contract) governs that arrangement, not your will. (You can, however, make your life insurance payable to your estate. Or if the beneficiary named in your policy dies before you do, the insurance money will go to your estate. Insurance money that becomes part of your estate will be distributed according to the instructions in your will.)

Veterans and Social Security death benefits and other government payments are controlled by specific laws and are not governed by your will. United States Savings Bonds go directly to the named beneficiary as do payable-on-death (P.O.D.) bank accounts.

An important subject is jointly held property. If you own property or an asset jointly with someone else, in many instances that property or asset will go automatically to the other person upon death. Common examples are a house, bank accounts, and stock certificates that are owned jointly by a husband and wife or brother and sister. Upon the death of one, those properties go directly to the survivor. However, there are different types of joint ownership. In addition, the laws governing jointly owned property may differ according to the nature of the property or asset. Discuss these matters with the lawyer.

Think about whom you want your property to go to or be used by after your death.

Depending upon the value of your estate, the variety and nature of the property in the estate, and other circumstances, you may want to provide for a small number of people or a large number of people.

As a general rule, you can leave whatever you want to whomever you want. Think carefully about whose welfare you should be concerned with and what you can realistically expect to accomplish.

Keep in mind that although you are planning the ownership or use of property, assets, and money, those items serve either or both of two functions: to meet needs or to provide opportunities. What you leave to a particular person should reflect the needs and opportunities that concern you regarding that person. Also keep in mind that you are planning for circumstances after your death. The needs and opportunities of the various people you are concerned about may be significantly affected by your death. Provide accordingly.

A note on disinheriting people—spouse, children, other relatives.

To disinherit someone means to leave that person nothing when you die. For a variety of reasons, a person making a will may want to disinherit someone who would otherwise be provided for.

You can, in your will, declare that you are specifically and intentionally leaving nothing to your spouse. However, in every state a surviving spouse has the legal right to "waive the will" and take whatever share of the deceased spouse's estate the surviving spouse would have received had the deceased spouse left no will. For example, suppose you live in a state in which, if you were to die without a will, your surviving spouse would receive one-half of your estate. If you make a will that explicitly leaves nothing to your spouse, your spouse can nonetheless waive the will and take one-half of your estate. The laws that allow a surviving spouse to do that are aimed at preventing one spouse from failing to provide for the surviving spouse. A will can be drafted and kept in secrecy. A spouse, sometimes for good reason but often out of misguided animosity, can make a will leaving nothing to the other spouse and the other spouse will not learn of this until the spouse who made the will dies.

There is at least one way to circumvent the laws which allow a spouse to waive the will of the other spouse and take property from the other spouse's estate even though the first spouse wanted to disinherit the other spouse. If there is little or nothing in your estate when you die, there will be little or nothing for your surviving spouse to inherit, even if he or she waives the will. But then there will be little or nothing for anyone else to inherit either. In some instances, a spouse simply gives away or transfers all of his or her property some time before his or her death so that there will be little or nothing for the surviving spouse to inherit.

A person can disinherit any or all of his or her children by specifically stating in his or her will that he or she has thought of each child (reciting the child's or children's names in the will) and has intentionally decided not to leave the child or children anything. Unlike your spouse, your children have no right to waive the will. However, if you try to disinherit a child by not mentioning that child anywhere in your will, certain state laws may come into operation which dictate that an unmentioned child (sometimes referred to as an "omitted heir") can receive that portion of the parent's estate which the child would have received had the parent left no will. Because of those laws, you must explicitly recite the name of the child or children you desire to disinherit.

Because of the legal technicalities involved in attempting to disinherit a spouse or a child, a lawyer should be consulted.

Relatives other than a spouse or child can be disinherited simply by not mentioning them in your will. For example, if you want to leave something to your sister but nothing to your brother, you can simply recite your sister's name and what she is to receive and omit any mention or reference to your brother. Of course, to make your desires unmistakably clear, you should mention your brother's name and declare that you are intentionally leaving him nothing. You can, if you wish, give your reasons, although giving reasons is not legally necessary.

Think about how you want your property to go to or be used by the persons named in your will.

Again, keep in mind that you are planning for the distribution of property, assets, and money to certain people after your death. Take into account each person's age, experience, present and future stations in life, their own assets, and other relevant factors. Often it is preferable to treat children equally. Sometimes, however, it is necessary to treat different children differently. One child may have special needs or special circumstances. The same may be true for relatives or friends you wish to provide for.

Consider whether a given individual should receive a particular property or asset outright or whether that property or asset should be sold and the money or proceeds given to that individual.

Also consider whether you should leave a certain property, asset, or sum of money to a particular individual directly or whether it would be better, for management and tax purposes, to have the property, asset, or money placed in a trust to be managed by trustees under your specific instructions for the benefit of that particular individual. (See Chapter 7.)

The nature of the property, asset, or money you wish to leave and the abilities and circumstances of the person or persons you want to leave them to must all be taken into consideration.

Remember, a will can be as detailed as you want it to be. People can be left specific items under specific conditions. For example, a husband may leave the summer cottage that is in his name alone to his wife but only for the rest of her life or until she remarries; upon her death or remarriage, the summer cottage goes to his children in equal shares.

A specific property, asset, or sum of money can be parceled out over a period of time rather than being received all at once. For example, instead of leaving a large sum of money to your prodigal son, you can have it distributed in manageable portions over several years.

Property and assets can be left to two or more persons jointly. For instance, you may leave a business or real estate to two persons, thus making them partners or joint owners, respectively.

The point is that it is not enough to simply state who is to receive your property after your death. How a person or organization receives property, assets, or money can be just as important as who receives it.

Think about the "what if's"—especially what if someone named in your will dies before you.

If you leave property to your three children in equal shares, what if your eldest daughter dies before you do? Would you want her share to go to her surviving brother and sister? If she is married, would you want her share to go to her surviving spouse? If she is married and has children, would you want her share to go to her surviving spouse and children or just to her surviving children (your grandchildren)? As you can see, several possibilities may have to be taken into consideration and accounted for.

Another "what if" involves the situation where you leave property or annual income to your surviving spouse. What if your surviving spouse remarries? Should the property or income then revert to your children? To someone else?

Of course, you can simply wait to see what events of this nature occur then make the appropriate changes in your will.

However, many people never change their will once it is made. In light of that fact, it would be wiser to account for at least the more likely "what if's" when you make your will.

Name a first and second choice for executor—someone to manage your estate after your death.

When you draft a will, it is important to name an executor—the person, persons, or institution (sometimes a trust company or bank) which will have the authority to manage your estate, conduct the necessary court proceedings and other legal matters involved in probating your estate, and make sure the instructions you put in your will are carried out.

If your estate is neither large nor complex, the executor would usually be your surviving spouse, an adult child or a close relative or friend. If the person you name as executor needs legal assistance or other advice in probating your estate or other matters, that person can consult a lawyer or other expert as the situation warrants.

Some lawyers encourage their clients to name the lawyer as

executor. Before agreeing to do so, ask yourself this question: If you name a lawyer as the sole executor of your estate, who is the lawyer's client? No lawyer should be without a client to whom the lawyer is responsible and accountable. That is why it is better to name a nonlawyer as executor. That person can hire a lawyer of his or her own choosing when the need for a lawyer arises.

If you feel that your lawyer's familiarity with your estate plan would make it worthwhile for the lawyer to be an executor, name the lawyer as a coexecutor along with your spouse, an adult child, or a close relative or friend. That way, the nonlawyer-executor can keep tabs on the lawyer-executor.

If your estate is very large or complex, it might be worthwhile to name a lawyer, a trust company, or a bank as a coexecutor along with your spouse, an adult child, or a close relative or friend.

It is wise to name a second choice as your executor. This is done because, when your death occurs, the person you named as executor may be unable or unwilling to serve as executor for any number of reasons. By naming a second choice for executor, you can avoid considerable confusion and loss of time in the probating of your estate and the settlement of your affairs. Often, people name their surviving spouse as first choice to be executor and an adult child or close relative or friend as the second choice.

Put other provisions in your will as needed.

Peculiar or unique family circumstances or problems should be dealt with in your will. Special provisions may have to be made for particular persons or organizations which you wish to name and provide for in your will. Special instructions may be needed so that your executor will know your exact intentions regarding the distribution of your property.

The best way to avoid disputes and court battles over your will is to make your will complete and clear. Often, a few additional words or clauses will avoid costly controversies and litigation.

A Note on the Formalities of a Will: Language, Format, Signing, and Witnessing Because of the formalities and intricate requirements established by law for a valid will, it is essential that you seek a lawyer's assistance in drafting your will. After all, the money you pay a lawyer to draft your will can save considerable expense, confusion, and possible legal battles. The lawyer will know the appropriate legal format and language for carrying out your plans and intentions.

The lawyer will also make sure your will is signed and witnessed in accordance with the current laws of your state.

Who Should Keep the Original Will and Where? There are usually a number of alternatives. Some attorneys advise their client to have the attorney keep the original will in his or her office while the client retains a copy for his or her own records and future reference. Many lawyers advise their client to have the attorney retain the original because doing so significantly increases the chances that the lawyer will later be hired to handle the probating of the deceased person's estate when the nearest kin comes to the lawyer's office looking for the will—and looking for legal advice on how to probate the estate.

Some people keep the original will in a safe-deposit box. Doing so can cause problems if you reside in a state which requires a court order before the executor-to-be or any other person can open the safe-deposit box to obtain the will. Also, in some states, a safe-deposit box containing a will cannot be opened unless a representative of the state estate tax bureau is present. These arrangements can cause delays.

In almost every state a person can, for a nominal fee, have the original will filed in the probate court. However, if you want to review the will at any subsequent time or change it, you will have to go to court to obtain it.

Generally, unless there is good reason not to, you should keep the original will and have your lawyer keep an unsigned copy. Be sure to keep your will in a safe, fireproof place along with other important papers. By keeping the original will, you can refer to it at any time, it will be more easily found by the persons who survive you, and you won't have to contact the lawyer or the probate court every time you want to read the will or every time you move.

Review Your Will Annually Review your will once a year, preferably around tax-paying time. Events may occur which make a change in your will necessary or highly advisable. Many people, however, do not think of changing their will at such times. A good way to avoid such oversights is to make a habit of reviewing your will once a year.

A Note on Marriage, Divorce, and Lost Wills In every state, marriage revokes a will. That means that your will becomes invalid automatically when you marry. The reason for that rule of law is that the law presumes that most people would change their will significantly once they marry. Often, however, people don't do so. Despite that, it would be unjust for the disposition of a married person's property to be governed by a will that was made before that person married and which that person almost surely would have changed after getting married had he or she thought about it.

Whether you have a will when you marry or not, that event is a good reason to have a will made or to reexamine and redraft your present will.

In some states, divorce revokes a will but only in regard to the divorced spouse. That is, the divorced spouse takes nothing under the will of the ex-spouse even though the will may specifically provide for the (now-divorced) spouse. Obviously, divorce is another situation in which a person would almost always change his or her will significantly. Again, however, many people simply don't do so. That is why some states have a rule of law which automatically revokes those provisions in a will which relate to an ex-spouse. In other states, however, divorce does not automatically revoke a will. In those states, if your will leaves all or a considerable amount of your estate to your ex-spouse and you fail to change the will after the divorce, your ex-spouse may inherit some or all of your property. Whatever your state law dictates, review your will if you are getting divorced or are divorced. Make sure your will reflects your present concerns regarding people and property.

Finally, if a person's will cannot be found after his or her death, it is presumed that he or she intentionally destroyed the will. Unless someone can locate a carbon or other copy of your will (perhaps from the lawyer who drafted the will), it may be impossible to convince the court of what your will provided. If your will cannot be found after your death and no legally adequate substitute is accepted by the court, your property will pass by the laws of descent and distribution. The careful planning and thought that went into your will will be wasted. Because of this, it is important to keep your will where it will be safe but also readily accessible after your death. People who hide their will or who forget where they put it are inviting confusion and expensive court proceedings upon their death.

Changing Your Will—Codicils Your will can be changed in any way you want and at any time. It is your will. In fact, your will should be changed on a number of occasions. Marriage and divorce are obvious examples of events in a person's life which warrant changing the will. Significant changes in your property holdings, changes in your relationships with persons named in your will, and changes in relationships with persons not named in your will may also warrant revising the will.

If the change you wish to make is minor or if the change can be put into effect without rewriting major portions of the original document, you should be able to change the will simply by having a lawyer draft a codicil.

A *codicil* is an amendment or supplement to a will. The codicil must be written, signed, and witnessed in the same manner as a will.

If the changes you wish to make are major or if trying to fit them into the present will would result in a confusing or inconsistent document, you should have a lawyer draft a new will. The new will should state at the outset that you are revoking your prior will and that the prior will is to have no force or effect.

DEALING WITH LAWYERS

In addition to the general points about lawyers in Chapter 1, keep in mind the following advice about dealing with lawyers with regard to your will and estate plan.

Not all attorneys are well trained and experienced in drafting wills and handling estate plans and related estate matters. The more complex your will and estate plan or the more substantial your estate, the more carefully you should act in selecting an attorney. Of particular importance, if your estate is substantial, is to select an attorney who has a solid knowledge of current tax law.

If you present a basic outline of what you want to do in your will, the attorney should be able to give you an estimate of what his or her fee would be to draft a will covering the points you mention and other usual matters.

Most attorneys charge a flat fee for a routine will. A flat fee for a routine will for a person of average means might cost anywhere from $25 to $250.

If the will is somewhat complex or if your estate is substantial, the attorney may charge an hourly fee. See Chapter 1 for a detailed discussion of flat fees and hourly fees.

7
Trusts

WHAT IS A TRUST?

A trust is a legal arrangement in which one person transfers legal title to assets or property to a second person under an agreement whereby the second person must invest and manage those assets and property for the benefit of a third person. The person who creates the trust is called the *settlor* (or the creator or donor). The assets or property which go into the trust are called the *corpus* (or principal or fund). The person or institution, such as a bank trust department, which holds legal title to and manages the assets or property is called the *trustee.* The person who is to be provided for out of the assets or property in the trust is called the *beneficiary*. Finally, the document which creates the trust and sets forth the terms and conditions of the trust is called the *trust agreement* (or trust indenture).

There are two types of trusts. A trust which takes effect while the settlor is living is called a *living trust* or an *inter vivos trust.* A trust which is contained in the settlor's will and which comes into existence upon his death is called a *testamentary trust.* Living trusts or inter vivos trusts are subdivided into two groups. A *revocable living trust* is one which the settlor can change or terminate more or less as he desires. On the other hand, an *irrevocable living trust* is one which the settlor cannot change or terminate once it has been created.

The purpose of a trust is to put money, assets, or other property in the hands of a person who is trained to invest and manage them wisely. That person, the trustee, is charged with distributing the income from those investments and possibly the investments themselves (or their cash value) to the beneficiary under specific conditions dictated by the settlor. For example, suppose a wealthy father wants to provide financial security or assistance to his wife, his daughter, and his son. Each of them being people in different circumstances, he must fashion an instrument which will provide the type of financial security or assistance he believes each of them deserves under terms and conditions he feels are appropriate. Starting with his wife, he knows that he will provide for her during his lifetime. His primary concern is her financial security after his death. Since his wife does not have considerable experience or training in managing large sums of money and diverse property holdings, he decides to set up a trust for her benefit and to put it in his will. Basically, the trust arrangement provides that, upon his death, a large sum of money, stocks, and bonds will be transferred to a particular bank's trust department. The bank trust department will hold legal title to the money, stocks, and bonds but it will be charged with the obligation to invest those funds and assets wisely, to distribute the income from those investments to the wife under specific terms, and, when necessary, sell some of those investments to pay certain major expenses of the wife. The details are spelled out in the trust agreement. This is a testamentary trust. It is a trust contained in the settlor's will and comes into existence upon his death.

Regarding his daughter, the father knows that she has been successful with her own business. She is capable and experienced in business and financial matters and is secure on her own at present. Nonetheless, he would like to work out an arrangement whereby some of his money and other assets are placed in a separate entity (so that he can lower his tax bracket) and so that those funds can accumulate interest and income until his daughter needs financial assistance or upon his death. On the other hand, the father doesn't want considerable assets and the interest and income to go to his daughter if she continues to be prosperous on her own. After all, his wife's needs or his son's needs or his own needs might take an unexpected turn for the worse some time in the future. In other words, he doesn't want the money and assets set aside for his daughter to be locked into an arrangement which he cannot subsequently change or terminate if the need arises. To accomplish this, the father establishes a revocable living trust. He names an attorney experienced in trust management as the trustee. He then transfers title to certain bank accounts, stocks, and bonds to the attorney (as trustee of the trust). Finally, an agreement is signed by the father setting forth when and under what conditions the daughter is to receive income from those investments or a portion of the investments themselves. In addition, however, the father expressly retains the right to revoke the trust (to terminate it) at any time and take back whatever money, stocks, and bonds are in it when he does so. This is a revocable living trust. It is a trust created while the settlor is living but subject to his right to revoke it.

Finally, his son presents an entirely different situation. Although in his late 20s, his son is mentally retarded and cannot grasp basic principles of money, income, and budgeting. Thus, the father wants to place a considerable amount of money and other valuable assets in the hands of someone who will then manage those assets and use the income and profits to provide for his son for as long as his son lives. To accomplish this, the father asks a specialist on mental retardation, who is familiar with his son, to serve as a cotrustee of a trust for the son. The father asks a lawyer with experience in trusts to serve as the other cotrustee. The father then transfers title to several bank accounts and numerous stocks and bonds into the names of the cotrustees. Finally, he signs an agreement containing detailed instructions as to how those investments are to be managed by the cotrustees and used to provide for his son until his son's death. Realizing that it would be wise to put the trust into operation during his lifetime (so that he can determine how well the specialist and the attorney manage the trust and provide for his son), the father creates a living trust. (He retains only the right to change trustees.) In addition, knowing that his son's mental retardation cannot be cured or significantly remedied and not being able to conceive of a situation in which he would want to reduce or terminate the trust as long as his son is alive, he makes the trust irrevocable. It will remain in existence as long as his son is living and as long as there are assets in it. This is an irrevocable living trust.

These are examples of the three types of trusts—the testamentary trust, the revocable living trust, and the irrevocable living trust. Although trusts can be used for a multiplicity of purposes and persons, all trusts take one of these three forms.

One of the major advantages of a trust is that the settlor can dictate elaborate terms and conditions to accomplish numerous purposes. Returning to our examples, the testamentary trust created by the man to provide financial security for his wife after his death might contain a clause declaring that the trust is to terminate if she remarries. At that point all monies and other assets in the trust are to be transferred to the trust for their mentally handicapped son. Likewise, the revocable living trust set up for the benefit of the daughter might provide that, should she marry and have children, the trustee would be authorized or required to use trust income and investments to pay for her children's education and other purposes. Finally, the irrevocable living trust set up for the benefit of the mentally handicapped son might provide that, upon the son's death, all monies and other assets remaining in the trust are to be donated to research and care facilities for mentally handicapped persons.

Trusts can be flexible as well as useful. Each trust is a separate legal entity, managed by trustees selected by the settlor who must provide for the beneficiary in strict accordance with instructions laid down by the settlor.

Some of the more common trusts which persons of average or above-average means utilize are:

- testamentary trust to provide for a surviving spouse and/or surviving children upon the death of the settlor
- living trust to provide for a handicapped, impecunious, or financially inexperienced or inept member of the family or other person
- testamentary or living trust to operate or otherwise provide for a charitable or nonprofit organization.

By contrast, a person would not use a trust if it is appropriate to simply give the money or other assets directly to the person you wish to provide for. For example, if the son in the previous example were not mentally handicapped, the father might decide to transfer money and other assets directly to him, either as an outright gift during the father's lifetime or as a bequest in the father's will. This shows that one of the chief purposes of a trust is to have a third person—the trustee—own and manage the trust assets and be responsible for providing for the beneficiary (according to the terms of the trust agreement).

If a person you wish to provide for can handle money or other assets competently and you would be comfortable relying on his or her judgment and discretion once the money or other assets are theirs—to do with as they please—a trust would be inappropriate. If, however, the person you wish to provide for is inexperienced at managing money or other assets, or if the person might not exercise good judgment and sound discretion if the money or assets were transferred directly to him or her, a trust may be appropriate. A trust brings the trustee into the picture. The concern of the settlor is, of course, to find a trustee who combines sound investment experience and judgment with concern for the beneficiary. The ability of the trustee to carry out the instructions and intentions of the settlor is at least as important as the value and nature of the assets and property put into the trustee's hands for that purpose.

WHY DO YOU NEED TO CONSULT A LAWYER?

Although what you wish to accomplish by means of a trust may be simple and straightforward, the necessary legal documents and procedures make the advice and services of a lawyer essential. An attorney with experience in preparing trusts may bring to your attention and resolve questions and problems you had not considered but which must be addressed. In addition, an attorney experienced in trusts can help you make sound decisions regarding what assets to put into the trust and how, the terms and conditions of the trust, the selection and qualifications of the trustee, and the tax consequences of creating a trust.

A trust is one part of your total estate plan. Whether you desire to set up a living trust or a testamentary trust, any trust you establish will bear upon how you should manage the assets and other properties in your estate during your lifetime and what you should try to accomplish through your will. An attorney can review the proposed trust and advise you how to implement that trust so that it fits effectively, especially for tax purposes, into your total estate plan. (See Chapter 6.)

Another reason to consult a lawyer before creating a trust is to have the lawyer explain your rights and obligations as settlor of the trust, the rights and obligations of the trustee, and the rights and obligations of the beneficiary. These matters vary greatly depending on the type of trust, its terms and conditions, and other factors. They are matters of which you must be cognizant if you are to understand what the trust will accomplish in terms of how it provides for the beneficiary, what restrictions it places on the trustee, and what financial, tax, and other consequences it will have on your estate.

Trusts are governed by many laws. Some deal with the legal requirements for a valid trust and the rights and liabilities of the settlor, the trustee, and the beneficiary. Other laws deal with taxation of trust income, assets, and distributions. Other laws deal with how trust agreements are interpreted, how many generations of persons can be provided for in a trust, what happens if the purpose of the trust is accomplished or defeated or otherwise terminated but the trust agreement does not adequately address that situation. As can be seen, trusts are governed by numerous intricate laws. The settlor of a trust needs the advice and services of an experienced trust attorney so that the trust is properly created and funded, so that the trustee is properly selected and empowered, and so that the purpose of the trust—providing for the beneficiary—is accomplished to the fullest extent possible under the law.

To create a valid trust and one which accomplishes its purpose successfully, the settlor must think out what it is he or she wants to do and how he or she wants to do it. In addition, many legal, financial, tax, and related matters must be considered. The following sections present a framework which will help you clarify your objectives and deal with the most important legal and related aspects of trust.

Determine whom you want to provide for and how.

As a practical matter, all a trust does is transfer legal title to money, securities, or other property to a trustee. The trustee is then obliged to invest and manage those assets or property and distribute the income therefrom and the investments themselves (or their cash value) to the person named as beneficiary in strict accordance with specific terms and conditions.

The first step in thinking about a trust is to decide whether a trust is the appropriate legal vehicle for what you want to accomplish. That can be determined by answering two questions: (1) Whom do you wish to provide for? (2) What are the advantages and disadvantages of using a trust to provide for that person?

For instance, if the person you want to provide for can manage money or other assets themselves, it may be appropriate to simply give some of your money or assets to that person if you are confident that he or she will use them wisely. Similarly, if you intend to provide for another person during your lifetime but want to provide for that person after your death and that person can manage money or other assets intelligently, it might be appropriate to bequeath that money or those assets to that person in your will. The important point is that a trust does not transfer legal title to funds or assets to the beneficiary. Legal title to the funds or assets is transferred to the trustee. The trustee invests and manages those funds and assets and distributes income or investments to the beneficiary under the terms and conditions of the trust agreement. Thus, there should be good reason why a trustee is needed. In addition, careful thought must be given to determining what funds or assets will be transferred to the trustee and what terms and conditions will govern the distribution of income and investments to the beneficiary.

It may be easy to determine whom you wish to provide for. How you wish to provide for that person requires determining whether a trust is the appropriate legal vehicle. The appropriateness of a trust centers on whether what you want to accomplish requires or would be best served by having a trustee own and manage the funds or assets and distribute income and investments to the beneficiary according to your instructions. Identifying and analyzing what it is about the person you wish to provide for that warrants the use of a trustee and detailed instructions will lead you to the next step in thinking about trusts.

Determine which type of trust would be appropriate and what terms and conditions should be written into the trust agreement.

As we saw in the first section of this chapter, there are three types of trusts—the testamentary trust, the revocable living trust, and the irrevocable living trust. Each has its advantages and disadvantages as to when it goes into effect and how much control, if any, the settlor retains. The answers to two questions will generally indicate which type of trust would be appropriate. First, should the trust become effective upon your death or should the trust come into operation during your lifetime? A testamentary trust goes into effect upon your death. Either type of living trust goes into effect when you sign the trust agreement and transfer assets to the trustees.

Second, if the trust is set up during your lifetime (a living trust), should you retain a power to revoke the trust whenever you feel it should be terminated or should the trust operate without being subject to your power to revoke it? A revocable living trust, as its name suggests, can be terminated by the settlor at any time. An irrevocable trust operates independently of the settlor for as long as the trust agreement requires (or as long as there are assets in the trust).

Determining what type of trust is appropriate also involves thinking about the terms and conditions which will govern the duties of the trustee. Of particular importance are those instructions which govern how and when the trustee is to distribute income or investments from the trust to the beneficiary or otherwise provide for the beneficiary (for example, by paying bills incurred by the beneficiary). In some cases, much can be left to the discretion of the trustee (subject to the right of the settlor and the beneficiary to object and sue the trustee if he or she abuses that discretion). In other cases, considerable care must be taken to spell out, in great detail, the duties of the trustee under a variety of anticipated circumstances.

In determining which type of trust to establish and deciding what terms and conditions to write into the trust agreement, the advice and services of an experienced trust attorney will be invaluable.

Determine what assets should be transferred to the trustee.

What you can expect to accomplish by means of a trust is limited to the value (present and future) of the assets or property you put into the trust. It is important to be realistic and cautious when creating a trust which, it is hoped, will provide financial security and assistance to the beneficiary for many years or even decades. Considerable thought should be given to what types of investments the trustee should be authorized to make and other restrictions on the trustee's authority to buy, sell, or convert investments and property.

Of course, it is important for you to determine the effects which transferring assets and property to the trustee will have on your own financial picture and estate. Different considerations apply depending on whether you will be setting up a testamentary trust, a revocable living trust, or an irrevocable living trust. The advice of an experienced trust lawyer and a knowledgeable tax expert are essential. (This is discussed later in this section.)

Determine who shall serve as trustee.

There are two types of trustees—professional trustees and nonprofessional trustees. A professional trustee is a person who is trained and experienced in trust management by profession, such as a bank trust department officer or a trust attorney. A nonprofessional trustee is any person who does not have professional training or experience in that position, such as the settlor's spouse or relative or a close friend or associate. The purpose of having a professional trustee is to gain the benefit of that person's training and experience in trust management. The purpose of having a nonprofessional trustee is to have someone serving as trustee who bears a personal relationship to the beneficiary. For example, a wealthy husband and wife may provide in their wills that, should they die together or upon the death of the survivor, if their children are minors, the wife's sister shall be appointed guardian of the children. All their assets will be placed in a trust with the children as beneficiaries. For trustees, the local bank trust department shall serve as one cotrustee and the wife's sister shall serve as the other cotrustee. This way, the trust will have the benefit of the financial and business acumen of the bank trust department but the interests and needs of the children will be protected and asserted by the wife's sister, who, as cotrustee, has duties and rights equal to those of the bank trust department.

The example above reveals that the choice of trustee (or trustees) depends largely on the expertise needed to manage the trust and the appropriateness of having someone with a personal relationship to the beneficiary as trustee (or cotrustee) despite that person's lack of financial experience. The example above also reveals that it is not uncommon to have a professional trustee and a nonprofessional trustee serve as cotrustees.

Review your rights and obligations as settlor and the rights and obligations of the trustee and the beneficiary.

Your attorney can provide you with an overview of the rights and obligations generally applicable to the settlor of a trust and those which generally apply to a trustee and a beneficiary. For example, as noted earlier, if the trustee violates the terms or conditions of the trust agreement or abuses the discretion granted to him or her under the trust agreement, either the settlor (if living) or the beneficiary can object and bring a lawsuit against the trustee to correct the situation. Trust agreements are enforceable in court. In fact, courts hold trustees to a high standard of conduct in fulfilling their obligations as set forth in the trust agreement, in their handling of assets in the trust, and in their dealings with the beneficiary.

Have your attorney inform you of the rights and obligations of a settlor, a trustee, and a beneficiary so that you will know where you stand, how a trust operates, and, particularly, what a settlor or beneficiary can do if they believe the trustee is not acting properly.

Review the tax consequences of establishing a trust.

The more substantial the assets you intend to transfer to a trust the more important it is to understand how trusts are taxed and the tax advantages and disadvantages of setting up a trust. Before establishing a trust with substantial assets, review with your attorney or a tax expert the consequences of taking those assets out of your present holdings (if you are going to establish a living trust) or the consequences of taking those assets out of your estate at the time of your death (if you are going to establish a testamentary trust).

Generally, since legal title to the assets and property in a trust is held by the trustee, the taxes on profits and income from the trust holdings are paid by the trustee (out of the trust). A trust is taxed as a separate legal entity. If income or other distributions are made to the beneficiary, he or she will pay taxes on the amounts received—unless the trust agreement specifies that such taxes are to be paid by the trustee (out of the trust). These are the general rules. There are exceptions and there are many detailed points about which your attorney or tax expert can advise you. As noted earlier, a trust consists of assets or property the legal title to which has been transferred to a trustee so that the trustee can manage them and use income and profits to provide for the beneficiary according to the settlor's instructions. In light of this, it is important to arrange the trust holdings and the trust agreement terms and conditions for distributing income and investments to the beneficiary in a manner which will minimize the settlor's taxes yet preserve investments and produce maximum income for the beneficiary.

DEALING WITH LAWYERS

In addition to the general points about lawyers in Chapter 1, keep in mind the following advice about dealing with lawyers with regard to drafting a trust.

The more substantial the assets you intend to place in a trust or the more complicated the trust, the more careful you should be to select an attorney with considerable experience in trust work. Of particular importance where substantial assets are concerned is to find an attorney (or other expert) who has a sound knowledge of tax law.

The best way to find an experienced trust attorney is to contact a few lawyers and ask each about his or her training, experience, and qualifications in trust work. Contact a bank trust department. Many bank trust departments have lawyers who advise their customers on trusts. Or the bank may refer you to private attorneys who are knowledgeable in trust work. You might also contact the probate court. Ask for the office of the clerk of the court. The clerk of the probate court may provide the names of several lawyers who handle trust work and whose ability the clerk respects. Also, talk to friends or associates who have established trusts recently. Ask them what they thought of the lawyer who drafted the trust. Or if you know someone who is the settlor of an ongoing trust, ask that person about the lawyer who drafted the trust.

After explaining to the attorney the trust you wish to set up, the attorney may quote a flat fee or an hourly fee. A flat fee is a set amount of money for which the attorney agrees to perform all necessary and customary work to prepare a trust. In a given community, a simple trust may cost \$200 to \$500, whereas a complex trust involving assets of great value may cost \$2,000 to \$5,000 or more.

Before agreeing to a flat fee or any other fee, make sure you understand what services the lawyer will perform for that fee and what additional services may be needed to put the trust in operation. For instance, the flat fee quoted by the lawyer normally covers the time and effort required on the attorney's part to draft the trust papers. Once those papers are typed and the document properly signed, the attorney's work—as covered by the flat fee—is over. However, the trust is not yet in operation. If you have established a testamentary trust, one contained in your will which takes effect upon your death, nothing more need be done for the present. However, if you are establishing an inter vivos or living trust, you must transfer money or other assets or property into the name of the trustee. This may require transferring names on bank accounts, stocks, bonds, deeds, or other titles. If you want the attorney, or someone else, to do that work, an additional fee will be required. Thus, before agreeing to a given flat fee or a given hourly fee, find out what work the attorney intends to do and whether there may be additional work necessary to get the trust operating and who should perform that additional work.

If the trust you wish to establish is a relatively simple one, the attorney's work will be largely a routine matter of putting the appropriate standard clauses into a trust agreement. If you feel the fee quoted by the attorney is too high for such routine paperwork, negotiate for a lower fee by emphasizing how uncomplicated the trust is.

Beware of attorneys who set their fee according to the value of the assets in the trust regardless of how much—or how little—time the attorney actually puts into the case. One way to gauge how time-consuming the lawyer's job will be is to keep track of how much time you spend with the attorney discussing the trust. If your case requires office consultations totaling an hour or less, chances are the trust will not require a great deal of time or effort for the attorney to prepare. If, on the other hand, your case requires a number of office consultations or if the attorney informs you that considerable research must be done to resolve questions of law, or if the attorney must put considerable time into such areas as tax advice, estate planning, and other financial advice, chances are the trust is far from routine and the attorney will have to put in considerable time and effort to prepare it properly. In that case, a sizable fee may be justified. Also, much of the financial and tax advice provided by the lawyer will be helpful in preserving the assets in the trust and minimizing the effects of taxes. Advice and information of that nature is usually well worth paying for.

Be aware also that lawyers who charge a percentage fee based on the value of the money and assets that are to go into the trust often receive grossly exorbitant fees by means of a percentage fee formula. For example, suppose one attorney quotes a fee of $50 an hour to draft an irrevocable living trust into which you intend to put $50,000. The attorney devotes 10 hours to the office consultations, research, drafting, and document review. The bill is $500. A second attorney, once he or she learns that the corpus of the trust is to be $50,000, quotes a fee of 3 percent of the corpus. That works out to $1,500. If that attorney also requires only 10 hours of work to draft the same trust papers, he or she is, in effect, receiving a fee of $150 an hour! On the whole, the best way to avoid exorbitant fees charged by means of a percentage fee is to insist on a flat or hourly fee.

Whatever fee you agree upon (after shopping around and selecting the best combination of lawyer and fee), discuss how the fee is to be paid. Work out an installment payment schedule; for example, pay one-third of the fee at the outset, another third at some point during the preparation of the trust papers, and the final third upon signing the trust agreement.

8

Inheritance and Probating a Deceased Person's Estate

WHAT DOES AN INHERITANCE INVOLVE?

In a strict legal sense, an *inheritance* is money or property received from the estate of a deceased person who did not have a will. When money or property is left to a person in a will, that money or property is called a *bequest*. (The person named in the will to receive the money or property is called a *beneficiary*.) For the purposes of this chapter, however, the word *inheritance* will include any money or property received from a deceased person's estate, whether or not there was a will.

If a person dies without a will, he or she is said to have died intestate. To govern such situations, every state has elaborate statutes called the laws of descent and distribution. These laws determine who shall receive the money and property owned by the deceased person at the time of his or her death. Naturally, those laws dictate that the deceased person's property goes first to his or her surviving spouse and children. If there are no surviving spouse or children, the deceased person's parents or brothers and sisters would then inherit his or her property. The laws of descent and distribution cover numerous situations and run through many levels of relatives. If a person dies without leaving any blood relatives, the laws of descent and distribution normally require that the deceased person's money and property be put into the public coffers (usually the state treasury).

If a person has a valid will at the time of death, he or she is said to have died testate. (The maker of a will is called the testator.) The will determines who inherits what money and property from the testator's estate. (The laws of descent and distribution come into operation only if the will is held invalid or if some money or property is not covered by the will.)

If a person dies without leaving a will, how can you determine whether you are entitled by the laws of descent and distribution to inherit money or property from that person's estate? Likewise, if a person dies leaving a will, how can you determine whether you were named in that will and what money or property was bequeathed to you? The remaining sections in this chapter discuss the answers to those questions. (This chapter also discusses the basic aspects of probating a deceased person's estate.)

It is useful to understand at the outset some basic points about inheriting money or property from a deceased person's estate. First, a good deal depends on whether the person who died had a will or died without a will. As noted, if there is no will, the distribution of the deceased person's money and property is strictly governed by the laws of descent and distribution. Before any money or property to which you may be entitled can be distributed, however, someone must be appointed by the appropriate state court to take charge of the deceased person's estate. Where there is no will, that person is called an *administrator*. One of the administrator's most important duties is to file an inventory in court listing all the money and property owned by the deceased person at the time of his or her death and the current value of all that money and property. Thus, for you to properly determine what, if any, money or property you are entitled to receive from the estate of a person who died without a will, you must first determine whether you are included by the laws of descent and distribution in the group of blood relatives who will inherit from the deceased person. You must then find out who the administrator of the estate is, determine the value of the money and property in the estate, and calculate what your share will be. But that is not all. You must also determine what procedures must be followed to make sure you receive proper legal title to your share of the deceased person's estate. Finally, you must determine what inheritance taxes, if any, will be assessed on what you receive.

Needless to say, inheriting money or property from the estate of a person who died without a will can be an involved process.

Inheriting money or property from the estate of a person who died with a will can also be an involved process. Unlike the situation where the deceased person had no will, where there is a will you must examine the will to determine whether you were named to receive a bequest and to determine the nature and value of the bequest. You must also determine whether the will is valid and whether anyone interested in the estate of that deceased person may challenge the validity of the will. For example, if a person who would have inherited from the deceased if there were no will is not mentioned in the will, that person may try to challenge the validity of the will. If the challenge is successful and the court declares the will invalid, the deceased person will be deemed to have died without a will. The laws of descent and distribution then come into operation and only the appropriate blood relatives will inherit.

Even if the will is declared valid, it may not be a simple, straightforward matter to obtain the bequest to which you are entitled under the will. For example, it may be some time before the estate is appraised and its value calculated. Also, debts of the decedent, funeral expenses, attorney's fees, taxes, probate fees and costs, and many other items must be paid before you receive the bequest. It is one thing to know that a person bequeathed money or property to you. It is something else to learn that it may be many months or even years before you receive that money or property.

When a person dies leaving a valid will, the person appointed by the court to take charge of the deceased person's estate is called an *executor*, if a man, or an *executrix*, if a woman. (Recall that, if a person dies without a will, the person appointed to handle the estate is called an administrator.) If you are entitled to receive money or property under a will, you must make sure the executor (or executrix) manages the estate properly and transfers title to the money or property bequeathed to you at the proper time and in the proper legal manner.

Thus, before you can receive money or property bequeathed to you in a will, you must first determine whether the will is valid or whether it will be challenged. Next, you must determine what was bequeathed to you and what procedures must be followed to have the money or property properly transferred to you. Finally, you must make sure that any taxes due on the bequest are paid.

Whether you inherit money or property from a person who died without a will or from a person who died with a will, numerous matters involving various legal aspects must be addressed and correctly resolved.

WHY DO YOU NEED TO CONSULT A LAWYER?

The numerous factors that must be considered and the various legal steps that must be taken to properly inherit money or property require the advice and assistance of an experienced lawyer. If the situation is uncomplicated, you may only need to consult a lawyer once or twice and have the lawyer check the paperwork done by the administrator or executor of the estate. If, on the other hand, the situation is complicated or confused, your lawyer may have to do considerable work to make sure you receive the full share to which you are entitled and that you receive it in the proper legal manner.

Many people are intimidated or bewildered by the laws and procedures that govern receiving money or property from a deceased person's estate. That is another reason why a lawyer's advice and assistance should be obtained—no matter how simple and aboveboard the situation may appear. It is worth emphasizing that, if you are entitled to receive a substantial amount of money or property from a deceased person's estate, it is wise as well as practical to consult a lawyer. The lawyer can make sure you receive the full inheritance coming to you, that you receive it as soon as possible, and that you receive it in the proper legal manner. Of course, if there are serious questions, problems, or controversies associated with the deceased person's estate, it is all the more important to obtain advice and assistance from an experienced attorney.

WHAT DOES PROBATING A DECEASED PERSON'S ESTATE INVOLVE?

The word *probate* generates considerable consternation and anxiety. Many people do not understand the basics of probate law and procedure. That lack of knowledge contributes to the anxiety most people associate with *probate.* The following discussion will improve your knowledge of what probate is and how it works. Hopefully, the following will also allay some of your uneasiness with this subject.

Probate means to prove the validity of a will. In most states, the courts in which wills must be filed upon the death of the testator (the maker of the will) are called probate courts. The purpose of filing a will in probate court when the maker of the will dies is to allow everyone interested in the deceased person's estate to examine the will and decide whether to accept it as valid or present grounds for challenging the validity of the will. For example, there may be serious doubts whether the maker of the will was mentally competent at the time he or she signed the will. Or someone may allege that the maker of the will was subjected to undue influence or coercion from an overbearing relative or friend or lawyer. In other cases, a person may challenge the will on the ground that it was not drafted and executed according to law. For instance, most states require that a will be signed by two witnesses. In addition, the witnesses cannot be people who are to receive anything under the will nor can they be married to anyone who is to receive anything under the will. (The purpose of that law is to make sure that the signature of the maker of the will is witnessed by at least two persons who are impartial and do not have a self-serving interest in the will.) Because of those legal requirements, a will may be declared invalid by the court if an interested party proves that one of the witnesses was to receive a bequest under the will or was married to someone who was to receive a bequest. Despite the good intentions of the people who drafted and executed the will and despite the fact that their mistake may have been inadvertent and not malevolent, if the will is not drafted and executed in strict compliance with specific laws, it stands a good chance of being held invalid in court.

Thus, probate involves filing the will in court and making it available to all persons interested in the deceased person's estate.

Probating a will also involves having the court appoint an executor to manage the deceased person's estate and act as the legal representative of the decedent. The court usually appoints the person named in the will to serve as executor. However, if that person doesn't want to or cannot serve as executor, the court must appoint someone else. In that case, the court will typically appoint the surviving spouse or an adult relative of the deceased or an attorney.

Before becoming an administrator (where there is no will) or an executor (where there is a will), a person must notify all persons interested in the estate that he or she is seeking to be appointed to that position. This gives all the people interested in the estate an opportunity to object and challenge that person if they can show good reason why that person should not serve as administrator or executor. An executor, as we have seen, must also notify all persons interested in the estate that the will is on file in the probate court so that they can examine it and decide whether or not to challenge its validity.

Probate courts also have jurisdiction over the estates of persons who die without a will. As we have seen, when a person dies without a will, the money or property that person owned at death must be distributed according to the laws of descent and distribution. To accomplish this, someone must be appointed administrator of the estate and take charge of the deceased person's money and property. Specific state laws dictate who the judge must consider in deciding who to appoint as administrator of the deceased person's estate. Typically, the surviving spouse is first choice, followed by surviving adult children, other adult relatives, and finally an attorney of the court's choice.

After the probate judge appoints an administrator (where there is no will) or an executor (where there is a will), the court retains jurisdiction over that estate. The administrator or executor is responsible to the court until the day the estate is closed out and the administrator or executor is discharged.

Administrators and executors have many important responsibilities and duties. The administrator or executor must file a bond declaring that he or she will act faithfully and honestly in managing the estate in a proper legal manner. In some instances the administrator or executor may also have to file a surety or other insurance policy which will reimburse the estate for loses if the administrator or executor mishandles funds or property, absconds with money or property, or otherwise mismanages the estate.

The administrator or executor must manage the deceased person's estate until it is distributed and closed out. This may involve paying funeral bills and other debts of the decedent, running or selling any business which the deceased person operated, paying income taxes due for the year of death, securing and maintaining the deceased person's possessions, taking over bank accounts, securities, and other financial assets, transferring the registration of an automobile to the appropriate person and otherwise conducting or closing out the decedent's financial and property affairs.

The administrator or executor must file in court an inventory listing all the deceased person's financial holdings and property. Any person interested in the estate can examine that inventory to determine whether the administrator or executor included everything that should have been included, whether the values listed are reasonable, and whether the administrator or executor has taken proper measures to preserve and protect the decedent's financial and property assets.

Every year until the estate is closed out, the executor or administrator must file an account describing all transactions involving the money and property in the estate. The purpose of these annual accounts is to allow persons interested in the estate to find out what the administrator or executor has been doing with the money and property in the estate and whether his or her actions are proper and legal. After the administrator or executor makes the final distributions and closes out the estate, he or she must file a final account. It is customary (in some states it is required) that the administrator or executor obtain receipts or vouchers from each person entitled to receive money or property from the estate stating that they received his or her proper share.

Of considerable importance is the responsibility of the administrator or executor to make sure that taxes due on the estate are paid.

Every state (except Nevada) levies estate taxes based on the value of the estate. Estate tax laws are intricate. Expert tax advice is necessary unless the value of the estate is so low that no taxes are due.

Many states also levy inheritance taxes against the persons who receive money or property from the estate. Inheritance taxes are based on the value of the money or property received and also on the relationship of the recipient to the decedent. For example, a brother of the decedent would pay lower inheritance taxes on an inheritance than would a cousin. Of course, there are minimum tax levels. If the value of the inheritance is below the minimum, no tax is due. Also, many people provide in their will that the executor shall pay inheritance taxes out of the funds in the estate. This way, the persons who inherit money or property will receive them with the inheritance taxes already paid.

There are many other responsibilities and duties of an administrator or executor. If the deceased person owned property in another state, the administrator or executor may have to file papers in the appropriate court in that state (this is called an ancillary administration). Or if the deceased person inserted trust provisions in his or her will, the executor may be responsible for setting up the trust, appointing the trustee, and transferring assets from the estate to the trust. If the deceased person was involved in a lawsuit (either as a plaintiff or as a defendant) at the time of his or her death, the administrator or executor may have to handle that matter as the legal representative of the decedent. These are some of the many developments that an administrator or executor may encounter.

WHY DO YOU NEED TO CONSULT A LAWYER?

As the previous section reveals, there are many important and intricate legal questions and procedures involved in probating a deceased person's estate. If there is no will, the operation of the laws of descent and distribution must be determined. If there is a will, its validity and its terms and conditions must be determined. Specific procedures must be followed to have an administrator or executor appointed. Once appointed, there are numerous duties and responsibilities the administrator or executor must discharge in accordance with strict and intricate laws. If the will is challenged or the actions of the administrator or executor are contested by someone interested in the estate, there may be a lawsuit.

If you or someone else is appointed an administrator or executor, chances are you have never served as an administrator or executor before and you are unfamiliar with and confused by probate law and procedure. Thus the need for a lawyer's advice and services.

Similarly, if you are interested in an estate as a potential inheritor of money or property, to properly understand what you are entitled to, how and when you will receive it, and related title and tax matters, you will need to consult an experienced attorney who can explain these matters and represent and protect your interests.

HOW TO THINK ABOUT LEGAL AND RELATED ASPECTS

The following sections present a framework which will help you understand your rights and obligations if you anticipate inheriting money or property or if you are involved in or have questions about the probating of a deceased person's estate.

Find out whether the deceased person had a valid will or left no will.

Whatever your concern may be regarding an inheritance or the probating of an estate, the first step is to find out whether the decedent left a valid will or died without a will.

If there is doubt or confusion as to whether the decedent had a will, considerable problems may develop. For example, people close to the decedent may know that he or she made a will but no one may know where to locate it. Or the deceased person may have drafted more than one will during his or her lifetime. For instance, a man may have had one will drafted when his children were young and later had another will drafted when the children had grown up. However, there may be questions concerning whether the second will was properly witnessed. Since each beneficiary's share varies under the two wills, there may be bitter contests over the wills. Divorce and marriage often drastically affect the way a court interprets and enforces a will. For these and other reasons, it is essential that every effort be made to locate the will, if it is believed that there is one.

Bring the will (or a copy) to a lawyer and have the lawyer explain your rights and responsibilities under the will.

If the decedent had no will (or no will is found), explain to the lawyer your marital or blood relationship to the decedent and have the lawyer determine what, if any, share of the deceased person's estate you are entitled to under your state's laws of descent and distribution. Note that those laws, except for the surviving spouse, follow blood relationships only. If you are the surviving spouse or a surviving child, you will inherit. If there are no surviving spouse or children, then parents, brothers and sisters, and other blood relatives inherit on successive levels. If you are only a friend of the deceased, no matter how close a friend you may have been, the laws of descent and distribution will not avail you of anything.

Determine who is to take charge of the deceased person's estate (that is, who will serve as administrator or executor).

If your interest in an estate centers on who is supposed to take charge of the decedent's estate, again, much depends on whether there is a will or not. If there is a will, chances are it nominates a particular person to serve as executor. If it does not (or if the person nominated in the will does not or cannot serve), the court will appoint an executor, often the nearest adult kin. Your lawyer can advise you more specifically on this matter.

If there is no will, the court will decide who shall serve as administrator of the estate. Normally, state law dictates that the judge must consider the surviving spouse as the first choice to be administrator. If the surviving spouse will not or cannot serve, state laws determine who the judge must consider next—usually, the nearest adult kin. By consulting a lawyer who is familiar with the laws governing administrators in your state you can get advice on the outcome and consequences of the situation.

If you are to serve as administrator or executor, consult a lawyer and find out about your duties and responsibilities.

If you are nominated in a will to serve as executor or otherwise apply to the court to be appointed executor, or (where there is no will) if you apply to the court to be appointed the administrator, it is important to obtain the advice and assistance of an experienced probate lawyer. The duties and responsibilities of an administrator or executor are considerable and they are comprehensively governed by state law.

A review of the earlier section, "What Does Probating a Deceased Person's Estate Involve?" will reveal some of the many tasks an administrator or executor must perform. Naturally, the more substantial the assets in the estate or the more complex the estate, the more essential it is to obtain legal advice and assistance from an experienced attorney. That advice and assistance will be needed to properly handle the legal and practical aspects of filing the will, establishing the validity of the will, representing the estate against challenges or lawsuits, drafting the inventory and annual accounts, managing the estate, notifying and paying creditors, paying taxes, distributing bequests, transferring title, closing out the legal and financial affairs of the decedent, and many other matters.

One matter you should be sure to discuss with the lawyer is what compensation you will be entitled to if you serve as administrator or executor. If you serve as an administrator, specific state laws determine your compensation. Normally, you must notify the court of the compensation you seek for your services as administrator and the court must approve your request before you can take money out of the estate as your compensation.

If you serve as an executor, the will may specify the executor's fee or compensation. If it does not, state law governs. Again, you will have to submit your request for compensation to the court and have it approved by the court before you can take money out of the estate as compensation for your services as executor.

Determine whether you are entitled to an inheritance, when you should receive it, whether there are any terms or conditions attached to it, and what taxes may be due on it.

If you have reason to believe that you are entitled to an inheritance from the estate of a deceased person because of your marital or blood relationship to that person (if there is no will) or because you are mentioned in that person's will, consult a lawyer.

If the deceased person left no will, it is usually a simple matter to determine how the laws of descent and distribution require that person's money and property to be distributed among which surviving blood relatives.

If the decedent left a will, the will must be filed in probate court. (Most states have criminal penalties for willful failure to file a will in court after the testator's death.) By examining the will with your lawyer, you should be able to determine whether the will is valid and what bequest you are entitled to.

In addition to determining what money or property you are to inherit, it is important to find out if there are terms or conditions attached to the inheritance. If you receive money or property by operation of the laws of descent and distribution, there will be no terms or conditions placed on the money or property. If, however, you receive a bequest under a will, there may be special provisos or conditions attached to the bequest. For example, a deceased spouse may leave most of his or her property in trust for the benefit of the surviving spouse but specify that the trust will terminate if the surviving spouse remarries. Or a father may leave a house and property to his adult children but only upon the condition that they allow the surviving mother to live there and that they care for her until her death. A wealthy relative may leave a considerable sum of money to a nephew or niece but stipulate that it is only to be used for a college education or some other specific purpose.

In addition to understanding the terms and conditions that may be attached to the inheritance you are to receive, you should get some idea when you will receive the inheritance and what, if any, taxes will be due on it. Even a relatively simple estate may take a year or more to close out. Most states allow creditors of the deceased to file claims against the estate within nine months or a year of the date of death. The administrator or executor would not want to distribute any inheritance until all filing dates for claims against the estate have passed. Of course, if litigation develops or other legal complications arise, the estate may drag on for two or three years or more. On the other hand, it is not uncommon for estates to be prolonged for years as a result of inattention or shoddy work by the lawyer handling the estate for the administrator or executor. The section "Dealing with Lawyers," below, discusses methods of preventing and combating that situation.

Have your lawyer advise you as to any inheritance taxes that may be due on your inheritance. As noted earlier, inheritance taxes are levied on the person who receives an inheritance. They are based on the value of the inheritance and the relationship to the decedent of the person who receives the inheritance. If the inheritance is below the minimum tax level, no tax will be due. In other instances, the decedent may have provided in the will that inheritance taxes would be paid out of the estate and not by the person who receives the inheritance. Your lawyer's advice should resolve this matter.

Finally, two brief observations should be made regarding your right to disavow an inheritance and the right of a surviving spouse to "waive the will" of the deceased spouse and take a share greater than that provided in the will.

First, you do not have to accept an inheritance if you do not want to. Although it is not common, a person may feel that receiving an inheritance would be inappropriate. You can disavow an inheritance. The money or property will then be distributed according to the laws of descent and distribution (where there is no will) or according to other clauses in the will. Perhaps the most common situation in which a person disavows an inheritance is when a wealthy son or daughter disavows his or her inheritance so that the money and property can be divided among his or her less-well-off brothers and sisters. You cannot, however, accept part of a bequest and disavow the rest. For example, if you are bequeathed $5,000 and a family heirloom you don't like, you can either accept both or disavow both. You cannot pick and choose.

Second, if you are the surviving spouse, be aware that in every state you have the right to waive your spouse's will and take that share of his or her estate which you would have received had there been no will. This rule was developed by the courts to prevent one spouse from purposely leaving the other spouse nothing or next to nothing in the will, which the surviving spouse would normally not find out until after the spouse's death. To correct that devious arrangement, the courts allow the surviving spouse to disregard the paltry share provided in the will and take that share he or she would have received under the laws of descent and distribution—typically one-half or two-thirds of the deceased person's estate.

DEALING WITH LAWYERS

In addition to the general points about lawyers in Chapter 1, keep in mind the following advice about dealing with lawyers on an inheritance or probate case.

The more substantial or complicated the inheritance or the estate, the more careful you should be to hire an attorney with sound experience in inheritance and probate work. Many lawyers handle inheritance and probate cases. However, many lawyers who do are not sufficiently astute or expert in those areas. Moreover, many lawyers have a bad habit of neglecting such cases for excessive lengths of time.

One source of recommendations for experienced lawyers consists of local bank trust departments. The people who work in bank trust departments are usually familiar with many local lawyers who handle inheritance and probate work. In addition, you might try contacting the probate court. Ask the clerk or registrar for the names of two or three lawyers who have reputations for diligent work.

Given the fact that many lawyers have a reputation for dragging their feet when handling inheritance and probate cases, it is important to know that you have the right to dismiss your lawyer if he or she seriously neglects or procrastinates on your case. You can then take your case to another lawyer. To avoid dissatisfaction of that nature, have your lawyer explain, in detail, what steps will be taken on your case, what each step is designated to accomplish, how long it should take, and who has control over how promptly it will be taken. It's one thing if your case bogs down because other interested parties filed a lawsuit; given the backlog in the court, it may be many months before you get into court. But it's something else if your case bogs down because your lawyer has neglected it for months and has no present intention of putting the necessary time and effort into it to get it moving. If, on the other hand, your attorney gave you time limits on the various steps involved in the case, when time begins to drag you can set up a meeting with the attorney and determine why delays have occurred and who is responsible for them. If you reach the point where the only way to get work done on your case is to take your case to another attorney, you may have to compensate the first attorney for work done on your case. Nonetheless, taking the case away from a neglectful lawyer and bringing it to a second lawyer can be an effective (and sometimes the only) way to get your case moving.

When you hire an attorney to handle an inheritance or probate case, you will most likely encounter one of three types of fees—the flat fee, the hourly fee, or the percentage fee. Flat fees and hourly fees are discussed in detail in Chapter 1.

The third type of fee which lawyers charge on inheritance and probate cases is the percentage fee—a percentage of the value of the inheritance or estate. For example, suppose you go to a lawyer because you have been bequeathed $20,000 in a recently deceased relative's will but other relatives have decided to challenge the validity of that will in court. The lawyer may quote a flat fee or an hourly fee. Or he or she may quote a percentage, perhaps one-third, of whatever inheritance you end up with. If the will is upheld in court and you receive the full $20,000, the lawyer will take one-third (or some other percentage) of that amount. (If the will is defeated and you get nothing, the lawyer may charge an hourly rate for the time put into the case.) If the lawsuit is settled out of court and you end up with $15,000, the lawyer will charge one-third (or some other percentage) of that amount.

The percentage fees lawyers charge to handle probate cases vary widely. In many areas, lawyers charge a "sliding scale" percentage fee. For example, a lawyer may charge 7 percent of the first $10,000 in the estate, 5 percent of the next $5,000 in the estate, 4 percent of the next $10,000, 3 percent of the next $50,000 and 2½ percent of any amount over $75,000. Thus, the lawyer's fee for a $50,000 estate would be $2,100. The fee for an estate worth $250,000 would be $6,225. The percentages used vary widely, even among lawyers in the same community. Many such sliding scales utilize percentages which yield far higher fees for the lawyer than the one illustrated here.

Needless to say, when a lawyer uses a sliding scale percentage fee, it can be difficult for the client to grasp how much money the lawyer will actually receive in attorney's fees. If a lawyer quotes you a percentage fee or a sliding scale percentage fee, have the lawyer calculate dollar figures you can understand so that you will know how much money the lawyer will receive before you hire that lawyer.

It is important to realize that percentage fees, more than any other type of fee, offer the lawyer opportunities to receive grossly excessive compensation in comparison to the time and effort the lawyer puts into the case. Also, the higher the lawyer's percentage, the lower your percentage. With these considerations in mind, shop around and negotiate for a percentage fee that you feel is reasonable under the circumstances and that is related not only to the value of the inheritance or the estate, but also to the time and effort the lawyer puts into the case.

The best approach might be to refuse to hire a lawyer on a percentage fee basis and insist on either a flat fee or an hourly fee. After all, both the flat fee and the hourly fee are based on the estimated or actual amount of time and effort on the lawyer's part. A percentage fee, as noted, is unrelated to the time and effort required of the lawyer to handle the case.

Whether the fee is a flat fee, an hourly fee, or a percentage fee, be wary of lawyers who try to charge a high fee simply because the value of the inheritance or the estate is substantial and regardless of how easy and uncomplicated the lawyer's job will be. A percentage fee is automatically tied to the value of the assets involved. Thus, it can easily yield a fee that is excessive when compared to the amount of time and effort expended by the lawyer. Some lawyers, however, try to charge an excessively high flat fee or an excessively high hourly fee simply because of the substantial value of the assets involved in the case and without regard to how much—or how little—time and effort it requires. By shopping around among several lawyers and negotiating for a lower fee by emphasizing how uncomplicated your case is (if it is uncomplicated), you should be able to obtain the services of an experienced attorney for considerably less than if, as most people do, you simply hired the first attorney you contacted and agreed to the first fee that attorney quotes.

Before a fee is agreed on, discuss the manner in which it is to be paid. At this point it is important to realize where the money to pay the fee will come from. If you are consulting an attorney in regard to an inheritance you believe you are entitled to, the lawyer may want you to pay a sizable retainer (an initial installment on the fee) at the outset. This will have to come out of your pocket. If you pay a flat fee or an hourly fee, you will most likely have to pay the remainder of the fee out of your pocket as well. The lawyer will want to be paid on a regular basis as your case progresses, whereas you must wait until the case is resolved to find out whether you receive an inheritance and how much it is. With a percentage contingent fee, the attorney will have to wait until the case is resolved to receive the fee. At that point, you can pay the attorney's fee out of the inheritance.

In an estate case, if you hire an attorney to provide legal advice and assistance because you are the administrator or executor of the estate, the attorney can take his fee out of the estate as a cost of administration. If, on the other hand, you hire an attorney to represent your interest in an estate, to file a lawsuit against an estate, or a similar matter, you will be personally responsible for paying the lawyer's fee. Only the lawyer who represents the administrator or executor of the estate is paid out of the assets in the estate. In many states a lawyer is not supposed to take a fee out of the estate until the fee has been submitted to the court and approved by the judge. In practice, however, many lawyers ignore or avoid that rule. They begin taking money out of the estate to pay their fee as soon as they are hired to handle the case. Of course, the higher the attorney's fee, the more money that must come out of the estate to pay that fee (that is, the fee for the attorney who represents the administrator or executor of the estate). The attorney's fee will be paid before the people who are to inherit from the estate receive their shares. Thus, the more money the attorney takes out of the estate in fees, the less money there will be to distribute to the people entitled to share in the estate. In light of this, if you are an administrator or an executor, be sure to shop around and negotiate for a reasonable fee as diligently as if you had to pay the attorney's fee yourself (rather than paying it out of the assets in the estate).

Whether the attorney charges a flat fee, an hourly fee, or a percentage fee, arrange to pay the fee in periodic installments. (The only exception would occur if the lawyer is charging a percentage contingent fee and agrees to take the fee only when your case has been resolved and only if it is resolved in your favor.) Otherwise, make sure the lawyer is paid in installments. If possible, have the installment payments tied to various stages in the case. For example, if the lawyer represents you in your efforts to make sure you get an inheritance you feel you are entitled to and you are paying a flat fee of $1,500, pay part of the fee, perhaps $500, at the outset. If your case is to be heard in court, have the second $500 installment due when the lawyer gets a court date. That will give him or her an incentive to get a court date as soon as possible. Have the final $500 installment due when your case is resolved. If the lawyer represents you in your capacity as administrator or executor of an estate and the lawyer is charging an hourly fee, have the lawyer send you monthly bills listing, in detail, the number of hours put in that month (with dates and times), the specific tasks associated with each hour of work, the name of the person (if someone other than your lawyer) who did the work, and the hourly rates (if your lawyer has an associate or assistant do some of the work, you should know about that and you should not be billed at that lawyer's hourly rate for a less experienced associate or assistant). By paying on a monthly basis, you can keep track of what work the lawyer is doing. If the lawyer fails to put any time into your case for a month or two or cannot substantiate the bills he or she sends out, you can more readily find this out and make the lawyer accountable for his or her neglect or misrepresentations. Thus, paying in installments makes the fee more affordable, gives the lawyer an incentive to work diligently on your case in order to receive the next installment, and makes it easier for you to keep track of your lawyer's work.

9
Adopting a Minor

WHAT DOES ADOPTION INVOLVE?

Adoption is a legal procedure by which one person legally establishes the relationship of parent and child with another person who is not his or her natural offspring. Although the majority of adoptions are by married couples, many states allow an unmarried couple or a single person to adopt.

To adopt, you must comply with the legal procedures established by the state in which the adoption is to occur. Typically, these procedures involve criteria set by law regarding the qualifications of the adopting parent, finding an infant or youth who is legally adoptable, determining who has legal authority to consent to the adoption (this can involve many parties—the natural mother, the natural father, a government or private agency, the child, and perhaps others), filing the appropriate papers in court, presenting one's case in court, undergoing an investigation by government or private agencies, and in other ways meeting the legal requirements necessary for an adoption.

Once the adoption has been finalized, you must think about several important legal consequences of adoption. Although the reasons why a person or couple want to adopt one or more children vary, the legal significance of adoption is the same—the adopting person becomes the parent of the adopted child. The adopting parent incurs most or all of the legal rights and responsibilities which natural parents have with regard to their children. These include the parental obligation to support the child, the parental right to guide and determine the child's upbringing, and parental liability for the unlawful or accidental acts of the child (in those states where parents are liable for the civil and criminal misconduct of their children). Adoption also has important consequences regarding the right of the adopted child to inherit from the adopting parent (and the right of the adopting parent to inherit from the adopted child).

Of course, adoption also involves the interpersonal and family aspects of bringing an infant or youth into one's life and into one's family in the special and unique status of child to parent.

WHY DO YOU NEED TO CONSULT A LAWYER?

Adoption is governed in each state by specific and sometimes intricate laws. These laws establish who may adopt, who may be adopted, what procedures must be followed, what court has jurisdiction to hear adoption proceedings, whose consent must be obtained for a valid adoption, what investigations must be made into the interests and needs of the child to be adopted and the background and circumstances of the adopting parent, what effects adoption will have on the rights and obligations of the natural parents and the rights and obligations of the adopting parent, and other important legal aspects of adoption.

Because of the detailed and sometimes complex nature of adoption proceedings, it is always best to have a lawyer advise and assist you. Adoption laws in many states have changed considerably in recent years. More changes will certainly be made in years to come as social and legal attitudes toward adoption change. Because of this, it is important to consult a lawyer who is familiar with your state's current adoption laws.

Even in cases where adopting a child is relatively routine and uncomplicated, you may not be aware of the varied and important effects of adoption on your rights and obligations as the adopting parent. A lawyer familiar with adoption law can advise you as to your rights and obligations in a number of areas. For example, in many states an adopted child gains the right of intestate inheritance from his or her adoptive parent but loses the right of intestate inheritance from his or her natural parents. (Intestate inheritance means receiving property as an heir of someone who died without a will.) In those states, an adopted child is considered an heir of the adopting parent and will inherit from the adopting parent if the adopting parent dies without a will. Once adopted, the child loses the right of intestate inheritance from his or her natural parents. By contrast, in other states, an adopted child does not gain the right of intestate inheritance from his or her adopting parent. Nor does the child lose the right of intestate inheritance from his or her natural parents. In those states, an adopted child would not inherit from his or her adoptive parents if they died without leaving a will, although the child would retain the right to inherit from his or her natural parents. Of course, if the natural parents die years after the adoption, it may be difficult or impossible to trace and locate the adopted child so that he or she will receive the inheritance. Whatever your state's laws are in this important area, a lawyer can advise you as to the steps you should take to make sure your adopted child is fully protected in your will and by other appropriate means.

Another important and rapidly changing area where you will need a lawyer's advice is the right of an adopted child to learn the identity of his or her natural parents. This and other aspects of adoption involve rights of privacy and related legal issues that have seen significant changes and developments in recent years. Another changing and controversial aspect of adoption includes the authority of public or private agencies to screen adoptive parents, to investigate the conditions under which the adopted child is raised, and, in certain cases, to revoke the adoption if the public or private agency objects to the manner in which the child is raised. Also, during the adoption process, steps must be taken to properly amend the adopted child's birth certificate and school records. All these matters, even if the adoption is uncontested and routine, involve questions of law which require the advice and assistance of an experienced adoption lawyer.

HOW TO THINK ABOUT LEGAL AND RELATED ASPECTS

If you think out the basic legal aspects of adoption before consulting an attorney, you can save the attorney a lot of time. By thinking ahead and planning ahead, you can avoid problems and delays and perhaps save considerable money on attorney's fees.

Determine your willingness and ability to raise the child as your own.

At various points during the adoption proceedings the public and private agencies involved and the judge who hears the case will inquire into your willingness and ability to raise the child as your own. You should be able to convince all concerned of your willingness to raise the child as your own and substantiate your ability to support the child in a proper manner and environment. Often, plans and decisions must be made early on as to the child's relationship with other children in the adopting parent's family, the child's schooling, his or her religious training, and many other matters. Your lawyer, given his or her experience in adoption cases, should be able to provide practical information and assistance on these matters.

Your willingness and ability to raise the child as your own should not be taken for granted. It will not be taken for granted by the various private parties and public officials who will be involved in the adoption. You will have to articulate and substantiate your intentions and ability to their satisfaction. Prior thought and planning can avoid problems and help insure a successful adoption.

Investigate the history of the child and determine who has present parental rights (natural parents, guardian, government agency or institution, private agency or institution).

In some cases, this area will involve only perfunctory inquiries. In other cases, it will present serious problems. For example, if a husband is adopting his wife's child from her previous marriage and the child's natural father is deceased, there will be little difficulty in determining the child's history and the fact that only the natural mother has present parental rights to the child. By contrast, if you are planning to adopt a child from a government or private agency or institution, you may know almost nothing about the child's background and history. In other cases, it may be difficult to determine who has present parental rights regarding the child and therefore whose consent to the adoption must be obtained.

Whatever efforts are required, make a thorough investigation of the history and background of the child to determine who has present parental rights. You will also want to learn as much as possible about the child's medical history (so that you can plan the child's medical care accordingly). You will also want to know the extent of the child's education (so you can place the child in the appropriate grade and school setting). You will want to know if the child has established close and important relationships with other persons such as relatives or other youngsters at the state or private facility where the child has lived for some time (so that you can help the child continue or sever those relationships, depending on the circumstances). There are many other areas regarding the child's background and upbringing that must be investigated as thoroughly as possible so that you will understand the child better and have a happy and successful relationship as parent and child.

Determine whose consent must be obtained or how to dispense with consent.

Some person or persons have present parental rights to the child you wish to adopt. In order to legally adopt that child, you may have to obtain the written consent of that person or those persons. This may require little more than having the natural mother and natural father sign consent forms. Or it may involve little more than having the appropriate official of the public or private agency or institution which presently has parental rights to the child sign such consent forms. In other cases, however, consent becomes a bitterly contested issue and the adoption proceedings may develop into a court battle over the issue of consent.

The following sections outline several important points regarding consent.

Consent Must Be Voluntary and Free from Duress, Fraud, or Mistake When a person who has present parental rights to a child gives his or her consent to the adoption of that child by another person or persons, that consent must be given freely and voluntarily. An adoption can be revoked if it is later shown that consent of the natural mother or father or the consent of the parental agency or institution was obtained by means of false or fraudulent information or by mistake.

If the consent of the present parents or guardians cannot be obtained freely and voluntarily, it may be necessary to go to court and have the judge dispense with the requirement of consent. For example, the consent of the natural mother or father can be dispensed with, by order of the court, if it is shown that the natural mother or father abandoned the child or seriously neglected or abused the child or engaged in other serious misconduct toward the child. The consent of a public or private agency can be dispensed with, by order of the court, if it is shown that they are withholding consent without good reason.

Because consent is crucial to an adoption, it is important to seek a lawyer's advice and assistance in this area.

Legitimate Child and Consent Normally, for the adoption of a legitimate child, consent must be obtained from the natural mother and the natural father if either or both have parental rights to the child. Even if the natural parents are divorced, usually the consent of both must be obtained and not just that of the parent who has legal custody of the child.

If a legal guardian has been appointed for the child, the consent of the legal guardian will normally have to be obtained. The consent of the natural parents may also have to be obtained.

If the child is presently in the custody of a public or private agency or institution, the consent of the natural parents may be required as well as the consent of the public or private agency or institution—unless the agency or institution has parental rights to the exclusion of the rights of the natural parents. For example, some parents who place their child in an adoption agency or institution sign papers which authorize the agency or institution to consent to an adoption without having to obtain any further consent or approval from the natural parents.

Illegitimate Child and Consent In most states the consent of the natural mother is the only consent necessary if the child is illegitimate and is with the mother. However, in some states the consent of the natural father to an illegitimate child is required in certain circumstances—for example, where the natural father has legally declared his paternity.

If the child is presently under the care of a legal guardian, the consent of the guardian and the natural mother may be required.

If the child is in a public or private agency or institution, the consent of the agency or institution and the consent of the natural mother may be required, unless the mother signed away her right to refuse an adoption approved by the agency or institution.

The laws pertaining to the consents necessary for the adoption of an illegitimate child have undergone major changes in many states. Here especially a lawyer's advice will be needed.

Child's Consent Every state requires that the child to be adopted give consent to his or her adoption if the child is over a specific age. The age at which the child's consent must be obtained is as low as 10 in some states and as high as 14 in others. If the child refuses consent to be adopted by a particular person or persons, the public or private agencies involved and the judge will inquire into the child's reasons and feelings. Depending on the child's age and ability, the court may grant the adoption if the child is withholding his or her consent for petty or misguided reasons or out of irrational motives. Or the court may honor the child's refusal to consent but allow the would-be adoptive parent to file for adoption later on if the relationship and the child's attitudes change.

Dispensing with Consent A judge may order that an otherwise required consent be dispensed with under specific circumstances. As noted, the consent of the natural mother or natural father may be dispensed with if the mother or father abandoned the child, neglected or seriously abused the child, or through other misconduct demonstrated their unfitness to keep the child. The consent of a public or private agency or institution which has present parental rights may be dispensed with if the agency or institution cannot show good and substantial reasons why the adoption should not be allowed. Finally, the consent of the child may be dispensed with if the child refuses to give consent for insignificant or misguided reasons.

Consent is often the crucial aspect of an adoption. Careful thought, investigation, and planning must be given to whose consent is necessary, whether and how that consent can be obtained, and, if consent cannot be obtained freely and voluntarily, whether and how that consent can be dispensed with.

Determine what adoption laws and procedures must be followed.

The following sections briefly outline typical adoption proceedings. Many adoptions are quite routine and involve only perfunctory paperwork, investigations, and a court appearance. Other adoptions, however, become complicated or bitterly contested and may involve legal questions or disputes which result in litigation.

Filing Court Papers Before an adoption becomes legally effective it must be approved by the appropriate state court. Your lawyer will advise you as to what information is needed to draft the necessary court papers and forms. By doing as much and finding out as much as you can yourself, you can minimize the lawyer's work and his or her fee. Be sure the lawyer explains the various papers and forms he or she prepares and files in court so that you know how your adoption is progressing, what steps have been taken, and what steps remain.

Probationary or Trial Period with the Child to be Adopted In many states, the adoptive parent or parents must care for the child for a probationary or trial period (typically six months or one year). At the end of that period a final hearing on the adoption is held in court. The probationary or trial period gives the adopting parent and the child an opportunity to determine whether their relationship can work out and what problems or matters must be taken care of. The probationary or trial period is often dispensed with if the adopting parent is married to one of the natural parents or if the child has lived with the adopting parent for a considerable amount of time.

Investigation by Court or Public or Private Agency Before the court approves an adoption, state law may require that an investigation be made by a particular state agency (usually the public welfare department or a state agency that deals with children's services or family services). In some states the investigation is made by a private agency. If the adopted child is under the authority or care of a public or private agency, that agency may conduct its own investigation or background check into the adopting parent in addition to any investigations by other public or private agencies.

These investigations focus on the willingness and ability of the adopting parent to care for and raise the child and on the needs and interests of the child. Favorable findings by the investigators are often crucial to a successful adoption.

A lawyer who is familiar with adoption proceedings in your state can explain who conducts these investigations, what you should do to prepare for them, your right to be informed of the findings of the investigators, and, if necessary, how to challenge unfavorable findings.

In some states these investigations are perfunctory or may be dispensed with if the adopting parent is married to one of the natural parents and the other natural parent is deceased or has given written consent to the adoption.

In other circumstances, however, the investigation is a critical part of the adoption. The judge who hears the adoption case may rely heavily on the findings, conclusions, and recommendations of the investigators. Because of this, it is important to have an experienced attorney to advise you and assert your interests.

Court Hearing An adoption is a legal decree granted by a court which establishes the relationship of parent and child between two persons who do not share that relationship by natural birth. It is necessary to appear in court even if the adoption is uncomplicated and uncontested. Unless the child is a small infant, the child may have to appear in court as well as the adopting parents and other interested parties. To the degree that the adoption is uncontested and uncomplicated, the court appearance will be perfunctory. In many states, the parties appear in the judge's chambers or another room other than the regular courtroom. Adoption hearings, unless contested, are usually conducted in private to preserve confidentiality and protect the privacy of the parties. If the necessary papers have been filed and all other procedures have been followed, the judge may ask some routine questions of the adopting parent and the child to be adopted (depending on the child's age and other circumstances), and then grant the adoption.

If the adoption is complicated or contested, there may be an extensive hearing at court and perhaps a trial on such issues as consent, the fitness of the present parents or guardians, the fitness of the adopting parent, and other matters.

The paramount concern of the judge is the best interests of the child. The judge who hears the adoption case has the authority to deny the adoption if he or she feels it would not be in the best interests of the child.

Your lawyer can explain what the hearing on the adoption would be like. Also, the lawyer can review the questions you may be asked by the judge or others at the court hearing so that your answers will be prepared and appropriate.

Think about the permanence of adoption and your rights and obligations as an adopting parent.

Except in unusual circumstances, an adoption cannot be revoked once it is granted. (One of the natural parents or a person who previously had parental rights may succeed in having an adoption revoked if they can prove that their consent to the adoption was obtained through fraud, duress, misrepresentation, or mistake. Or other challenges to an adoption, such as allegations that the adopting parents are unfit, may result in the adoption being revoked. However, such revocations are rare.) Normally, once the adoption is granted, the adopting parent and the adopted child are parent and child for the rest of their lives.

Because of the importance of an adoption and because it establishes a permanent relationship of parent and child, such an undertaking should not be embarked upon without careful thought.

Once an adoption is granted by the court, the adoptive parent has a legally binding obligation to support the adopted child identical to that of a natural parent. Although it is of little concern to most adopting parents, if you live in a state where a parent can be held liable for the criminal or civil misconduct of a child, you will be that child's parent in the eyes of the law and may be subject to lawsuits arising out of the actions of your adopted child. (However, most states that make parents liable for the civil or criminal misconduct of their children limit the number of situations in which parents can be held liable and also limit the amount of money for which parents can be sued as a result of intentional or accidental injuries or damage caused by a child.)

Because of the important legal effects and consequences of adopting a child, it is worthwhile to have your lawyer explain the more significant consequences of adoption. One area you should review with the lawyer is discussed in the following section.

Think about inheritance—when you adopt is a good time to make a will or change your will.

In most states an adopted child inherits from his or her adopting parent in the same manner as a natural child. Moreover, if the adopted child dies before the adopting parent, the adopting parent inherits from the adopted child in the same manner as if a natural child had died. In other states, however, the opposite is true; an adopted child continues to have the right to inherit from his or her natural parents and not through his or her adopting parent. In still other states, there is some confusion regarding the inheritance rights of an adopted child.

To avoid or at least minimize any confusion regarding the inheritance aspects of adoption, have your lawyer explain the laws in your state regarding the adopted child's right to inherit from you and others in your family and vice versa.

An excellent way to handle the question of inheritance is to make a will (if you don't already have one) or change your present will so that it reflects exactly how you want the adopted child to be provided for after your death.

DEALING WITH LAWYERS

In addition to the general points about lawyers in Chapter 1, keep in mind the following advice about dealing with lawyers on an adoption case.

It is very important to find a lawyer who is familiar with your state's adoption laws. Adoption laws and procedures are undergoing significant changes in a number of states. Although many lawyers will take an adoption case, some are not sufficiently knowledgeable or up to date on adoption law and procedure. Ask each lawyer you contact how many adoptions he or she has handled and how recently.

In addition to the sources of names of lawyers to contact recommended in Chapter 1, you should also contact adoption agencies and perhaps the clerk of the family court, probate court, or other court in your jurisdiction which hears adoption cases.

If your adoption case is uncontested and otherwise routine, the attorney may quote a flat fee or an hourly fee. These types of fees are discussed in detail in Chapter 1.

10
Becoming a Guardian or Conservator

WHAT IS INVOLVED IN BECOMING A GUARDIAN OR CONSERVATOR?

Some people, due to age, illness, mental disability, or otherwise, are unable to competently handle their financial, business, property, and related matters. Some people, in addition, need someone to act as their legal custodian and have legal authority over them. Guardianships and conservatorships are the two positions recognized by law which authorize one person, the *guardian* or *conservator*, to manage the financial, property, and business affairs of the incompetent person, called the *ward*, and, where appropriate, have custody of the ward. (More than one person may serve as guardian or conservator of the same ward. They would be called *coguardians* or *coconservators.*)

In most states, there are various types of guardianships and conservatorships. Some guardianships include custody of the ward and other prerogatives over the ward as well as authority to oversee and manage the ward's financial, property, and business matters, whereas a conservatorship usually involves only the latter powers and not custody of the ward or related prerogatives over the ward.

The most common guardianships and conservatorships are those established to provide protection for minors, mentally retarded persons, persons with other mental disabilities or illnesses such as senility, and people who are profligate with their income and assets, known as spendthrifts. A special type of guardianship, called a *guardian ad litem*, exists when one person is appointed by a court to protect the interests of an incompetent ward with regard to a particular lawsuit or legal proceeding.

Since the specific duties and responsibilities of a guardian or conservator depend largely on the nature of the disability of the ward which requires the appointment of a guardian or conservator, it is useful to review the five most common types.

Guardian of a Minor—with or without Custody If the natural parents of a minor die, or if they abandon the child, are declared by a court to be unfit to have custody of the child, or for some other reason lose custody of the child, the court may appoint another person to be the child's guardian. Depending on the child's age and circumstances, the court may also grant the guardian custody of the child.

When a person becomes the guardian of a minor child, he or she has legal authority and responsibility to oversee the care, upbringing, education, and all other aspects of the child's life. If the guardian is granted custody of the child, the guardian may determine where the child will reside and how the child will be brought up—within limits. A guardian does not have all the rights or all the responsibilities of a natural parent. For example, in most states, if a minor child earns income or performs work, the natural parent has the right to that money and any other benefits of the child's labor. Of course, a natural parent also has a legal obligation to provide for and support a minor child. By contrast, a guardian—even with custody—does not have a right to money earned or any other benefits produced by the ward's efforts or labor. They remain the ward's, although, the guardian can manage them for the ward's best interest. By the same token, a guardian does not have an obligation to provide for and support a ward out of the guardian's own money or assets. The guardian may use money or property or assets belonging to the ward to provide for the ward. If the ward has no money or assets, the guardian may apply, on the ward's behalf, for whatever public or private assistance is available. Any assistance received (and any funds, property, or assets of the ward held by the guardian) must be used by the guardian for the benefit of the ward. Thus, the guardian must use the ward's assets and benefits solely to care for the ward and not for the guardian's personal use, but the guardian does not have to and cannot be made to use his or her own funds or assets to provide for the ward (although many guardians do so voluntarily).

There are other important differences between the relationship of a minor to a natural parent and that of a minor to a legal guardian. A natural child inherits from his or her parents (if they die without a will), whereas a ward does not inherit from his or her guardian (where the guardian leaves no will). (Of course, both natural parents and a guardian may provide for a child in their will.)

A natural parent may determine the religion into which his or her child will be indoctrinated. A guardian, normally, must raise the child in whatever religion the child's parents had chosen.

A child cannot sue his or her natural parents because of the way the parents provide for the child, as long as they provide minimally decent care and support. On the other hand, since a guardian is appointed by a court to serve the ward's best interests, a ward or someone acting on behalf of the ward can take the guardian to court if the guardian neglects the child's needs, abuses the authority to manage the money or assets of the ward, or otherwise mistreats the ward. In general, courts are much more reluctant to interfere with the relations between a natural parent and child than to intercede between a guardian and a ward.

In these and other areas there are significant differences between the rights and obligations of a parent regarding a natural child and the rights and obligations of a guardian regarding a ward.

Depending on the circumstances, the guardian may or may not seek custody of the minor ward. If the minor will be living with the guardian, it is appropriate to seek legal custody. Even though the minor may not live with the guardian, it might be necessary or appropriate for the guardian to have legal custody of the minor so that the guardian will have the authority to determine where the child will reside and how the child will be cared for—for example, at a boarding school, a public or private home, or a foster care facility. Having custody of a minor does not necessarily mean that the minor must or will live with the guardian, although most wards do live with the guardian who has custody of them.

If the ward will not be living with the guardian and other arrangements have been made which do not require that the guardian have legal authority to determine where the child will reside, a person may seek appointment as a guardian but without custody.

A guardianship of a minor terminates when the minor reaches the age of adulthood. In many states, if the minor marries before reaching the age of adulthood, that would also terminate the guardianship. When the guardianship of a minor ends, the funds, assets, and property of the ward held by the guardian at that time must be transferred to the ward.

Testamentary Guardian—with or without Custody Parents who have minor children often provide in their wills that, should they die while any of the children are minors, a designated person (or persons) shall be nominated to serve as guardian of the minor child or children. (See Chapter 6.) Typically, a close relative or friend or couple are so nominated. The parent who makes the will, however, can only nominate a guardian for the minor children. Upon the parents' death, the will must be filed in the appropriate state court. The person or persons nominated to be guardians must appear in court and seek the approval of the court before they can become lawfully appointed guardians. Any person interested in the welfare of the minor children may object to those persons being appointed guardians. It may happen that a person or persons who seemed good choices as guardians when the will was drafted may not be good choices under the circumstances at the time of the parents' death. The guardians nominated in the will may have moved away from the community where the children live, they may have lost contact with the parents and the children, or they may be too old or preoccupied with other matters to properly serve as guardians. Any number of circumstances may occur which make the persons nominated in the will inappropriate to serve as guardians. For these reasons, the court has the authority to hear anyone interested in the children's welfare and then decide who would best serve their needs and interests as guardians. Of course, the courts give strong preference to the persons named in the parents' will to be guardian if those persons are still willing and able to serve as guardians upon the death of the parents.

Usually, *testamentary guardians*—that is, guardians named in the will of the deceased parent—seek and are granted custody of the minor children if the circumstances warrant. Having legal custody does not necessarily mean that the wards will live with the guardians, although that is often the case.

Testamentary guardians generally have the same rights and obligations toward the ward as do nontestamentary guardians. Those rights and obligations were outlined in the previous section—but with one major difference. When a parent drafts a will and nominates a person to serve as guardian of minor children, the parent may include in the will special provisions regarding the manner or conditions under which the guardian shall serve. For example, many parents provide in their wills that all or a large portion of their estate shall be placed in trust for the benefit of the minor children and that the person who serves as guardian shall also serve as trustee of the trust. (See Chapter 7.) Nor is it uncommon for a parent to provide in the will that the person who serves as guardian must be willing to take the children into his or her own family and home and raise them as their own and shall forfeit the position of guardian if he or she fails to do so. Or a parent may provide in the will that the guardian must follow specific instructions regarding the children's education, religious training, social behavior, travel, or other matters.

Generally, a guardian who is nominated and appointed under a will must comply with whatever provisions are set forth in the will pertaining to the guardian's duties—as long as those provisions are reasonable and lawful. It does happen that a parent will attempt to empower the guardian with authority over the minor that a guardian cannot lawfully exercise. For example, the parent may try to empower the guardian with authority to refuse consent for the ward to marry until the ward reaches at least the age of 21 even though state law would permit the ward to marry, without the permission of the guardian, at age 18. In this situation, the provision in the will is contrary to state law and the guardian need not abide by it.

There may be other provisions in the will of the parent which govern matters of concern to the testamentary guardian. The will may specify what compensation the guardian shall receive for his or her service. The will may recite certain conditions governing how the guardian must handle specific financial, property, and business matters pertaining to the children. Here, the duties of the guardian may overlap those of the trustee of a trust set up for the children. As noted, a parent often names the same person to serve as trustee of the trust as was nominated to serve as guardian.

The will of the parents must be carefully examined to determine the rights, duties, and responsibilities of the testamentary guardian. Of course, the guardian must also comply with standards established by state law. Every guardian (and conservator) is appointed by a court. Legally, a guardian (or conservator) is an officer of the court and is accountable to the court for his or her action and decisions on behalf of the ward.

Normally, a testamentary guardian serves until the minor reaches the age of adulthood or otherwise (as through marriage) legally becomes an adult. (By contrast, parents often direct in the will that the trust established for the benefit of the children shall continue until the youngest child reaches the age of 21 or 25 or older.) When the conditions for termination of the guardianship are met, the property and assets held by the guardian on behalf of the ward must be transferred to the ward outright or under whatever terms are specified in the will of the parent.

Guardian or Conservator of a Mentally Retarded, Mentally Ill, or Mentally Handicapped Person—with or without Custody Whether a person has a congenital mental disability or one caused by an injury, illness, emotional trauma, or senility, that person, if incapable of properly handling his or her money, property, and business affairs, needs someone to oversee and take charge of those matters. If the mental disability is such that the person cannot manage personal and daily care without close direction, the person designated to manage his or her financial, property, and business affairs may seek legal custody as well. As with other types of guardianships with custody, legal custody of a mentally handicapped person does not necessarily mean that the mentally handicapped person will live with the guardian. Custody is authority to determine how and where the ward shall be cared for. The ward may be placed in a private or public residence or facility. Having legal custody allows a guardian to make such arrangements and sign consent and authorization papers on behalf of the ward where the ward does not have sufficient mental competency to do so for himself or herself.

When a person is appointed by a court to act as the overseer of a mentally handicapped person's money, property, and related matters, the name used is either *guardian* or *conservator*. In many states, a conservator has authority only to oversee and manage the ward's money, property, debts, contracts, and similar matters. If, in addition to that authority, custody is to be granted to the overseer or if the overseer is to have authority to consent to residential care, medical treatment, and similar matters, the overseer is usually called a guardian. In this chapter, the terms *guardian* and *conservator* are used with those distinctions in mind—a conservator is usually limited to authority to manage money, property, contracts, and business matters for the ward whereas a guardian, in addition to those powers, also may have custody of the ward or authority to consent to residential care of the ward and medical care or treatment and, to some extent, control the personal and interpersonal life of the ward.

The guardian or conservator of a person with a mental handicap, like any other guardian or conservator, may use the ward's income and assets to provide for the ward. This includes authority to use public or private financial assistance received by or on behalf of the ward. Also, as with any other type of guardian or conservator, a guardian or conservator of a mentally handicapped person must comply with strict standards established by law and enforced by the courts. Any person, such as a relative or friend of the ward or someone familiar with the ward, may go to court if he or she feels the guardian or conservator is neglecting or abusing the ward's needs and interests.

On the other hand, a guardian or conservator has no legal obligation to use his or her money or assets to provide for the ward. In fact, the guardian or conservator may deduct from the ward's income or assets fair compensation for his or her services as guardian or conservator. Such compensation, however, must be approved by the court. Many guardians and conservators who are relatives or friends of the ward take little or no compensation for their services.

The guardian or conservator of a mentally handicapped person often faces the difficult task of determining what is best for a person who is either largely or totally incapable of considering his or her own welfare in a rational and practical manner. Advice and assistance from trained and experienced professionals may be appropriate. The cost of such assistance may be charged to the accounts held on behalf of the ward. Even with assistance from professionals and others personally concerned with the ward, problems may develop between the guardian or conservator and the ward. Few persons assume such demanding responsibility for the care and protection of another as does a guardian or conservator of a mentally handicapped person. Because of this, you should give serious consideration to the task ahead before seeking appointment as the guardian or conservator of a mentally handicapped person.

If the mental disability is removed, cured, or overcome and the ward becomes capable of handling his or her financial, property, business, and personal matters and taking care of him- or herself, the conservatorship or guardianship can be terminated. Any funds, property, or assets held at that time by the conservator or guardian must be turned over to the ward.

Guardian or Conservator of a Spendthrift State laws recognize that some adults, for whatever reason, lack the ability to handle their financial, property, and business affairs with even a trace of frugality or caution. The term *spendthrift* is used to refer to such profligate people who, due to immaturity, emotional problems, addiction to drugs, alcohol, or gambling, or for whatever other reason, spend money foolishly and otherwise handle their financial and property affairs with a singular lack of discipline and foresight. Such cases are particularly harmful when the spendthrift has a spouse or children.

In serious cases of this nature, a court may grant a guardian or conservator legal authority to take charge of that person's money, property, and business dealings and manage them for his or her benefit and protection. People interested in the spendthrift's money or property must thereafter deal with the guardian or conservator.

As with any other guardian or conservator, the guardian or conservator of a spendthrift must always act in the best interests of the ward and can be brought to court by any interested person who can show that he or she is abusing the position of trust and authority or not properly protecting the ward. As with other guardians and conservators, the guardian or conservator of a spendthrift is not obliged to use his or her own funds or assets to provide for the ward, is entitled to receive compensation for services rendered on behalf of the ward, and must comply with all legal requirements and procedures relating to filing accounts and other papers detailing the assets and property of the ward and how the guardian or conservator has managed those assets and property and other matters.

Since a guardianship or conservatorship of a spendthrift is based on the ward's inability to handle financial and business matters with even minimal self-control, if the spendthrift at some point can show that he or she has reformed his or her wayward manner, the guardianship or conservatorship may be terminated. The guardian or conservator will then be relieved of authority to supervise the affairs of the spendthrift.

Guardian Ad Litem *Ad litem* means during or in relation to a lawsuit or other legal proceeding. A *guardian ad litem* is a person appointed by a court to protect the interests and rights of another person during a lawsuit or legal proceeding because the other person is incapable of protecting his or her own interests due to age, mental disability, or some other condition. For example, if a trust is established for the benefit of a minor child or a person with a mental handicap, the court may appoint a guardian ad litem to look after that person's rights and interests when the trustee files the annual account in court. The guardian ad litem is appointed to review the records, actions, and decisions of the trustee and make sure that the trustee has acted in the best interests of the beneficiary.

In some divorce cases, particularly where there is doubt as to whether one or both parents are acting in the best interests of the children, the court may appoint a guardian ad litem to look into the situation and report to the court regarding the children's welfare and circumstances and make recommendations as to custody, child support, visitation by the noncustodial parent, and other matters.

A guardian ad litem may be appointed in an adoption case to investigate and report on the child to be adopted and the adopting parents and what, in the guardian ad litem's judgment, would be in the best interests of the child.

In a civil lawsuit, if there are minors or mentally handicapped persons involved who do not have legal representation, the court may appoint a guardian ad litem to look out for the interests and protect the rights of such persons.

In some cases the court is not sure that all persons with an interest in a particular lawsuit or legal proceeding are represented before the court. The court may appoint a guardian ad litem to represent such unknown or unascertained persons. For example, if a person dies and it is unclear whether minor children or others may have an interest in his or her estate, the court may appoint a guardian ad litem to see that the estate is probated properly, to make every effort to determine whether there are minors or others who have an interest in the estate, and, if so, to protect the rights and interests of those persons and do what is necessary to have them receive the share of the estate they are entitled to.

Most guardian ad litems are attorneys appointed by the court to make sure the appropriate legal procedures are followed in a given case, such as probating a deceased person's estate or filing a trustee's annual account—or, in other cases, to investigate the circumstances relating to a person who does not have proper legal representation before the court and, due to age or mental disability or some other factor, cannot provide adequate legal representation by his or her own means.

In some cases, however, if a nonlawyer comes forward or otherwise displays an interest in asserting and protecting the rights of a minor or mentally disabled or other person in a given lawsuit or legal proceeding, the court may appoint that nonlawyer as a guardian ad litem. The nonlawyer guardian ad litem can then hire an attorney to provide legal advice and assistance as needed.

A guardian ad litem's duties relate only to a particular lawsuit or legal proceeding. The duties and responsibilities of a guardian ad litem depend largely on the nature of the lawsuit and whose rights and interests the guardian ad litem was appointed to protect. Usually, the guardian ad litem must file a report of his or her actions, decisions, and findings in court.

A guardian ad litem is entitled to compensation for his or her services either from the property or assets of the person he or she was appointed to represent or from the monies or property involved in the lawsuit or legal proceeding.

When the litigation or legal proceeding ends or when the rights and interests of the person for whose protection the guardian ad litem was appointed have been resolved, the guardian ad litem will be discharged.

WHY DO YOU NEED TO CONSULT A LAWYER?

The preceding sections outlined the basic duties and responsibilities of a guardian and conservator. It is apparent that to properly discharge the duties of a guardian or conservator, you must be familiar with legal procedures and requirements that are often complex and intricate. The procedures that must be followed to be appointed a guardian or conservator, the requirements relating to maintaining and filing in court accounts of actions taken and decisions made on behalf of the ward, the liability of the guardian or conservator, compensation for services rendered, under what circumstances the guardianship or conservatorship will end, and other critical matters all require the advice and assistance of a lawyer experienced in the legal and practical aspects of guardianship and conservatorship.

You should also be aware that the courts hold guardians and conservators accountable to a high standard of honesty, fairness, and responsibility in their dealings with the ward. A guardian or conservator may be found personally liable for abusing the ward, failing to use the ward's funds and property solely in the best interests of the ward, or in any other way abusing his or her position of trust as a guardian or conservator of a person who is not competent to manage his or her own affairs. In order to enable any interested person and the court to review the actions and decisions of the guardian or conservator to be sure that he or she is acting properly, a guardian or conservator must file reports, called *accounts*, usually every year, which disclose all money and property held on behalf of the ward, all income and profits, all expenditures, purchases, sales, and other disbursements, and related information regarding the actions and decisions of the guardian or conservator. Any person interested in the welfare of the ward may challenge the decision or actions of the guardian or conservator in court and may seek to have the guardian or conservator removed and held personally liable for serious errors or transgressions.

Because of the specialized legal procedures that are a necessary part of becoming a guardian or conservator, it is essential to seek the advice and assistance of an attorney. By obtaining the services of an attorney who is experienced in working with guardians and conservators and their wards you will also receive the benefit of the attorney's practical experience as well as his or her legal expertise. There will be many decisions regarding the ward's money, property, contracts, care and custody, and other important matters on which an experienced attorney can provide useful advice, information, and assistance.

If the guardianship or conservatorship is uncomplicated and more or less routine, you may not need a great deal of assistance from an attorney. Nonetheless, an attorney can make sure that the appropriate court papers are drafted and filed and that you learn how to keep the necessary records of your actions and transactions on behalf of the ward. Moreover, the attorney can explain, in words you can understand, your rights and responsibilities as a guardian or conservator under the laws of your state. Most people have only the vaguest concept of what a guardian or conservator is and is supposed to do. By consulting a lawyer who is experienced in this area, you can become informed of the many important legal and practical aspects of the job you are undertaking as a guardian or conservator.

If the guardianship or conservatorship is complicated, and especially if it will involve litigation, there is all the more reason to seek legal advice and assistance. The various laws and procedures which apply to guardians must be complied with. You may find yourself inadvertently at odds with those laws and procedures unless you are informed of your duties and liabilities and review your actions and decisions with a lawyer so that the appropriate legal requirements are handled properly.

HOW TO THINK ABOUT LEGAL AND RELATED ASPECTS

The following sections outline important aspects of serving as a guardian or conservator and useful information on finding and working with a good lawyer. After reading these sections, you will be more aware of your duties and responsibilities as a guardian or conservator, how to handle those duties and responsibilities, and how to handle lawyers.

Determine why the ward needs a guardian or conservator and why you should serve in that capacity.

It is important to analyze why the ward needs a guardian or conservator so that you file for the appropriate type of guardianship or conservatorship and make sure to find out from the lawyer and others exactly what your rights, responsibilities, and liabilities will be under the circumstances facing you as a guardian or conservator.

It is usually not difficult to determine why the ward needs a guardian or conservator. On the other hand, understanding your duties and responsibilities as guardian or conservator and understanding the needs and interests of the ward may require considerable and continued thought and effort. For example, there is a considerable difference between a guardian of a minor without custody and a guardian of a minor with custody. The same is true of being a guardian of a mentally handicapped person without custody as opposed to having custody of the ward. More personal and more difficult decisions and actions must be taken if one has custody of the ward than if one doesn't. In addition, each ward has special needs and interests. Being the guardian of a small infant is one thing; being the guardian, with custody, of a rambunctious adolescent is a different matter. Being the guardian or conservator of a senile relative who has little money or assets other than a regular social security check is very different from being the guardian or conservator of a brother who was a successful businessman with considerable financial and property holdings but who suddenly became mentally deranged and can no longer manage his sizable and complicated business affairs.

Answering the questions of why the ward needs a guardian or conservator and what are the ward's needs and interests raises another question: why should you be the person to serve as guardian or conservator? What is it about your relationship to that person that makes it necessary or appropriate for you to be the guardian or conservator? What knowledge or ability do you have and what information and assistance will you need in discharging your duties? It is essential to be candid and realistic in assessing the situation. Being a guardian or conservator means assuming considerable responsibility for another human being. Properly handling that responsibility begins with understanding why that person needs a legally appointed guardian or conservator, what that person's needs and interests are, what resources and ability you bring to the job, and what advice and assistance you will need from a lawyer, a financial advisor, medical or mental health professionals, or others.

Determine whether you should seek legal custody of the ward and, if so, where and by whom the ward will be cared for.

As noted earlier, there is considerable difference between being a guardian without custody and having custody of the ward. If you have custody of a minor or a mentally handicapped person, you must determine and make arrangements regarding where and how the minor or mentally handicapped person will live, how and by whom he or she will be cared for, and what kind of a relationship you should develop and maintain with the minor or mentally handicapped person.

It should be reiterated that having legal custody of a ward does not mean that the ward must live with you and your family. Having legal custody means that you have the legal authority to determine the residence, living conditions, and daily and long-term care of the ward. For example, if necessary or appropriate, a guardian with custody of a minor may enroll the minor in a boarding school where the officials and employees of the school will look after the daily care, education, and social activities of the minor. Similarly, a guardian with custody of a mentally handicapped person may place the ward in a public or private facility that provides medical, psychological, and other professional care as well as board, room, and hygienic and other daily needs of the ward.

On the other hand, if by necessity or choice the ward will live with you and your family, other considerations and arrangements must be attended to. The daily and long-term care of the minor or the mentally handicapped ward will necessitate numerous and continuous decisions and actions on your part. Much will depend on your previous and present relationship with the ward. Much will also depend on the previous and present relationships between the ward and the other members of your family with whom the ward will be living. Considerable thought and planning should be devoted to becoming and being a guardian with custody, especially if that means taking the ward into your own home and family.

Find out about the funds, property, and other assets you will be managing on behalf of the ward, how to manage them, and what records and reports are required.

As guardian or conservator, you may be responsible for managing the funds, property, and other assets of the ward. If the ward has an uncomplicated financial situation, that part of your job may be relatively easy. If, on the other hand, the ward has considerable assets or involved finances, your job will be more demanding.

You must also determine how to manage the ward's finances, property, and other assets with the best interests of the ward in mind: how to set up guardianship or conservatorship accounts, how to secure title and ownership of property in your name or control as guardian or conservator, how to keep accurate and thorough records of income, expenditures, purchases, sales, and other disbursements, and how to file and pay taxes due on the ward's income and property.

As guardian or conservator, you must file accounts in court, usually every year, listing all funds and assets held on behalf of the ward and all transactions involving those funds and assets for the time period covered by the account.

In managing the ward's money and property for the ward's personal welfare, you may also have to secure medical and other insurance for the ward, secure public or private assistance to which the ward is entitled such as Social Security, public welfare, veterans benefits, private pension or retirement benefits, and similar matters.

Find out about the legal and practical aspects of being a guardian or conservator—particularly your rights, obligations, and liabilities and how to obtain compensation for your services.

Each state has specific laws which govern the rights, obligations, and liabilities of guardians and conservators. Your lawyer can review and explain those laws and how they apply to you and your ward. An experienced lawyer can provide practical information and assistance as well as legal advice.

Among the many specific matters you will need to determine are: What procedures must be followed to be appointed a guardian or conservator by the court? What are your rights and obligations regarding the ward if you have custody? How should you provide for the daily and long-term care and needs of the ward? How can you best use the ward's income and assets and any public or private assistance that he or she is entitled to? What records must be kept and what accounts or other documents must be filed in court? What special circumstances must you deal with because of the particular needs of the ward or the particular conditions under which you serve as guardian or conservator? (For example, if you are a testamentary guardian, you must examine the will for special provisions governing your duties and responsibilities.) Under what conditions might you be held liable for violating the procedures or legal standards which govern guardians and conservators? Finally, as discussed in the next section, find out when and under what circumstances or conditions the guardianship or conservatorship will be terminated.

It is important to understand the standard of conduct to which a guardian or conservator is held by law. A guardian or conservator is a *fiduciary*—a person who serves in a legal position of trust and responsibility for the benefit of another person. All fiduciaries (such as executors, trustees, and attorneys, as well as guardians and conservators) are held to strict standards of fair dealing, diligence, and integrity in their management of the affairs of the person whose welfare they are charged with protecting and providing for. You can be held personally liable for violating the fiduciary trust which you assume as a guardian or conservator of another person. For example, a guardian who takes money out of the ward's account to buy clothing for him- or herself can be held personally liable for that misappropriated money. Similarly, a guardian who uses the ward's property as collateral for a loan and then uses the borrowed money for personal indulgences may also be held personally liable for abusing his or her authority as guardian.

A good way to understand your job as guardian or conservator is to have the lawyer who advises you explain the various papers and documents which must be prepared and filed in court. Also, have the lawyer explain your authority, under your state's laws, to give consent for matters relating to the ward such as consent for medical treatment, residential care, travel, and other matters that may arise in taking care of the ward. Also find out about your authority to review any contracts or legal obligations—such as bills—pertaining to the ward. Usually a ward, because of his or her age or mental disability, does not have legal capacity to enter into binding contracts for goods or services or other legal obligations. You, as guardian or conservator, may enter into contracts or incur legal obligations on behalf of the ward. Have the lawyer explain how to handle the situations in this area that might arise with your ward.

Finally, have the lawyer explain what procedures you must follow to receive compensation for your services as guardian or conservator. Although many guardians and conservators who are relatives or friends of the ward do not ask for any compensation, if you feel entitled to compensation (especially if your job as guardian or conservator involves considerable work and worry), have the lawyer take the necessary steps to secure reasonable compensation for your services. As with all other expenses related to the ward's needs, your compensation comes out of the money or assets held on behalf of the ward. Normally, any compensation you seek must be submitted to and approved by the court.

DEALING WITH LAWYERS

In addition to the general points about lawyers in Chapter 1, keep in mind the following advice about dealing with lawyers in a guardianship or conservatorship case.

The more complicated or involved the guardianship or conservatorship or the more substantial the assets of the ward, the more careful you should be to select a lawyer with proven experience.

If the ward is receiving assistance, education, training, or other care from a public or private agency, ask people at these agencies for the names of lawyers they have encountered on other guardianship or conservatorship cases and whose work they respect. Guardianship and conservatorship cases are usually processed in the family court or the probate court for the county where the ward resides. It might be useful to contact one of these courts and ask a clerk for the names of respected lawyers who handle such cases.

On guardianship and conservatorship cases, lawyers usually charge a flat fee or an hourly fee. (See Chapter 1 for a discussion of what you should know about lawyers' fees.) If your case is uncomplicated and routine, stress those factors to the lawyer and ask for a lower fee if the fee initially quoted by the lawyer seems unreasonably high. If there is no one challenging or objecting to you being the guardian or conservator, if it is clear the ward needs a guardian or conservator, and if there is not much money or assets involved, emphasize those points and negotiate for a low fee. If those conditions apply to your case, the lawyer's job will consist largely of drafting and filing routine papers and appearing at a perfunctory hearing in court. This is not the demanding and difficult work a lawyer must go through to prepare for and handle a contested or complicated case for which the lawyer deserves a substantial fee.

Since most guardianship and conservatorship cases take several months (or longer if it is contested or complicated), arrange to pay the fee in installments. You should not pay the entire fee at the outset, as some attorneys may try to get you to do. Pay part of the fee when you hire the lawyer. Make another installment when all the necessary papers have been properly filed in court. Pay the final installment when you go to court or when the guardianship or conservatorship is granted by the court.

In many situations, you should be able to have the lawyer's fee and related expenses paid out of the ward's assets or accounts. Your lawyer can follow the procedure necessary under your state's laws to accomplish that. Since you will be serving as guardian or conservator on behalf of the ward, it is only reasonable and proper that your expenses—including the lawyer's fee—should be paid (or reimbursed) out of the ward's money or assets.

11 Employment-Related Injury, Illness, or Disability

WHAT IS INVOLVED IN AN EMPLOYMENT-RELATED INJURY, ILLNESS, OR DISABILITY CASE?

Most employment-related injuries, illnesses, and disabilities are covered by Workers' Compensation laws (in some states they are called Employer Liability laws). These laws are administered by a board or commission instead of courts. Employees who are not covered by Workers' Compensation laws normally must initiate a conventional lawsuit against the person responsible for their injury, illness, or disability, usually the employer, a co-worker, or a third party. The Workers' Compensation system and the conventional lawsuit process are discussed in more detail below.

Most states have comprehensive laws requiring almost all employers to carry insurance which automatically pays compensation and other benefits to employees who suffer an injury, illness, or disability that is caused by or results from working conditions. In exchange for this comprehensive employment-related injury, illness, and disability insurance coverage provided by the employer, employees lose the right to sue their employer in court (for whatever compensation the employee could win—if the employee wins the case). Under Workers' Compensation, the employer is not subjected to conventional lawsuits by every injured, ill, or disabled employee. This avoids lawsuits which could involve protracted and expensive litigation and which might result in a judgment against the employer which would be financially difficult to meet. That situation is replaced, under Workers' Compensation, with a set premium the employer must pay to buy insurance that will cover the business for all employee injury, illness, and disability cases. Replacing each employee's right to sue his employer with comprehensive insurance has also improved the situation for employees in important ways. Prior to Workers' Compensation, employer liability was an unpredictable, all-or-nothing proposition. The employee-plaintiff had to prove fault on the employer's part or on the part of some person for whom the employer was legally responsible. The employee also had to endure the expense, delays, and other aggravations of initiating and pressing a conventional lawsuit. The vagaries of lawyers, judges, and juries lead to an inconsistent and haphazard handling of employer liability cases. Under Workers' Compensation, employees lost their right to sue the employer (or some other legally liable party) for whatever they could get the judge or jury to award in their favor—if they won the case. No doubt, some employees did win money judgments that were considerably larger than the compensation they would receive under Workers' Compensation. But other employees won little or nothing. Under Workers' Compensation, most of those unlucky employees would have received compensation and other benefits. Although the level and nature of the compensation and other benefits provided by many Workers' Compensation systems are barely adequate and often paltry, the Workers' Compensation system of employer-paid comprehensive injury, illness, and disability insurance is faster in providing compensation and benefits to employees than the private lawsuit process and protects more employees than the private lawsuit process. Unlike the private lawsuit process, when an employee files a claim for Workers' Compensation he or she does not have to prove fault on the part of the employer or any other person. In fact, under most Workers' Compensation systems, an employee can recover full statutory compensation and benefits even if his own negligence or carelessness caused or contributed to the injury, illness, or disability (although the employee may be barred from receiving compensation and benefits if his or her conduct was intentional or reckless).

An important feature of Workers' Compensation is that claims for compensation and benefits are handled initially by an administrative system. Under most Workers' Compensation systems, claims and disputes are heard much sooner than would be the case if the employee had to resort to the civil courts by means of a private lawsuit. Also, since the administrative officials who hear Workers' Compensation cases handle only those types of cases, they develop an expertise in this area. By contrast, judges in the civil courts are confronted with many different types of cases. And juries have little or no opportunity to develop any expertise at all. Because of the administrative procedures used in Workers' Compensation cases, they are often less complicated, less time-consuming, less risky, and less costly for the employee—and for the employer—than the conventional lawsuit process.

In contrast, an employee who is not covered by Workers' Compensation will encounter and must endure the often complicated, time-consuming, risky, and costly process of initiating a conventional lawsuit against his employer, a co-worker, or a third party. Unlike the Workers' Compensation system, in which an employee need only prove that his or her injury, illness, or disability was caused by or arose out of work conditions, an employee who is not covered by Workers' Compensation must prove much more. To begin with, if the employee caused or contributed to his or her injury, illness, or disability, he or she may have no case against anyone. Such legal doctrines as "contributory negligence" and "assumption of the risk" still apply to conventional lawsuits in many states. Those doctrines do not apply to most Workers' Compensation systems; an employee can usually collect under Workers' Compensation despite many types of conduct on his or her part which would bar him or her from recovering in the conventional lawsuit process.

If a co-worker or a third party for whom the employer is not legally responsible caused the employee's injury, illness, or disability, the employee will have to sue that co-worker or that third party. Generally, an employee not covered by Workers' Compensation can sue the employer only if the employee can prove that the employer was directly or primarily at fault. *Fault* means that the employer violated a legal standard of conduct owed to the employee. Similarly, if the employee must sue a co-worker or a third party, he or she must prove that the co-worker or third party was at fault—violated a legal standard of conduct—which caused the employee's injury, illness or disability. Under Workers' Compensation, fault is not an important or difficult issue most of the time. The employee must prove only that the injury, illness, or disability was caused by or arose out of working conditions. It doesn't matter who—the employer, a co-worker, a third party—caused the injury, illness, or disability. Nor does it matter whether that other person was at fault. In a sense, Workers' Compensation is largely a "no-fault" system; if the injury, illness, or disability is work-related, the employee is automatically entitled to compensation and benefits. (The only major exception is where the employee's own intentional or reckless conduct caused his or her injury, illness, or disability.)

If an employee covered by Workers' Compensation can prove that his or her injury, illness, or disability was work-related and that it was not caused by his or her own intentional or reckless conduct, he or she is entitled to compensation and benefits that are determined by the tables and formulas contained in the Workers' Compensation statutes. Essentially, that compensation and those benefits are geared to the employee's wage or salary, the extent and nature of the injury, illness, or disability, the number of dependents, and whether the employee receives other private or public assistance. Once the Workers' Compensation hearing officer finds in the employee's favor, the employer's insurer must pay the required compensation and benefits. This is very different from the situation faced by an employee who is not covered by Workers' Compensation and who must initiate a conventional lawsuit. As noted, that employee must prove that the employer or a co-worker or third party was at fault. He or she must also prove what his or her losses and expenses have been and will be and seek an amount of money that will compensate him or her for those losses and expenses. The employee must then try to collect that amount of money—if the judge or jury finds in his or her favor—from the employer, co-worker, or third party. Often, the length of time it will take to get into court, the risk of something going wrong at court, and the pressing nature of the employee's dire circumstances force the employee to settle the suit against the employer, co-worker, or third party. On the other hand, if the employee has a solid case and can wait to go to trial to win a substantial judgment, or negotiates a handsome settlement, he or she may win more money than he or she would have received under the generally meager Workers' Compensation system.

In sum, there are considerable differences in the legal and practical problems faced by employees who are covered by a no-fault Workers' Compensation system as opposed to the problems faced by employees who must initiate a conventional lawsuit and prove that some other party was at fault.

Despite these considerable differences, all work-related injury, illness, and disability cases have common aspects, whether they are handled through a Workers' Compensation administrative system or through the courts. For instance, the employee must gather sufficient evidence to prove the cause, nature, extent, history, and prognosis of the injury, illness, or disability. He or she must present accurate proof or reasonable estimates of medical care and treatment, medication, physical therapy, rehabilitation services, and related needs and expenses. Compensation and benefits under Workers' Compensation must be calculated by consulting the statutes or, if the employee is not covered by Workers' Compensation, he or she must calculate an amount of money which will compensate for wages lost and other expenses related to the injury, illness, or disability. Allowances for dependents must be determined. If there is a scar, loss or impairment of a bodily function, or disfigurement, a monetary value must be calculated so that compensation for that can be sought. Under

Workers' Compensation, employees may be restricted or barred from bringing a claim for pain and suffering. Employees not covered by Workers' Compensation are not restricted from suing for pain and suffering. This is a very important difference between the legal rights of employees covered by Workers' Compensation and the legal rights of those who are not. As is well known, pain and suffering often comprise one of the most important elements in a lawsuit for an injury, illness, or disability. If an employee receives private or public wage loss, unemployment, accident, illness or disability benefits, or other insurance coverage or public assistance, he or she must determine how those benefits will affect his or her claim under Workers' Compensation or his or her lawsuit. Under many Workers' Compensation systems, the employee is entitled to full Workers' Compensation benefits even if he or she also receives private insurance. On the other hand, if the employee receives public assistance—such as Social Security disability payments—the Workers' Compensation benefits may be reduced by the amounts he or she receives from that or other public assistance programs. An employee not covered by Workers' Compensation can sue the liable party for all losses and expenses resulting from the injury, illness, or disability and does not have to reduce the amount he or she is suing for by amounts received from private insurance or public assistance. However, when the employee receives a money judgment or settlement, he or she may have to reimburse the insurance companies and the public agencies that extended such benefits.

Under Workers' Compensation, an employee may be faced with the choice of receiving the statutory compensation and benefits for the duration of his ailment or incapacity or accepting a settlement with the employer's insurer. Such a settlement is sometimes referred to as a *lump sum.* A lump-sum settlement is a specific amount of money which the employee receives all at once and in return for which he or she foregoes all future claims for any other compensation or benefits.

A somewhat different choice may be faced by an employee who is not covered by Workers' Compensation and who sues his or her employer, a co-worker, or a third party in court. That employee, depending on the soundness of his or her case, may have the alternatives of either waiting for a trial and taking the risk of getting whatever the judge or jury awards—if they find in his or her favor—or making an out-of-court settlement with the other party (or the insurer) which will provide an amount of money now but for which he or she must agree to dismiss the lawsuit and forego all future claims against the employer, co-worker, or third party with regard to that injury, illness, or disability.

The advantages and disadvantages of staying on Workers' Compensation or accepting a lump-sum-settlement, going to court, or accepting an out-of-court settlement are unique to each case and each employee's circumstances. Experienced legal advice is essential.

As can readily be seen, recovering compensation for a work-related injury, illness, or disability requires a thorough knowledge of personal injury law and employment liability law including, where applicable, Workers' Compensation. It also requires experience in the practical and financial aspects of dealing with a work-related injury, illness, or disability and recovering as much compensation and benefits as possible from all available sources.

WHY DO YOU NEED TO CONSULT A LAWYER?

Whether your employment-related injury, illness, or disability is covered by Workers' Compensation or requires a conventional lawsuit may be easy to determine. How to proceed once that has been determined will be considerably more complicated and difficult to decide.

If your employment-related injury, illness or disability is covered by Workers' Compensation, you must notify your employer of your claim in writing within a specific period of time. That notice must meet statutory requirements. If your employer's Workers' Compensation insurer does not contest your claim, you would still be wise to consult a lawyer and review the situation to make sure you receive the full amount of benefits and compensation to which you are entitled under your state's Workers' Compensation laws. Unless you seek advice from a lawyer familiar with those laws, you may be short-changed on wage-loss compensation, medical expense payments, payments for your dependents, or other benefits.

If your employer's Workers' Compensation insurer rejects your claim, you will certainly need the advice and assistance of a lawyer who is familiar with the Workers' Compensation system in your state. When an insurer denies an employee's claim, the employee must file papers with the state Workers' Compensation commission. He or she must also gather evidence to prove that the injury, illness, or disability was employment-related, establish the nature, extent, history, and prognosis of the injury, illness, or disability and seek the full amount of compensation and benefits provided in the Workers' Compensation statutes. In some cases, the attorney may be able to convince the insurer to reverse its initial denial of the employee's claim without going through administrative hearings. If that cannot be done and the insurer intends to contest your claim as far as possible, you will need an attorney to make sure your case is presented in the strongest manner and in compliance with various and complicated rules of evidence and procedure. An employee whose Workers' Compensation claim is denied by the insurer is usually in a difficult position: he or she is not able to work because of the injury, illness, or disability but the insurer will not voluntarily pay Workers' Compensation benefits while he or she is out of work. This necessitates getting a hearing before a Workers' Compensation officer as soon as possible to seek temporary or interim benefits until a full hearing on the merits of the claim can be scheduled. Many Workers' Compensation laws provide expedited hearings for temporary or interim orders.

If your injury, illness, or disability is not covered by Workers' Compensation, you must seek compensation for your losses by initiating legal action against the employer, a co-worker, or a third party. For example, if you develop a lung disease or disability because of the contaminated air you breathe at work, you will sue the employer. If, on the other hand, you are injured at work by a salesperson from another company who carelessly cuts you while demonstrating a new sheet-metal cutting device, you would sue the salesperson and his or her employer. Whether you sue your employer, a co-worker, or a third party, you will need expert legal advice as to whom to proceed against and how. Unlike employees covered by Workers' Compensation, an employee who is not covered by Workers' Compensation must utilize the civil courts. In many jurisdictions, the employee must wait many months or even years to get into court. Unless you have sufficient private insurance, you may have to rely on public assistance during the time you are out of work and waiting for your case to be assigned a trial date. During that period, the party you are suing (or the insurer) may be open to settlement negotiations. Given your difficult circumstances, you may not be in a position to hold out for an adequate and fair settlement. Without the advice and assistance of an experienced attorney, your dire circumstances and unfamiliarity with the law and accepted standards may lead you to shortchange yourself. If the other party (or the insurer) does not agree to settle out of court, you will certainly need a lawyer to handle the pretrial and trial proceedings. Proving the cause, nature, extent, history, and prognosis of your injury, illness, or disability, proving what compensation you deserve, and collecting any money judgment in your favor are all matters which require the assistance of an experienced trial attorney.

While you are suffering from an injury, illness, or disability, your physical and mental condition may be worsened by anxieties over how you and your family will cope financially. How will the medical and other bills be paid? How will you make up for lost paychecks? What kind of therapy and rehabilitative services do you need? What compensation will you receive for scars, disfigurement, or loss or impairment of a bodily function? What private insurance or public assistance are you entitled to and how do you go about obtaining them? Understandably, distress over these matters may worsen your physical and mental condition and interfere with your ability to make sound decisions. That distress may also impede your recovery and rehabilitation. The only way to reduce your anxieties and distress regarding the complicated legal questions and problems confronting you and your family is to have an experienced attorney working on your side.

HOW TO THINK ABOUT LEGAL AND RELATED ASPECTS

The following sections review important points to think about to make sure you handle your case properly and effectively.

Determine exactly what or who caused your injury, illness, or disability and in what way it is employment-related.

Determining what or who caused your injury, illness, or disability and how it is work-related is a prerequisite to determining who is legally liable and how to go about receiving compensation and benefits.

In most cases, it is easy to determine what or who caused or contributed to the injury, illness, or disability. If your employer failed to repair a broken stair or a defective machine and you were injured, the cause of your injury is clear. Similarly, if you live in a healthy and relatively pollution-free environment—except at work—and you develop an illness or disability which can be traced directly to material in the air you breathe at work, the cause of your illness or disability is clear. On the other hand, if you develop a vision problem or a nervous disorder, it may be difficult to determine whether it was caused by conditions at work or by conditions at home or elsewhere. In some cases potential causes are present at work but others exist at home or other places where you spend time. In these cases, it may be necessary to consult medical and other experts to assist in determining the cause of your injury, illness, and disability and to what degree a condition related to your employment is the cause or a contributing factor.

Determine who is legally liable for your injury, illness, or disability. Are you covered by Workers' Compensation or must you initiate a lawsuit against your employer, a co-worker, or a third party?

It will usually be a simple matter for an attorney to determine whether your injury, illness, or disability is covered by Workers' Compensation or not. If it is covered, the attorney can explain what papers must be filed, what steps can be taken immediately to apply for compensation and benefits, what long-term steps will be necessary, and what the overall prospects for your case are. In a sense, if you are covered by Workers' Compensation, it doesn't really matter who is responsible for your injury, illness, or disability as long as it is employment-related and was not caused by your own intentional or reckless conduct. For example, if an employee intentionally inflicts a wound on him- or herself, or if he or she becomes drunk and injures him- or herself in a mishap at work, he or she may not be able to collect under Workers' Compensation. Since he or she is the cause of his or her own injury or disability, there is no one else to sue or collect from. If, on the other hand, an employee's injury, illness, or disability is caused by the employer, a co-worker, or a third party (such as a visitor, a government official or inspector, or an independent contractor), he or she can collect under Workers' Compensation. (If the injury, illness or disability is caused by a third party, the employee has the option of suing that third party directly and foregoing Workers' Compensation or accepting Workers' Compensation and letting his or her employer's insurer sue the third party.) An employee can recover compensation even if no one is at fault for the injury, illness, or disability—as long as it is employment-related. For example, if the employee is injured at work in a storm or natural disaster, he or she is covered.

If the employee is not covered by Workers' Compensation, he or she faces many different questions and problems. First, he or she must determine who, if anyone, was at fault for the injury, illness, or disability. In the private lawsuit system, the plaintiff must show that the defendant was at fault—that the defendant violated a standard of conduct owed to the plaintiff. For example, if you are injured in a storm or a natural disaster, you cannot sue your employer or anyone else if they were not at fault in some manner. You must be able to prove in court that your employer, a co-worker, or a third party caused your injury, illness, or disability and did so in a manner which makes them liable to you. For example, if you develop a nervous disorder because of stress and pressure at work, it may be difficult to prove that your employer or a co-worker or a third party caused that nervous disorder in a manner which makes them legally liable to you. Moreover, in the private lawsuit system, you may lose your case or have any award in your favor diminished if you contributed to your injury, illness, or disability. That is, if you are at fault, you can't sue someone else; if you are partially at fault, you may win a judgment against the other party but only for that portion of your losses and expenses which represents that other party's share of responsibility for your injury, illness, or disability.

If you can prove that your employer or a co-worker or a third party caused your injury, illness, or disability, you can initiate a lawsuit against the liable party. This involves filing papers at court, pretrial research, investigation, and preparation and a trial of the facts, issues, and merits in court, unless your case is settled out of court.

Keep an accurate and complete record of your injury, illness, or disability.

You must be able to substantiate the nature, extent, history, and prognosis of your injury, illness, or disability. Whether you are covered by Workers' Compensation or must proceed by a conventional lawsuit, what you receive in compensation and benefits will depend largely on what you can prove about your injury, illness, or disability. What does it involve? How long has it lasted and how long will it continue? What does it prevent you from doing? How much pain and suffering must you endure? Are there scars, disfiguration, or loss or impairment of a bodily function? Will you recover completely or only partially? Will it prevent you from resuming your job? You must also be able to prove medical and many other expenses incurred for care and treatment—doctor bills, hospital bills (in-patient and out-patient), physical therapy, prosthetic devices, counseling, and rehabilitation services. Other losses resulting from the injury, illness, or disability must be dealt with; for example, if an injury at your regular job makes it impossible for you to continue a second job, you must seek compensation for losing that secondary source of income. If there are psychological or mental disorders caused by the injury, illness, or disability, you must be able to substantiate them. Did you require psychiatric or similar counseling or care? Were you prevented from leading a normal emotional and mental life because of the injury, illness, or disability?

Substantiating these matters requires consulting the appropriate medical authorities and other health care professionals whose records and reports will set forth their expert observations, tests, and opinions as to the nature, extent, history, and prognosis of your injury, illness, or disability. In addition, however, there is much you can do to maintain accurate and complete records which can be just as effective—if not more effective—in substantiating your case. Keep a diary or journal from the outset. Record the cause, the nature, the extent, and the progress of your injury, illness, or disability; all pain and suffering, loss or impairment of bodily function, scars or disfigurement, and emotional or mental disorders should be noted in detail. Visible manifestations of the injury, illness, or disability should be photographed. For example, if you are hospitalized or placed in a cast or traction or must use a crutch or prosthetic device, have a series of photographs taken which represent the course of your injury, illness, or disability from its onset to the present. If at all possible, have photographs taken of the premises, object, or condition which caused the injury, illness, or disability and where it took place. The more flagrant or shocking the premises or condition, the more powerfully those photographs will speak on your behalf. Reports from medical, hospital, and other professionals are often technically worded and clinically unemotional. Your own personal diary or journal recounting what you have gone through and what you have to look forward to will have considerable impact on anyone who hears your case. Of particular importance is the powerful and convincing impact of photographs. A series of photographs showing where and how the injury, illness, or disability arose and a second series of photographs showing your condition throughout the course of the injury, illness, or disability will bring home to the hearing officer, the judge, or the jury what happened, where and how it happened, what you had to go through and endure, and what condition you are now in compared to before the injury, illness, or disability. Photographs are perhaps the least expensive yet most convincing method of preserving an account of your injury, illness, or disability in a manner which everyone can understand and sympathize with.

Determine what compensation and benefits you may claim and how to obtain them. Also find out what procedures and timetables are involved.

The type of compensation and benefits you claim will depend on whether you are covered by Workers' Compensation or not. If you are covered, the Workers' Compensation statutes must be consulted. They contain various tables and formulas for computing the compensation and benefits to which you are entitled given the nature, extent, history, and prognosis of your injury, illness, or disability, your wage or salary, and number of dependents. If you are not covered by Workers' Compensation, you will need expert legal and medical assistance in determining how much to sue for to compensate yourself for the injury, illness, or disability and related losses and expenses.

Whether you will be proceeding under Workers' Compensation

or through a conventional lawsuit, your calculations must start by establishing how much money you were making at the time of the injury, illness, or disability and what expenses and losses can be attributed to that injury, illness, or disability.

In addition to the compensation you are entitled to under Workers' Compensation or by suing the liable party, you must determine what, if any, private insurance and public assistance is available. If you have private accident, illness, or disability insurance, find out how to collect on your policy. If you qualify for unemployment compensation, Social Security disability, veterans' benefits, welfare, or other public assistance, find out how to apply. Chances are that you will need all the financial assistance you can find. In addition, medical and rehabilitation care and treatment programs, counseling, job training, and other services may be available through private insurance companies or public agencies.

The private and public assistance you are entitled to is especially important if it will be some time before you start receiving Workers' Compensation benefits. It is even more important if you are not covered by Workers' Compensation and must sue to receive compensation from the liable party. Unfortunately, in many jurisdictions, it takes many months or even years to get into court on a personal injury case. During that period you will most likely be in dire need of financial and other assistance. You should contact a lawyer familiar with employment liability law. Also contact your labor or employee organization representatives, your local, state, and federal elected officials, the claims officers at private insurance companies and public assistance agencies, and all other persons who can assist in making sure you receive the benefits and compensation to which you are entitled while waiting to collect Workers' Compensation or waiting to go to court.

Find out what procedures must be followed to obtain compensation and other benefits and how long those procedures may take. If you are applying for Workers' Compensation benefits, there may be a standard procedure, especially where your employer's insurer does not contest your claim. If your claim is contested, time-consuming proceedings may be involved. Contested Workers' Compensation claims usually center on one or all of the following three issues: (1) the employer's insurer denies that your injury, illness, or disability is work-related; (2) coverage is not denied but the amount or type of benefits is contested; (3) you may want to settle your claim in a lump sum and the insurer may want to as well but an acceptable figure cannot be reached. In the first two instances, you must take steps to get before a hearing officer as soon as possible so that you can start receiving temporary or interim benefits until a full hearing on the merits of your case and other issues can be scheduled. In the third situation, you will be faced with a choice. On the one hand, you can receive regular compensation while you are out of work due to the injury, illness, or disability but you cannot engage in other income-producing work. If the insurance company finds out that you are working somewhere "on the side" while collecting Workers' Compensation, the insurance company may reduce or cancel your compensation. They will argue that you are capable of going back to your regular job. By contrast, if you settle your claim with the insurance company for a lump sum, they will no longer be interested in your case. You can then engage in whatever income-producing work or activities you are capable of without risking the loss of the lump-sum settlement money—unless the insurance company tries to rescind the lump-sum settlement, arguing that your outside work proves that you misrepresented the nature and extent of your injury, illness, or disability.

If you are not covered by Workers' Compensation and must initiate a lawsuit against the liable party, it is all the more important to understand what procedures must be followed and how long they may take. As noted, it may take many months or even years to get into court. In that case, you must apply for whatever private and public assistance you can get while waiting to go to court or work out an out-of-court settlement. The time it may take to get into court and the risks inherent in any trial are two factors which often militate in favor of accepting an out-of-court settlement. Experienced legal advice is essential in this area.

Determine when and under what circumstances your Workers' Compensation benefits will end and the advisability of a settlement. Or determine how a money judgment from your lawsuit or a settlement should be used.

Generally, if you recover from your injury, illness, or disability and are able to return to work, your benefits and compensation under Workers' Compensation will terminate at that point.

If you are not covered by Workers' Compensation, the amount of money you may sue for, at least to cover lost wages, is limited by the length of time your injury, illness, or disability kept you out of your normal employment. But that is only with respect to lost wages. You may sue for future as well as present medical expenses and other costs. If the injury, illness, or disability prevents you from returning to work at the same pay level as previously, you can sue for the difference between what you will make and what you would have made had you not suffered the injury, illness, or disability.

If you receive private or public assistance, determine when and under what conditions those sources of assistance will end. Also find out whether you must reimburse those sources out of any compensation or settlement you receive.

You should understand some basic points about settlements. A *settlement* is a sum of money for which you agree to release the other party from liability for future claims relating to your injury, illness, or disability. That is, in exchange for a given amount of money, the other party is absolved of any further obligation or liability to you. Because of this, it is important to review settlement opportunities and offers carefully with your lawyer. Find out not only the gross or total amount of the settlement, but what expenses and other items will be deducted from the settlement money and how much—or how little—you will end up with in dollars and cents. Your lawyer's fee may take a large chunk out of the settlement money. Unpaid bills for doctors, hospitals, laboratories, and other medical professionals may have to be paid out of the settlement. If you are obligated to reimburse private insurance companies or public assistance agencies for the money they extended to you, those amounts must be paid out of the settlement money. Because of these numerous and sizable deductions, do not be overly impressed or misled by a large gross settlement figure; the net—what you will actually end up with after all deductions are made—is what you should be concerned with.

In considering the advantages and disadvantages of a settlement, also consider what you will do with the net settlement money you receive. How long will it last? Can you bank or invest some of it? Will it realistically compensate you for the effects of the injury, illness, or disability? No settlement can restore you to the condition you were in prior to the injury, illness, or disability. A settlement is money. Money can only purchase goods and services. You must think in terms of what goods and services you will need for past, present, and future care and related needs. What those goods and services will cost is what you want from a settlement.

DEALING WITH LAWYERS

In addition to the general points about lawyers in Chapter 1, keep in mind the following advice about dealing with lawyers on a Workers' Compensation case.

In every community or county there are usually a number of lawyers who handle employment-related cases on a regular basis. You may be able to get the names of three or four such lawyers by asking your co-workers, union officials, or members of your employee organization. Talk to people you know who have been injured at work. Ask them about the attorney who represented them.

Whatever the nature of your employment-related injury, illness, or disability, your objective is money—hopefully, enough money to compensate you for lost wages, medical bills, and all other expenses which result from the injury, illness, or disability. As noted earlier, all money can do is buy goods and services. You want that amount of money which will buy the goods and services necessary to provide proper care and treatment and attain the highest level of recovery. With this in mind, you want to make sure that as much of the money you receive as possible can be used for those purposes. You want to hire a good attorney who will do a good job, but you do not want your own needs to be inadequately provided for because of the size of the attorney's fee. This can happen where your case is a relatively small one—moneywise—but the attorney's fee takes a large chunk out of what little money you do receive. It can also happen when you have a major case and win a substantial amount of money but the attorney's fee, which is often a percentage of the money won, is so huge that it diminishes your share of the money judgment or settlement to a paltry amount.

In some states, the Workers' Compensation statutes set maximum fees which lawyers may charge on Workers' Compensation cases. Ask your lawyer what those statutory maximum fees are (if they apply to your case). To double-check, contact you state's Workers' Compensation commission. They will provide you with that information. Be aware that these statutes set maximum fees—there is nothing preventing you from negotiating with the lawyer for a fee that is lower than the maximum allowed by statute.

If you have a Workers' Compensation case but the lawyer's fee is not regulated by statute or if your case is not covered by Workers' Compensation, you are likely to encounter one of three different types of fees: the flat fee, the hourly fee, or the contingent percentage fee. (See Chapter 1 for a detailed discussion of flat fees and hourly fees.)

If your case is likely to result in a money award from a judge, jury, or administrative hearing officer, or in a settlement, the attorney may quote a contingent percentage fee. That means that the attorney's fee will be a percentage of the money awarded or the settlement. The contingent percentage fee also means that, if you lose your case and collect nothing, the attorney will not charge a fee for his or her services since there is no pot of money to take the percentage out of. Percentage fees may be 20, 33-1/3, or 40 percent and even higher, depending on the attorney, the difficulty of your case, statutory limits, your ability to shop around and negotiate for a lower percentage, and other factors.

A major problem with contingent percentage fees is that they are not directly related to the amount of time and effort the attorney puts into your case. They are, however, directly related to the amount of money won on your case. The more money won, the higher the attorney's fee, regardless of how much—or how little—time and effort the attorney puts into the case. As noted, the percentages charged by attorneys may range from 20 to 40 percent or higher. Be wary about having such a high percentage of the money that is to compensate you for your losses and suffering go to the attorney without any guarantee that the amount received by the attorney will be proportionate to the time and labor required on your case. This is even more true with settlements. If your case is settled for a substantial amount of money—perhaps several thousand dollars or tens of thousands of dollars—an attorney's fee of one-fourth or one-third of that amount will usually be exorbitantly disproportionate to the amount of time and labor he or she put into your case. You can counter that possibility by shopping around and negotiating with lawyers. By contacting a few lawyers you can get an idea what the "going rate" percentage fees are in your community. You can then shop around and negotiate for a lower percentage. Emphasize that the more routine and uncomplicated your case is, the lower the attorney's percentage should be. Also, the larger the total amount of money you receive, the lower the attorney's percentage should be. After all, for an attorney to receive one-third of $5,000 is one thing; for an attorney to receive one-third of $50,000 may be grossly exorbitant.

Suppose you contact two attorneys both of whom tell you that they would charge a one-third percentage fee for a case such as yours. You can counter that oversimplified and often exorbitant percentage with the following:

> *If your case involves a court trial or full administrative hearing, the attorney can charge according to the following scale:*
>
> 30 percent of the first $10,000
>
> 25 percent of any amount from $10,000 to $20,000
>
> 20 percent of any amount from $20,000 to $50,000
>
> 15 percent of any amount over $50,000.
>
> *If your case is settled out of court or without a full administrative hearing, the attorney can charge according to the following scale:*

25 percent of the first $10,000

20 percent of any amount from $10,000 to $20,000

15 percent of any amount from $20,000 to $50,000

10 percent of any amount over $50,000.

The percentages listed above would lead to considerable savings on attorney's fees. Suppose your case goes to trial and you are awarded a jury verdict of $25,000. If you agreed to pay the attorney a one-third percentage fee, the lawyer would take out one-third of $25,000, which is $8,333. You would be left with $16,667. If, on the other hand, you insisted that the attorney abide by the percentages listed above, the attorney's fee would be only $6,500 and you would be left with $18,500. Small changes in the percentages can mean a big difference in how much the lawyer takes and how much you are left with. On the other hand, if your case is settled out of court for $25,000 and you had agreed to pay the attorney the "going rate" of one-third, the lawyer would get the same $8,333 and you would be left with $16,667—despite the fact that the attorney put considerably less time and effort into your case than would have been required had there been a trial or a full administrative hearing. The recommended percentages listed above utilize a lower scale of percentages when the case is settled out of court. If you were successful in getting the attorney to agree to those percentages, his or her fee would be only $5,250 (compared to $8,333) and you would be left with $19,750 (compared to $16,667). Again, small changes in the percentages can mean that a considerably greater portion of the money you win stays with you.

One advantage you have when negotiating for a lower scale of percentage fees is that since the fee is a percentage of the total money won, the lawyer still has every incentive to work hard on your case. The more the attorney wins for you, the more he or she gets by means of the percentage. Use that fact in conjunction with the principle that the lower the lawyer's percentage, the higher your percentage.

In many states the attorney's fee on Workers' Compensation cases is subject to review by the Workers' Compensation commission to prevent excessive fees. Unfortunately, many such commissions and hearing officers simply rubber-stamp the "going rate" charged by most attorneys in that community. If the going rate is exorbitant or unrelated to the amount of time and effort put in by the lawyer, there may be little effective supervision. Nonetheless, Workers' Compensation commissions and hearing officers sometimes reduce an attorney's fee where it cannot be justified or where it exceeds the statutory maximum. If you feel that your attorney's fee is excessive, contact the Workers' Compensation commission directly and find out how to have your case reviewed.

When negotiating with the lawyer over the fee, if you have a routine, clear-cut case, emphasize that point. If it is a relatively simple matter to get medical and other opinions as to the cause, nature, and extent of your injury, illness, or disability and if other matters, such as adding up bills and calculating the compensation and benefits you should seek, are not difficult, emphasize those points during your discussions over the fee. An attorney should not receive a high fee for a case that involves little more than putting the basic information on standard forms and then presenting your case at a perfunctory administrative hearing or routine court appearance. This is even more true if your case is settled without a formal administrative hearing or out of court.

Although under most Workers' Compensation systems the employee must pay his attorney's fee, there are some circumstances in which the Workers' Compensation commission may be authorized to order the employer to pay part or all of the employee's attorney's fee. This may happen if it is shown that the employer or his insurer contested your case without plausible grounds for doing so or where your injury, illness, or disability was caused by grossly improper conduct on the employer's part. Have your attorney investigate the possibility of having part or all of his or her fee paid by the employer.

If you will bear the burden of the attorney's fee, emphasize to the attorney that you have to pay his or her fee out of the money you receive as compensation.

Finally, make arrangements to pay the lawyer's fee in installments—if it is a flat fee or an hourly fee. Have the installments geared to your compensation. Although the attorney may want an amount of money at the outset, as a retainer, do not make a substantial payment at that time if it would seriously strain your financial resources. Arrange to pay the attorney's fee in periodic installments over the course of your case. If the attorney's fee is a percentage of the money won on your case, the attorney will not receive his or her fee until the check for the money judgment or settlement comes in.

Keep in mind that an attorney usually won't take your case unless he or she feels confident that you have a good case and will win some money. If you must be willing to wait until you are awarded compensation, the attorney should be willing to wait that long and longer—until you can afford to pay the fee without serious financial strain.

12 Collecting Money Owed to You

WHAT IS INVOLVED IN A DEBT COLLECTION CASE?

Depending on the nature of the debt, your relationship to and prior dealings with the debtor, and the debtor's reasons for not paying, a debt collection case may involve several or all of the following:

- pursuing informal methods of convincing the debtor to pay
- pursuing formal legal proceedings, that is, initiating a lawsuit in the appropriate court, to get the debtor to pay
- determining how to prove in court that the debtor is obligated to pay the debt
- determining how to prove in court the amount owed
- determining what charges, interest, or penalties you may seek from the debtor for nonpayment or late payment
- determining what collateral or other security exists and how you can take over that collateral or security and apply it to the debt
- deciding whether and how you can put an attachment or other court control order on the debtor's property or assets until the debt is paid or the litigation resolved
- countering any arguments or defenses the debtor advances to justify nonpayment
- going to trial (if an out-of-court settlement or agreement cannot be reached)

- if you win a judgment against the debtor, determining how to collect that judgment (by either obtaining a court order requiring the debtor to pay or having a sheriff levy against the debtor's property and assets by forced sale or auction)

- dealing with your own financial obligations while the debt remains unpaid

- finding out about tactics and methods which you, as a creditor, are prohibited by law from using in your efforts to get the debtor to pay.

Informal methods of collecting money owed involve efforts to convince the debtor to pay without or at least before initiating a lawsuit or other formal court proceeding. After personal contacts and entreaties fail, many people to whom others owe money contact a lawyer. Some debtors begin payment once they know the creditor has consulted an attorney. Others wait until formal legal proceedings are initiated or may hold out until a judgment is entered against them in court and collection procedures are undertaken. Much depends on the debt and the debtor's reasons for not paying. Many debtors respond favorably to a letter on a lawyer's stationery. A typical lawyer's letter states that the attorney has been hired to represent you, that the attorney believes from what you have said that the debt is valid and enforceable, and that the matter can and should be settled without formal court proceedings. If the debtor begins repayment by a certain date, no further action will be taken. However, legal proceedings will be initiated if the debtor does not make good-faith efforts to repay by the date stated in the letter. If the debtor disputes the debt, the amount owed, or some other matter, the letter will instruct the debtor to contact your attorney to discuss the matter.

As a general rule, you should exhaust informal methods of convincing the debtor to pay before resorting to formal and perhaps expensive court proceedings. After all, your objective is not only to obtain full payment but to do so with the least amount of expense, aggravation, and time. On practical grounds, it may be advisable to compromise with the debtor if the debt is small and work out a mutually acceptable settlement rather than pursue expensive legal proceedings that may cost as much or more than the amount owed. Even with a substantial debt, the cost of legal proceedings must be compared to the likelihood that those proceedings will be successful and the debt will be recovered.

Mailing the debtor a letter written by a lawyer trying to convince the debtor to pay works in many instances. It is almost always worth the effort. If it is likely that the debtor will leave town and take whatever property or assets he or she owns with him or her, your lawyer may be able to file papers in court immediately to get an attachment or other court control order against the debtor's property preventing him or her from selling or removing that property or requiring the debtor to post a bond or other surety while litigation is in progress.

If informal methods do not work, legal proceedings can be initiated. If the debt is within the limits of the local small claims court, it may be advisable to file a complaint against the debtor and have the matter heard there. If the facts are not complicated and do not involve complex legal issues, you should be able to handle the case yourself without having a lawyer present at court. However, you should consult a lawyer initially, explain your situation, and ask the lawyer for advice and information about how to handle your case in small claims court.

If the debt is too large for small claims court, you will need the assistance and advice of an attorney to prepare the appropriate legal papers, file them in the appropriate court, and have notice served on the debtor. Although the debt may be a simple matter, the legal issues and procedures involved in filing a lawsuit, serving the debtor with notice, proving your case in court, and collecting a judgment against the debtor may be complicated and fraught with practical difficulties. The advice and assistance of an experienced debt collection lawyer will be invaluable.

The most critical aspect of collecting money owed by formal legal proceedings is proving in court that money is owed and the exact amount due. Many people lend money or sell goods on credit and accept the other person's word that he or she will pay back the amount owed within a certain amount of time. If the matter ends up in court, how can you prove that you lent that person a specific amount of money or sold that person a given item to be paid for by a given date? A person who welches on a loan or sale may perjure him- or herself in court and deny that there was a loan or sale for which he or she agreed to pay you a given amount of money. Unless you have the basic terms in writing and signed by the debtor, the judge or jury may have difficulty deciding whether you or the debtor is telling the truth. In reality, it is unlikely that a judge or jury will find in your favor and order another person to pay you a substantial amount of money unless you can prove—by means other than and in addition to your own testimony—that there was a loan or sale and that the debtor owes you a specific amount of money. (In most states, loans or sales involving more than a specified amount of money are unenforceable by the courts unless there is a written document signed by the debtor.) You must be prepared to prove in court the validity of the debt and the amount owed. As noted, in addition to your own testimony regarding the transaction or agreement that gave rise to the debt, you must produce documents, witnesses, correspondence, statements, and all other available evidence to prove to the judge or jury that the debtor owes you a specific amount of money.

You must determine what late charges, penalties, or interest you are allowed by law to collect from the debtor. Also, determine what collateral or other security is associated with the debt and how you may take over that collateral or security and apply it to the debt. If you file a lawsuit, find out whether you can seek an attachment or other court control order against the debtor's property or assets so that you will have sufficient property or assets of the debtor available at the termination of the lawsuit to collect against. An experienced debt collection attorney can explain these matters in more detail and in a manner appropriate to your situation.

Under some circumstances, a debtor has the right to pay back only a small portion of the money owed even if he or she admits the obligation. This occurs when the debtor files for bankruptcy or when the debtor files a debt-repayment schedule under Chapter 13 of the federal Bankruptcy Act. Those procedures allow people to have their debts canceled or repaid only partially if they are insolvent. Many times the creditor receives only a small portion of the money owed from a person who files for bankruptcy or for a Chapter 13 Plan. Of course, if the creditor is a business, the business can write off the unpaid balance of the debt as a "bad debt" on its taxes.

In the majority of debt collection cases, the creditor can readily prove in court the loan or sale out of which the debt arose. Usually, there is a written loan or sales agreement signed by the debtor which sets forth the amount of the debt, the interest rate, if any, the repayment and collateral terms, and other matters. In the majority of cases, the debtor does not deny the validity of the debt where there is a signed loan or sales agreement. Also, in most debt collection cases the debtor does not file for bankruptcy or a Chapter 13 Plan or any other debt relief procedure.

What, then, is the creditor's major concern?

In most cases, after informal means of getting the debtor to pay have failed and the creditor initiates formal legal proceedings, the creditor is worried about the costs of going to court and the likelihood of successfully collecting a judgment against the debtor. The costs of going to court include paying a lawyer and court fees, waiting to get a court hearing, taking time off from work to go to court to testify, possibly encountering delays or continuances, and waiting for the court to announce a decision. If for some reason, the judgment is against you, you must either appeal, which will involve additional costs, or accept the fact that you have lost and will never collect that debt. If the decision of the court is in your favor, you must then determine how to get the debtor to pay the judgment. (Of course, the debtor may appeal, requiring you to incur further costs and delays.)

Is it worth the risk of not winning and the risk, if you do win, of not being able to collect the judgment against the debtor?

If the debtor does not start paying the debt when the court announces that it has found in your favor, you may have to go back to court for a hearing at which the court will examine the debtor's circumstances and order him or her to pay you a given amount each week or month. If that is not an appropriate procedure, you may have to obtain an execution or similar document which certifies your right to collect the unsatisfied judgment by having the debtor's property seized and sold. An execution does not authorize *you* to seize the debtor's property and sell it to pay the debt. An execution authorizes a sheriff or other court officer to levy against the debtor's property. To *levy* means to seize property of the debtor and give the debtor notice that that property will be sold at a public sale or auction unless the debtor pays you the amount specified in the execution by a certain date. Needless to say, filing a lawsuit, conducting a trial or hearing, winning a judgment against the debtor, converting that judgment into an execution, and then taking the execution to the sheriff to have it levied on is an expensive and time-consuming process. On the other hand, many debtors do begin payment when they are informed that the court has issued a judgment against them. Other debtors may not begin payment immediately but do so when they learn that you have converted the judgment into an execution and the sheriff has begun efforts to levy on that execution.

There are other legal devices you can use, in conjunction with a lawsuit, to get the debtor to pay. In some situations, as noted, an attachment can be put on the debtor's house, car, or other property preventing him or her from selling that property until the debt is paid (if you win the case). Also, as noted, some courts have special procedures you can use after you have won a judgment if the debtor does not begin payment. You can have the debtor ordered to appear in court—and be arrested and brought to court if he or she fails to do so voluntarily—so that the judge can determine what income and financial assets the debtor has and order the debtor to make weekly or monthly payments on penalty of going to jail if he or she doesn't pay. In addition, in many states, the court has authority to issue orders requiring the debtor's employer to pay you a specific amount directly out of the debtor's salary or wage.

Using the courts to collect a debt is often effective. Also, under some circumstances, the court will order the debtor to reimburse you for some or all of the costs of taking the debtor to court. (See the section "Dealing with Lawyers" for further information on having the debtor ordered to pay your court costs and lawyer's fee.) On the other hand, going to court can be an expensive, aggravating, time-consuming process that ends in futility. The debtor may not have sufficient income to pay the debt. Or the debtor may not have property or assets that can be sold to pay the judgment. Or you may lose your case in court because of some deficiency in the evidence you submit, or because of a procedural oversight, or because the judge or jury sympathize with the debtor or do not believe you.

Going to court to get a debt repaid, like loaning money or selling goods on credit in the first place, is never a sure thing. Having an experienced debt collection lawyer represent you, however, can substantially increase the odds in your favor.

WHY DO YOU NEED TO CONSULT AN ATTORNEY?

Because of the complexity of the laws and procedures involved in collecting a debt and because of various practical considerations that come into play, the advice and assistance of an attorney who is experienced in debt collection cases is essential.

Given the attorney's experience with creditors, debtors, and the courts, the attorney should be able to size up the debtor and devise alternative methods of handling the situation. The attorney should be able to outline a series of steps to get the debtor to pay. For example, the attorney may start with a letter to the debtor written on the lawyer's professional stationery as described at the beginning of the previous section. If the attorney's first letter does not work, he or she may follow it with a second, more strongly worded letter or a phone call. In many cases, debtors resist paying because of personal animosity or other ill feelings toward the creditor. An attorney may be able to placate the debtor and convince the debtor to pay the debt. If those efforts do not work, the attorney can confront the debtor with the legal consequences that may occur if the debtor is brought to court and found liable for the debt and for unjustifiable refusal to pay the debt on time.

The attorney can review with you the various court proceedings that can be used, how much each procedure may cost, how long it may take, what it will involve, what can be done if the debtor refuses to pay even after that procedure is used, and what the likelihood for success is with respect to each proceeding. You and your attorney can then devise a plan for proceeding against the debtor in light of these alternatives.

The first thing the attorney may want to know is whether the debt is personal in nature or a business matter. If the debt is one between erstwhile friends or acquaintances, it may be wise, at least initially, to pursue efforts to settle the matter out of court. Even if the debt is easily provable in court, there must be some reason why your friend or acquaintance is not paying. If you and your lawyer can determine why the debtor is not paying, it may then be possible to have your attorney discuss the matter with the debtor and work out a mutually acceptable agreement to get the debt paid. If the debtor's reasons for nonpayment are ignored, attempts at forcing the debtor to repay may only harden the debtor's resolve not to pay. Also, if the debtor is your erstwhile friend or acquaintance, it is better to try to work out an understanding instead of, or at least before, initiating formal legal proceedings.

If, on the other hand, the debt is a business matter between a customer and a business or a client and a professional, other approaches may be more appropriate. Of course, it would still be good policy to make every effort to determine why the debtor is not paying the debt by having your lawyer contact the debtor to discuss the matter. If the debtor is having financial troubles and cannot pay the debt in full, a revised installment payment schedule may be the solution. If the debtor claims that there were defects in the goods he or she purchased or deficiencies in the professional services he or she received, those matters should be investigated. If there is legitimacy to the debtor's claims, a compromise may be reachable. Also, if the debtor's counterclaims are mistaken or groundless, but he or she cannot be persuaded to pay, you will then be aware what the debtor may say in court and can prepare a defense to those allegations.

Be sure to seek a lawyer's advice and assistance if the debtor has retained a lawyer or has initiated legal proceedings against you. If the debtor has hired an attorney to sue you for allegedly selling a defective product or providing deficient services or using illegal terms or tactics with regard to the loan or sale, you will need the advice and assistance of an attorney who is familiar with the laws and procedures that govern those matters. In recent years numerous proconsumer and prodebtor laws have been established by legislatures, the courts, and administrative agencies. It is important to consult an attorney so that you do not unwittingly violate one or more of those laws in your dealings with the debtor or in your efforts to get the debtor to pay the debt. Many creditors have ruined their chances of having the debt paid not because they could not prove the debt but because the terms or tactics they used violated consumer protection laws or debtor's rights laws. Many of those laws give the consumer/debtor grounds for suing the creditor. The advice and assistance of an attorney who is familiar with creditor and debtor laws is needed to avoid those pitfalls.

When you are considering hiring an attorney, you must take into account the cost of hiring an attorney to try to get the debt paid. You must then compare the cost of hiring a lawyer and trying to get the debt paid to the amount owed and the likelihood of recovering part or all of it. It is one thing to hire an attorney and, after informal methods have failed, initiate litigation and get an attachment on the debtor's property where the debt is $10,000 and the debtor has a house and a good job and has lived in the community for many years. The debt is substantial and there is good reason to believe you will be able to collect if you win the case in court. By contrast, if the debt is $2,000 and the attorney's fee and court costs may be $1,500 and the debtor has no substantial assets and no steady income, you may never be able to collect from the debtor even if you win the court case. You will have spent $1,500 to collect $2,000 unsuccessfully. You will then be out a total of $3,500.

Consult two or more lawyers to get various opinions as to how good your case is and, just as importantly, how likely it is that you will collect part or all of the debt if you win the case. It may be wisest not to spend money on an attorney if the chances of collecting the debt are too low. Of course, if the attorney charges a fee that is contingent on collecting money from the debtor, it may be wise to pursue the matter even if the odds are not good. (See the section "Dealing with Lawyers" for an explanation of contingent attorneys' fees.)

Because of the considerations noted in the preceding paragraph, it is important, at your initial conference with the attorney, to gain an understanding of what steps the attorney recommends, how much each step will cost, and what the likelihood of success will be. From a money point of view, you must determine whether the cost of going after the debtor by a given means is worth the risk and cost of being unsuccessful. If a given method is relatively inexpensive and has a good chance of being successful, it may be worth pursuing. By contrast, if another method is expensive and is not likely to be successful, why pursue it?

Of course, there is always the matter of principle. As a matter of principle, debtors should pay their debts. Similarly, they should be required to do so by law when they do not do so willingly. In reality, however, some debtors do not repay their debts. Also, attorneys and the courts are sometimes unsuccessful at getting them to do so.

Your best course of action is to consult an experienced debt collection attorney. Find out what the available informal and formal procedures are, then decide how to proceed against the debtor.

HOW TO THINK ABOUT LEGAL AND RELATED ASPECTS

The following sections review important points to think about when determining how to collect money owed to you.

Make sure you understand the terms of the debt and find out, if possible, why the debtor isn't paying.

Before an appropriate plan can be developed for dealing with the debtor, you and your attorney should have a clear understanding of the debt. Whether the debt is personal in nature or strictly a matter of business between strangers may have considerable bearing on how to go about collecting it. Whether the debt is personal or a business matter may relate to why the debtor is not paying. If it is a personal debt, there may be misunderstandings or ill will on the part of the debtor. Correcting those misunderstandings or dispelling that ill will may be the key to getting the debtor to pay without resort to expensive legal proceedings. In fact, initiating legal proceedings without first exploring informal methods may make matters worse by antagonizing the debtor or escalating the animosity between debtor and creditor.

If the debt arose out of business or commercial dealings between strangers, it is less likely that personal animosity or ill will is motivating the debtor to refuse payment. It may be that the debtor feels—perhaps with some justification—that the product purchased on credit was defective or that the services received on credit were deficient and that the bill shouldn't be paid. Perhaps the debtor feels that his or her consumer rights were violated or that your end of the bargain or agreement wasn't fulfilled or performed. Disagreements or misunderstandings such as these can sometimes be resolved without litigation.

Often a debtor does not pay and alleges that financial problems make it difficult or impossible for him or her to pay. If the debtor can substantiate his or her financial difficulties, it may be wise to take a conciliatory approach and try to work out a revised payment schedule the debtor can afford. Although it may take longer to get your money back under such an arrangement, it may be the least costly way of doing so. If you conduct expensive and time-consuming court proceedings only to have the judge order the debtor to pay according to such a revised schedule, you will have spent considerable money to accomplish what you might have been able to do without court proceedings. Also, if the debtor is in serious financial difficulty, trying to force payment by legal proceedings may result in the debtor filing for bankruptcy or a Chapter 13 plan or the debtor may leave town or take some other drastic step which jeopardizes your chances of getting any money at all.

If the debtor does not claim a legitimate reason for not paying and there is no apparent reason or circumstances that prevent payment, you and your lawyer should review the various informal procedures that may be effective given the situation. Some debtors fail to pay their debts out of irresponsibility; when they learn that you have hired an attorney and are willing to take them to court, they may take their responsibilities more seriously.

When reviewing informal and formal procedures to get the debtor to pay, you must determine how to prove the existence and amount of the debt in court and disprove any defenses or counterclaims the debtor may make. If the debt and related matters can be proven by a document, you may have a strong case. If, on the other hand, some issues boil down to a contest of your word against the debtor's, your attorney may have to confront you with the fact that credibility battles are never a sure thing. The judge or jury may or may not believe you.

Determine what informal methods of dealing with the debtor are advisable, what each would involve, and the cost and likelihood of success.

As a general rule, unless you expect the debtor to leave the community or sequester his or her property, you and your attorney should initiate informal contacts and communications before resorting to formal legal proceedings. Your attorney may be able to get through to the debtor where you have failed. Or once the debtor learns you have hired an attorney, the debtor may contact your attorney. At that point, your attorney and the debtor may be able to work out a mutually acceptable resolution.

Your attorney may begin by sending a letter to the debtor stating your side of the case and asking the debtor to begin payment immediately or justify his or her nonpayment. If payment is not forthcoming, your attorney can confront the debtor with a more strongly worded communication advising the debtor that if he or she does not pay, you will have no alternative but formal legal proceedings.

Find out useful information about the debtor during your efforts at informal resolution of the matter. For example, if the debtor has a history of nonpayment, it may not be advisable to devote too much time or effort to informal approaches. If you or your attorney can find out about other creditors for whom this debtor has been a problem, you may gain helpful information about how to handle the debtor.

Some debtors refuse to pay a debt in the expectation of using the costs and inconveniences of litigation as a bargaining lever against the creditor. By threatening to hold out and not pay unless the creditor brings him or her to court, the debtor may hope to win a compromise or settlement under which he or she will not have to repay the full amount of the debt. Another tactic is to stall as long as possible—usually until you get to the point of initiating a lawsuit—then the debtor will pay a small amount and promise to pay the rest soon or on a regular basis. Shortly thereafter, however, the payments stop. When you go after the debtor again through formal legal proceedings, he or she makes another small payment and again promises to make regular payments. In this manner, the debtor may drag out the repayment process and hope that at some point, far short of full payment, you will give up in disgust. To deal with such hard-core debtors, you will need the advice and assistance of an experienced attorney who has dealt with people like this before and who knows how to spot their tactics and counter them.

Determine what formal court proceedings are available, what each will involve and cost, and the likelihood of success. Also find out about interest or penalties you may be able to charge the debtor, taking over any collateral or security, putting an attachment on the debtor's property and how to collect on a judgment if you win the lawsuit.

A lawyer's advice and assistance is essential if you must initiate court proceedings to collect a debt. Even if the debt is small and you can sue in small claims court, contact a lawyer and find out what to say at court and how to present your case in a convincing manner. If the debt is substantial and suit must be filed in one of the state trial courts or in federal court, you will need a lawyer's advice and assistance to prepare and file the necessary papers and documents and to adhere to the intricate rules of procedure and evidence that must be followed to prove and win your case.

Have your lawyer explain what documents will be needed to prove your case, how long it may take to get into court for a hearing, what testimony you will have to give and how much time you may have to spend in court, what will happen if the debtor does not show at court or, if he or she does show, how to handle the situation if the debtor contests every issue and raises counterclaims. Also determine what will happen if the jury or judge finds in your favor, that is, how do you enforce a favorable judgment and get the debtor to pay? Ask what measures can be taken as soon as papers are filed in court to put an attachment or other court control order on the debtor's house or bank account or car or other property to freeze those assets and prevent the debtor from removing them or selling them before the lawsuit is resolved. Of course, the judge may be reluctant to grant an attachment if the debt is small compared to the value of the property you want to attach or if the debtor has a sound reputation in the community and is not likely to skip town because of this lawsuit. Nonetheless, in numerous cases debtors have escaped with their property after making the creditor conduct costly and time-consuming court proceedings, which the creditor won, only to find there was no way the creditor could collect on the judgment against the debtor. An attachment could have prevented that. Also, some debtors would rather pay the debt or at least work out a mutually satisfactory settlement rather than have an attachment put on his or her property.

Find out how long the court proceedings may take. If you need to have the debt paid soon for your own financial purposes, it may be disheartening to learn that it may take many months or a year or more to get into court and that, even if you win the case, it may take more months to get the debtor to pay or have a sheriff seize the debtor's property to be sold to pay the debt.

Find out the cost of litigation—particularly the lawyer's fee. Be aware that the type of fee the lawyer wants to charge may indicate how sound a case he or she thinks you have. Many attorneys charge a contingent percentage fee to represent a creditor on a debt collection case. The attorney's fee is contingent on getting money from the debtor. If the attorney's efforts are successful in getting money from the debtor, the attorney will take, as the fee, a given percentage of the money recovered. If the attorney's efforts prove futile, he or she will not charge for his or her time and services but only for such costs as filing fees and related expenses. By contrast, an attorney may want to charge a flat fee or an hourly fee. A flat fee is a specific amount of money for which the attorney will handle the case. An hourly fee is a set hourly rate the attorney will charge for each hour put into the case. Be aware that attorneys will often charge a contingent percentage fee if they feel there is a good chance of getting money out of the debtor. Why else would they take the risk of receiving no fee if they cannot get the debtor to pay?

Conversely, if a client's debt collection case doesn't look too promising, the attorney will want to make sure he or she gets a fee—even if no money is recovered from the debtor. The attorney can get a sure fee by charging a flat fee, which the creditor usually must pay at the outset or soon after the attorney takes the case, or by charging an hourly fee, which the client pays as the case progresses. Either way, if the lawyer's efforts are unsuccessful and no money is recovered from the debtor, the attorney will have received most or all of his or her fee by the time the creditor realizes that. This avoids the difficult task of trying to get the disgruntled creditor to pay the attorney's fee after the creditor realizes that the attorney's efforts have been fruitless.

With this in mind, be careful how much money you agree to pay an attorney to initiate proceedings against a debtor. Also, pay close attention to the type of fee the attorney wants to charge. A contingent percentage fee may be the only way of making sure you won't have to pay the attorney unless the attorney's efforts are successful. (Read the section "Dealing with Lawyers" for further information on attorney's fees.)

Discuss with the attorney the counterarguments the debtor may make. These involve such matters as allegations that the debtor never agreed to the sale or loan, that the product sold was defective or the services rendered deficient, or that you violated the debtor's rights or the terms of the loan or sale. Be candid in your discussions with the lawyer on these matters. The lawyer must be prepared to combat the debtor's counterclaims in court.

Also ask the attorney about any interest, late charges, or other penalties you can charge the debtor either under the terms of the sale or loan or under the laws of your state. If you receive payment from the debtor six months or two years after it was due, you should receive compensation for the lost use of that money during that period. Find out from the attorney how you can take over the collateral or security associated with the sale or loan, if there is collateral or other security. You may be able to have the property or asset held as collateral or security sold to pay part or all of the debt. The terms of the sale or loan must be examined as well as state law to make sure proper procedures are followed.

Finally, keep your mind open to an out-of-court settlement even after filing a lawsuit. An out-of-court settlement can save you considerable time and expense. Do not let formal legal proceedings ruin opportunities for working things out on a mutually agreeable basis.

Devise a plan or series of steps to maximize your chances of success while minimizing the costs. Also, learn about the debtor.

You are concerned with money. No doubt, principle is also involved. Nonetheless, your objective is to get back all or as much of the money owed as possible. You also want to avoid spending a disproportionate amount of money in your efforts to collect the debt.

With this in mind, work with your attorney to devise a plan to deal with the debtor. It is usually wise to develop alternatives, such as a series of increasingly serious measures. For example, a letter from the attorney to the debtor demanding payment may be the first step. The next step may be a second letter or telephone communication from the attorney advising the debtor that if payment does not begin immediately, legal proceedings will be initiated. The next step would then be filing a lawsuit and serving the debtor with notice. In conjunction with the lawsuit, an attachment may be sought against the debtor's property. At this point, it may be wise to pursue the dual course of not only preparing for trial but also pressing for an acceptable out-of-court settlement. If necessary, you must conduct a trial and, if you win, take appropriate measures to collect the judgment against the debtor.

If a substantial amount of money is involved, you want to maximize your chances of recovering as much as possible while minimizing the costs. Having your lawyer or a professional investigator check into the debtor's background may be well worth the cost if the investigation reveals useful information. For example, the debtor might pay up rather than have an attachment placed on property which the debtor didn't think you would find out about. Or the debtor may be making false claims about the product or services associated with the debt. An investigation may uncover information that will enable you to combat the counterclaims or arguments the debtor makes in court. For example, the debtor may claim that the automobile you sold him or her doesn't operate properly. A professional investigator, however, may be able to take photographs of the debtor using the car at various times with no apparent problems.

An investigator may uncover information about previous nonpayment tactics used by this debtor with other creditors. By contacting those other creditors, you and your attorney may be able to learn successful techniques for getting the debtor to pay and otherwise protecting your rights as a creditor and increasing your chances of getting the money repaid.

Find out what you are prohibited by law from doing in your dealings with the debtor.

Certain communications or tactics on the part of a creditor may be illegal under state or federal laws. Also, it may be illegal to charge certain interest rates, late fees, or other penalties. Notice requirements, time periods, and other procedures may have to be followed exactly in order to comply with consumer rights laws and debtor's rights laws.

It is essential that you seek legal advice and assistance from an attorney who has a thorough knowledge of current consumer rights and debtor's rights laws. This is necessary so that you do not unwittingly violate the debtor's rights or overlook required procedures and thereby jeopardize your right to collect the debt.

Also have the lawyer explain the laws which govern repossession, wage garnishment, foreclosure on security or collateral, discrimination, unfair and deceptive business practices, credit investigations and reports, privacy, and other areas that apply to your case. Those matters may give rise to issues which the debtor can use at court to block your efforts at collecting the debt. Mistakes on your part, though innocent and due to ignorance of the law, may nonetheless jeopardize or even ruin your case. Also, you may spend more time and money defending yourself against the debtor's charges of unlawful tactics or improper business practices on your part than you spend trying to collect the debt. This is why it is important to seek the advice and assistance of a lawyer at the outset.

DEALING WITH LAWYERS

In addition to the general points about lawyers in Chaper 1, keep in mind the following advice about dealing with lawyers on a debt collection case.

Given the various legal and practical aspects of trying to collect a debt, it is important to hire an attorney experienced in these types of cases. In addition to a knowledge of applicable laws, the attorney should have the kind of experience that has instilled a grasp of what procedures and techniques should work and which would be futile or unlikely to succeed. The attorney may have developed, through experience, an ability to approach a debtor and convince the debtor to pay. The attorney should be able to pursue opportunities for a favorable out-of-court settlement but also have the knowledge, skills, and ability to conduct a trial, if necessary.

Before hiring a given lawyer, have the lawyer explain the steps he or she would recommend, how much time and money each step would involve, and the likelihood of success. Don't hire a lawyer who promises to get all the money owed from the debtor but who refuses to explain how he or she intends to do that. Hire a lawyer who is willing to explain the law, assess practical considerations, and answer your questions and who shows concern for your objectives and judgment.

Make sure you get a clear explanation at the outset about the fee. After all, you must compare the amount of money owed to the cost of hiring a lawyer to collect it. Also, bear in mind that the type of fee the lawyer charges may reflect how the lawyer assesses your chances of getting money from the debtor.

Lawyers usually charge one of three types of fees on debt collection cases: a flat fee, an hourly fee, or a contingent percentage fee.

A flat fee is a specific amount of money for which the lawyer agrees to perform the customary and necessary legal services to try to collect the debt. After the lawyer has learned the facts of the situation, he or she may be able to gauge roughly how much time and effort the case will require. The lawyer may quote a flat fee that will cover his or her services. Before agreeing to a flat fee, make sure you understand what services the fee covers. Does the flat fee cover only nontrial work? Does the flat fee cover the lawyer's services if the case goes to trial? If you go to trial and win a judgment against the debtor, but the debtor doesn't pay immediately, does the flat fee cover the attorney's services in getting the sheriff after the debtor or bringing the debtor back into court for not paying the judgment? Get answers to these questions so that you know what the flat fee covers. If the flat fee covers all these possible actions, you are fully covered. If the flat fee quoted by the lawyer covers only some of these steps, you must get an estimate of how much the other steps may cost before you can assess how much the case may cost and whether it is worth it. If you go to court, lose your case, and file an appeal, the flat fee quoted by the lawyer does not normally cover the cost of an appeal. An appeal will require an additional, separate fee.

An hourly fee is a set rate the attorney charges for each hour he or she puts into your case. (See Chapter 1 for a detailed discussion of hourly fees.)

The third type of fee charged by lawyers on debt collection cases is the contingent percentage fee. The word *contingent* means that the attorney will charge a fee only if money is recovered from the debtor; if no money is recovered from the debtor, the attorney will not charge for his or her time and services. (You will, however, be responsible for such expenses as the court filing fee, the fee for having court papers served on the debtor, and related expenses.) The *percentage* means that the attorney will charge a given percentage of the money recovered from the debtor as his or her fee. The percentages range from 20 to 40 percent and even as high as 50 percent. The contingent percentage fee was developed to allow a creditor to hire an attorney without having to pay a lot of money to the lawyer before finding out whether any money will be recovered from the debtor. Under the contingent percentage fee, if the lawyer's efforts are successful, the lawyer takes a given percentage of the money; if the lawyer's efforts are not successful, the creditor does not pay for the lawyer's time or services.

The most important thing to understand about the fees lawyers charge on debt collection cases is that the type of fee may indicate what the lawyer really thinks about your chances of getting money out of the debtor. The next most important thing to realize is that contingent percentage fees frequently lead to grossly exorbitant fees for the attorney.

If the lawyer feels that your case is not a good one—that you don't have a good chance of getting money out of the debtor—the lawyer must make sure he or she will get a fee. In these cases, the lawyer will quote a flat fee or an hourly fee. A flat fee is normally paid by the creditor at the outset of the case or within a short period thereafter. An hourly fee is paid on a monthly or other periodic basis. In either case, the lawyer will have received most or all of his or her fee before you find out whether any money will be recovered from the debtor. By contrast, if the lawyer feels there is a good chance of getting money out of the debtor, he or she may quote a contingent percentage fee. Since the percentages charged are very high, the attorney can look forward to taking a huge portion of the money recovered from the debtor. Why else would an attorney run the risk of receiving no fee if no money is recovered?

Perhaps the most sensible approach would be to offer the attorney a fee that is partly a flat fee and partly a contingent percentage fee—but one with low percentages scaled to the amount of money recovered. Some examples and background may be useful in understanding this approach. Suppose someone owes you $10,000. The lawyer quotes a one-third contingent fee. That means that he or she will receive nothing if the case produces no money. On the other hand, if the debtor pays the full $10,000, the lawyer will take one-third—$3,333.33. Note that the attorney receives that amount regardless of whether the case goes to trial or whether it is settled out of court—regardless, in fact, of how much or how little time and effort the attorney actually puts into the case. For instance, suppose the attorney puts 10 hours into the case on interviewing you, preparing letters to the debtor, investigating the debtor, reviewing documents, filing a lawsuit, seeking an attachment, and other procedures. Before going to trial, however, the debtor decides to pay up. The attorney receives a fee of $3,333.33 for 10 hours of work: in effect, a fee of $333.33 an hour! Even if the case goes to trial, the attorney may spend 3 hours in trial preparation and 3 hours at court and perhaps another 4 hours on the case before the debtor agrees to pay up (rather than have his or her property sold by the sheriff). The attorney has now put a total of 20 hours into the case for a fee of $3,333.33; in effect, a fee of $166.66 an hour! You can see how contingent percentage fees can reap exorbitant profits for the lawyer (especially if the case is successfully resolved without a lengthy trial).

To avoid exorbitant contingent percentage fees, offer the attorney a two-part fee: a flat fee combined with a descending scale of percentages contingent on recovery. By *descending scale of percentages* is meant a scale under which the attorney receives a lower percentage for higher money values involved. Under standard contingent percentage fees, the attorney takes a straight percentage regardless of how much money is involved. If the attorney recovers $5,000 from the debtor and is charging a one-third fee, the attorney receives $1,666.66. If the attorney recovers a $50,000 debt, his or her fee will be $16,666.66. Suppose the attorney put 20 hours of work into each case. That would mean that the attorney was, in effect, receiving $83.33 an hour on the $5,000 debt case but $833.33 an hour on the $50,000 debt case! Should an attorney receive such an inflated fee simply because more money—but not more time or effort—is involved? A descending scale of percentages corrects that situation.

If you are trying to recoup a $10,000 debt, present the attorney with this fee package: a $500 flat fee to cover several hours of the attorney's time (perhaps 10 hours at $50 per hour) plus 20 percent of any money recovered from the debtor. If the full $10,000 is recovered, instead of paying the attorney a fee of $3,333.33, leaving yourself only $6,666.67, you will pay the attorney only $2,500 (the $500 flat fee plus 20 percent of $10,000) and leave yourself with $7,500. The difference between the fee favorable to the attorney and the fee favorable to you is $833.34.

Similarly, if you hire an attorney to collect a $50,000 debt, offer to pay the attorney $2,500 as a flat fee to cover initial efforts and procedures (perhaps 33 hours at $75 an hour) plus 20 percent of the first $10,000 recovered, 15 percent of any amount between $10,000 and $20,000, and 10 percent of any amount between $20,000 and $50,000.

If you had agreed to the simplistic and exorbitant one-third contingent fee, the attorney would take $16,666.66 of the $50,000 recovered and you would be left with only $33,333.34. By contrast, under the fee described in the previous paragraph, the attorney would receive $9,000 and you would be left with $41,000. The difference between the fee favorable to the attorney and the fee favorable to you is $7,666.67.

To summarize, if an attorney tries to get you to pay a simplistic one-third or 40 percent or 50 percent contingent fee, counter with the following formula:

Pay a flat fee of 5 percent of the debt, then insist that the lawyer receive, in addition, a percentage according to the following scale:

If the case is settled out of court:

20 percent of any amount up to $10,000

15 percent of any amount between $10,000 and $20,000

10 percent of any amount between $20,000 and $50,000

5 percent of any amount over $50,000.

If the case goes to trial:

25 percent of any amount up to $10,000

20 percent of any amount between $10,000 and $20,000

15 percent of any amount between $20,000 and $50,000

10 percent of any amount over $50,000.

If the attorneys you consult insist on a flat fee or an hourly fee, recall that they may be doing so because they do not think you have a good chance of getting money from the debtor and they want to make sure they get a fee whether money is recovered from the debtor or not. With that in mind, try to get the lawyer to agree to the combination 5 percent flat fee with the descending scale of percentages listed above. If the attorney does not agree to such a fee, that may be a sign that he or she doesn't think your chances of recovery are good. It may be better at that point to consult other attorneys. If you cannot find an attorney who would take your case for the 5 percent flat fee with the descending scale of percentages, you probably have either a poor case or poor chances of getting money out of the debtor. If that is the situation, it may be better to consult a tax lawyer or tax consultant and determine whether you can write that debt off your taxes as a "bad debt."

Even if you cannot get an attorney to agree to the 5 percent flat fee with the descending scale of percentages fee outlined previously, there are techniques you can use to negotiate for a lower fee. For example, emphasize that you should not have to pay the same fee regardless of whether the case goes to trial or is settled out of court. If the lawyer offers a flat fee of $4,000, respond that $4,000 may be appropriate if your case goes to trial. After all, trial work requires considerable preparation and involves difficult and demanding work on the lawyer's part. If the case is settled out of court, however, the lawyer shouldn't get the same amount of money as he or she would have had the case gone to trial. Offer to pay the $4,000 *only* if the case goes to trial; offer to pay $2,500 if it is settled out of court.

If your case is routine and uncomplicated, that is, the debt is easily provable in court and the debtor has no legitimate defenses or counterclaims, emphasize that fact. A lawyer may be justified in charging a high fee for a difficult, complicated case but not for a routine, uncomplicated case. For example, if the lawyer quotes a fee of $2,500 but you feel that is too much for your routine, uncomplicated case, offer to pay the attorney $1,500 and no more than that unless unanticipated difficulties or complications arise.

During the negotiations over the fee, keep in mind that most lawyers would rather have your case for a fee that is somewhat lower than they would like than have no case and no fee at all. Do you think a lawyer would let a $1,500 fee go out the door because of the lawyer's misplaced insistence on a fee of $2,500? If you show the lawyer that you won't accept the fee quoted and are willing to contact other lawyers, you may be surprised how accommodating the lawyer will be.

Finally, have your lawyer investigate any laws or procedures by which the court can order the debtor to reimburse you for part or all of your expenses—including your attorney's fee. Most states have laws or rules of court which authorize the judge to assess against the debtor the cost of bringing the debtor to court, if you win the case. The judge may be able to include your filing fees, notice fees, and part or all of your attorney's fee in the judgment against the debtor. Be sure your attorney utilizes those laws and procedures if they are available in your case. After all, if the debtor is the one who is wrongfully making you go to court to collect the debt, he or she should be required to pay your costs of going to court—including your lawyer's fee—as well as the debt.

13
Motor Vehicle Personal Injury

WHAT DOES A MOTOR VEHICLE PERSONAL INJURY CASE INVOLVE?

You will be concerned with one or both of two issues regarding a motor vehicle accident which results in personal injuries. First, what is the nature and extent of your liability, if any, for the accident? Second, if you have suffered personal injuries, what must be done to receive compensation for those injuries?

The first issue requires a knowledge of the legal concept of "liability" and how it applies to motor vehicle accident cases. Liability means that a person can be shown to have violated a legal duty which he or she owed to another person. If one person violates a legal duty owed to a second person, the second person can sue the first person for compensation for the injuries and losses that resulted. Everyone has a duty to exercise due care in the operation of a motor vehicle. If someone drives recklessly and hits your car, causing you serious bodily injury, that person is liable to you. By driving recklessly, that person violated the legal duty to exercise due care while operating a motor vehicle. Suppose, on the other hand, you and another motorist proceed, from different streets, into the same intersection simultaneously because the traffic lights are not functioning properly and both of you have green lights. Your cars collide. In that situation, the other driver did not violate the duty to exercise due care any more than you did. He is no more liable to you than you are to him. The city, however, may be liable. City officials have a duty to the public to correct any dangerous condition such as malfunctioning traffic lights. You would have to prove that city officials knew or should have known that the traffic lights were malfunctioning and that they failed to take reasonable and timely measures to correct the situation. If you and the other motorist arrived at the intersection only minutes after the traffic lights began to malfunction, it may be difficult to establish that the city should be held liable for something it couldn't have done anything about at the time. It could also be argued that you and the other motorist were at fault for proceeding into the intersection without being on the lookout for each other. Had either or both of you been more careful, the accident might not have occurred.

The failure to exercise due care under the circumstances is the basic element of liability under negligence law. Negligence is the most common basis for lawsuits arising out of motor vehicle accidents. Operating a motor vehicle requires more attentiveness, caution, and control than many other tasks. The duty of due care required of every motorist takes that into consideration. In addition, there are many criminal laws, ordinances, and rules of the road which drivers are required to obey. Violation of those laws, ordinances, or rules of the road may establish that you or the other motorist did not exercise due care and may be held liable for the accident. Of course, conduct that goes beyond negligence, such as driving recklessly or with the intent to injure someone, would also make that person liable for an accident.

Liability is associated with fault. Of course, some accidents are not caused by human error or fault, as when a gale wind sweeps a car off a highway or bridge. Other accidents are caused by human beings but no one can be said to be at fault, as when a person has a heart attack at the wheel of a car and veers into another car—although the driver could be found liable if he knew of his susceptibility to heart attacks but drove the car anyway. Under negligence law, you can be held liable for what you can reasonably foresee.

Most accidents do not involve human fault or error and someone is liable. However, determining who is liable may or may not be easy. If you are stopped at a red light and are hit from the rear by a drunken driver, that driver's liability is clear. But suppose you are moving from the outside lane to the middle lane of a superhighway at the same moment that another motorist is moving from the inside lane to the same middle lane and your cars hit one another? Who is liable? Are you both equally liable?

Many states apply a rule of negligence law called contributory negligence. *Contributory negligence* means that if you acted in a negligent manner—if you failed to exercise due care—and your negligence contributed to some extent to the accident, you cannot sue the other party, even though the other party was also at fault and even though the other party may have been more at fault than you. The rationale behind the contributory negligence rule is that if you had not been somewhat negligent the accident might not have occurred.

Other states have avoided the often unfair results of the contributory negligence rule by replacing it with a rule called comparative negligence. Under the *comparative negligence* rule the jury assigns a percentage of negligence (or fault) to each party that failed to exercise due care. For example, suppose you are entering an intersection and your car is struck by one of two cars that were engaged in an illegal drag race. The jury may find that the motorist who hit you is 75 percent at fault and the other drag racer is 25 percent at fault. Whatever judgment you are awarded by the jury must be paid 75 percent by the driver who hit you and 25 percent by the other drag racer. The advantage of comparative negligence is that it attempts to apportion liability according to the degree of each party's negligence or fault.

Unlike contributory negligence, under comparative negligence a person who was himself negligent may still sue the other party if the other party was more at fault. For example, suppose you are driving down an exit ramp off a superhighway. You are traveling at 40 miles per hour even though the posted speed limit for the exit ramp is 25 miles per hour. A second car is tailgating you just 15 or 20 feet behind your rear bumper. Suddenly, a third car appears heading directly at you—the driver apparently mistook a turn and is driving up the exit ramp the wrong way right at you. You slam on the brakes. The car tailgating you collides into the rear of your car. The third car coming up the exit ramp the wrong way swerves into the guard rail and comes to a stop. After hearing everyone's version of what happened, a jury decides that the third car coming up the exit ramp the wrong way was 70 percent at fault, the car tailgating you was 20 percent at fault, and you were 10 percent at fault for speeding. You can sue either or both of the other drivers because they, individually or together, were more at fault than you. On the other hand, although you were somewhat negligent, neither of them can sue you, because you were less negligent than either of them. If you do sue both of the other drivers, the third motorist must pay 70 percent of the award and the second must pay 20 percent. You lost 10 percent of the award because you were 10 percent negligent. By contrast, under a strict contributory negligence system none of these drivers—not even you—would be able to sue either or both of the others because all three of you contributed some degree of negligence.

Many states have replaced this "fault" or liability system, to a limited extent, with a no-fault system. *No-fault* simply means that your insurance company must provide you with compensation and benefits, up to certain limits set by statute, regardless of who was at fault for the accident. No-fault systems are intended to provide minimum compensation and benefits for all injured parties in a relatively quick manner by requiring insurance companies to provide money to pay medical and other bills, up to specified limits, before issues such as fault and liability are resolved—which often takes many months or years.

No-fault systems, however, do not eliminate the fault or liability system. If your medical and related bills surpass a certain level, or if your injuries involve any of a number of serious conditions (such as loss of a limb or bodily function, serious bone or spinal damage, etc.) or if other conditions are met, you may sue the other party under the traditional fault or liability system by means of a lawsuit.

If you are injured in an automobile accident, determining how to receive compensation for your injuries will be of critical importance. Much depends on the nature of the fault and no-fault systems in your state. All states have fault systems which center on private lawsuits. Some states also have no-fault systems under which claims are made with your own insurance company regardless of whether a lawsuit has been or will be filed. As explained above, there are considerable differences between a fault system which utilizes the contributory negligence rule and a fault system which utilizes the generally fairer comparative negligence rule.

If your state has a no-fault system, you may be able to collect a limited amount of compensation or medical bill coverage fairly soon after the accident by filing a claim with your own insurance company. Whether you are limited to that recovery must be determined. As noted, if a person's medical and related bills surpass a specific amount (such as $500 or $1,000) or if the injury fits into any of a number of serious categories (such as loss of a limb or fractures) or if other conditions are met, you can seek further compensation by initiating a lawsuit. Determining this is important. Under many no-fault systems a person cannot receive compensation for pain and suffering. The no-fault benefits cover only medical and other bills. The only way to seek compensation for pain and suffering is to sue the other party under the fault system by means of a lawsuit. If your state has a no-fault system, you may not be able to initiate such a lawsuit unless your circumstances fall into one of the special categories which take you out of the no-fault system and allow you to sue under the fault system.

To obtain compensation under the fault system you must sue

the other party. His or her insurance company will automatically come into the picture. Your lawsuit may be settled out of court. Most are. If not, it will go to trial before a judge and jury.

Determining whether you are liable for someone else's injuries or how to collect compensation for your own injuries requires a knowledge of insurance. With regard to your liability for someone else's injuries, whether you have insurance, whether it covers you, and how much it covers make all the difference in the world. If you have suffered injuries, whether the other person has insurance, whether that insurance covers him, and how much it covers also make all the difference in the world. A few examples will illustrate. Suppose you are found liable for a motor vehicle accident. A jury awards the other party a money judgment against you for $100,000. Your insurance policy, however, has a single-accident limit of only $50,000. Where does the other $50,000 come from? From you. The other party may go into court to have you ordered to sell your property or assets to pay that $50,000. On the other hand, suppose the same accident and the same jury verdict of $100,000 against you, but you had the foresight to purchase $250,000 in auto insurance for a single accident. The insurance company will then pay the entire $100,000 judgment. Quite a difference.

With regard to collecting compensation if you are injured, suppose you receive $2,000 in personal injury protection from your own insurance company under your state's no-fault law. Your total medical and related expenses, including lost wages, amount to $15,000. Suppose further that you have to endure considerable pain and suffering and your attorney estimates that a case like yours could win a jury verdict in your favor of around $75,000 or more. Then your lawyer explains the bad news. First, you may have to wait one to three years to get into court. Second, the person who struck your car and caused your injuries is uninsured. He is also unemployed and broke. What do you do? On the other hand, suppose the same personal injuries suffered by you, the same medical and related expenses and lost wages of $15,000, and the same likelihood of being awarded a $75,000 jury judgment, but the person who caused your injuries is heavily insured and his insurer agrees to settle the case for $65,000 only a few months after the accident. Again, quite a difference.

The preceding paragraphs provide a cursory look at two major issues involved in every motor vehicle personal injury case: liability (under fault and no-fault) and compensation (under both systems and under various fact patterns with regard to insurance). Every personal injury arising out of a motor vehicle accident must be examined from the perspective of those two issues. Though many other factors may enter the picture, your main concerns are whether you are liable for someone else's injuries and how to receive compensation if you are injured.

WHY DO YOU NEED TO CONSULT A LAWYER?

As noted in the previous section, in a motor vehicle personal injury case, you will be concerned about one or both of two issues; how to obtain compensation for any injuries you may have suffered and how to handle your liability for someone else's injuries if that person has grounds for believing you were at fault.

Whether you are concerned about obtaining compensation for your own injuries or about your liability for someone else's injuries, advice and assistance from an experienced attorney is essential.

Most motor vehicle insurance policies stipulate that the insurance company will provide an attorney if you are sued civilly as the result of a motor vehicle accident. That may sound like you get a lawyer for free. Other considerations, however, should be kept in mind. After all, the lawyer provided by the insurance company works for the insurance company—not for you. For example, if you failed to report the accident properly or failed to comply with any other terms of the insurance policy, the insurance company's lawyer may use that information to deny coverage. If the insurance company can find some way to deny coverage, they may be relieved from paying any judgment that may be entered against you. Another example of how the insurance company's attorney may not act in your best interests is when you do not have a large amount of coverage, say only $10,000 or $20,000. The insurance company may decide that it isn't worth their time and money to defend your case fully. They may try to settle your case or take other measures that you do not agree with and that may be contrary to your own interests.

The most important reason for not relying solely on the insurance company's lawyer is that you have little or no control over that lawyer. You do not hire him or her; you do not give him or her instructions on how to handle the case; you do not pay his or her bill and you cannot fire him or her.

For all these reasons, it is wise to consult a private attorney on your own. For your own best interests, it may be essential to have your own attorney working on the case—an attorney you can hire or fire and who will follow your instructions and look out for your interests. True, you will be responsible for the attorney's bill, but that attorney will be responsible and accountable to you, not to the insurance company.

It is very important to hire your own attorney if your liability may be greater than your insurance coverage. For example, suppose you have a $50,000 insurance policy. If, however, the person who is suing you is successful, he might get as much as a $100,000 judgment against you. The insurance company will be responsible for only $50,000. You will be responsible for the other $50,000. How the insurance company wants to handle your case, how they weigh the advantages and disadvantages of going to trial versus settlement, and other matters may be different, in many important ways, from how your own attorney—who is looking out for your interests—wants to handle the case and how he or she would weigh the advantages and disadvantages of trial or settlement. Keep in mind that for an insurance company to lose a case and pay $50,000 is something that happens every day. It is entirely different for you to lose a case and be personally responsible for paying a $50,000 judgment.

The insurance company has its lawyer there to protect it. You should have your own lawyer there to protect you.

It is also essential to consult a lawyer because of the many laws that apply to motor vehicle personal injury cases. Criminal laws, motor vehicle regulations, and local ordinances may be involved. Tort law is also involved. A *tort* is a civil wrong involving damage or injury to a person's body, emotional or mental well-being, reputation, or personal property for which the injured person can sue in a civil court. Motor vehicle personal injury cases usually involve torts based on negligence (the failure to exercise due care under the circumstances). Defending yourself against a tort lawsuit based on negligence requires a sound knowledge of the applicable laws and procedures. What happened—the accident—may be fairly simple to determine. The laws and rules of procedure that govern lawsuits, settlement negotiations, and court trials, on the other hand, are intricate and complex. These laws and procedures change from year to year. An experienced attorney's advice is essential.

If you have suffered injuries, you will be concerned with the legal procedures and other steps involved in seeking compensation for your injuries. This requires a knowledge of fault and no-fault recovery systems and a knowledge of various public and private sources of compensation and assistance, including your own accident, disability, or medical insurance, Workers' Compensation (if the motor vehicle accident is employment-related), unemployment compensation, welfare, Medicare, Medicaid, and others.

Given the attorney's experience with dozens of motor vehicle accident cases, he or she can make sure you receive proper medical and related care and treatment. Many people forego necessary or recommended medical care or treatment because they do not seek proper medical advice, are afraid of being stuck with the bill, or unwittingly disregard the necessity or advisability of certain treatment. An attorney, given his or her experience in these cases, can refer you to qualified doctors and other medical professionals to determine what care and treatment you need and what it will cost. The attorney can also coordinate the insurance coverage and financial assistance to which you are entitled in order to pay for that care and treatment. For example, in some employment-related motor vehicle accidents, the injured employee collects Workers' Compensation benefits but never thinks of suing the other driver. In many of these cases, the Workers' Compensation benefits are paltry compared to what the injured person could obtain by suing the other motorist and collecting from his or her insurance company. Similarly, some motor vehicle accidents involve products liability issues. That is, the manufacturer of one of the motor vehicles may be responsible for the defect which caused the accident. Many people receive only a meager settlement from the other driver's insurance company and nothing at all from the manufacturer's insurer because they unwittingly forego suing the manufacturer of the defective car and collecting considerably more money. A third example of how your own lawyer can look out for your best interests involves cases where an injured person carried "underinsured" or "uninsured" motorist coverage but did not file a claim for benefits under that coverage out of ignorance or oversight. Your attorney, on the other hand, will want to look at your insurance policy if there is any possibility that the other party does not have adequate insurance. By utilizing the "underinsured" and "uninsured" provisions in your own insurance policy, your attorney may be able to recover thousands more dollars than you would otherwise have received.

There is a final reason for having your own attorney working to protect your interests. A major anxiety-causing aspect of any personal injury case is the fear and apprehension that surrounds the accident and its aftermath. You may be in a constant state of distress worrying about whether you might be found liable or at fault in some way and what that would mean, financially and otherwise. If someone sues you, what can you do to defend yourself? On the other hand, if you are injured, you will be worried about how to pay medical and other bills if you are out of work, how to make sure the responsible party compensates you for your injuries and losses, how to prove that the other party is liable, how long it will take, and how much it will cost. These questions can cause tremendous anxiety and distress. Your worries and apprehensions can be allayed considerably if you know you have an experienced attorney working diligently on your case with your best interests in mind.

HOW TO THINK ABOUT LEGAL AND RELATED ASPECTS

The following sections explain important points you should keep in mind and think about regarding your motor vehicle personal injury case.

Determine who is liable for the accident and resulting injuries.

In the majority of motor vehicle accidents, liability depends on whether one or more persons acted in a negligent manner. Did one or more persons fail to exercise due care under the circumstances? Of course, if a person causes a motor vehicle accident through reckless or intentionally hazardous driving, liability is clear. Most accidents, however, center on conflicting stories as to who did what and on contradictory allegations as to who was negligent and to what degree.

In some accident cases, it is relatively easy to determine who is liable. The facts of the accident may indicate liability. For example, as a general rule, any rear-end collision is presumed to be the fault of the party in the rear. Or if there are impartial witnesses, their testimony may resolve differences of opinion between the motorists involved. Physical evidence such as tire marks, the location of glass and metal, or the position of the vehicles may indicate how the accident occurred and which driver was at fault.

On the other hand, in many accident cases liability is difficult to resolve because each motorist claims that the other was at fault and there is no impartial witness or objective physical evidence by which to resolve the conflict in allegations. Also, it is not uncommon for both drivers to be partly at fault. In that situation, it makes a considerable difference whether you live in a state which uses the contributory negligence rule or in a state which has adopted the comparative negligence rule. Under the contributory negligence rule, you cannot sue the other party if you were at fault to any extent, whereas under the comparative negligence rule you may sue the other party even if you were partly at fault as long as the other party was more at fault than you.

Unless the other party and his or her insurance company are willing to admit (or at least not deny) fault, you may have to convince a jury that the other party is at fault. This requires introducing evidence in court which supports your version of what happened and refutes the other party's version of what happened. Of critical importance is your ability to explain the manner in which the accident occurred and substantiate your version with convincing evidence.

Report, investigate, and photograph the accident as soon as possible and as thoroughly as possible.

Since most motor vehicle accidents occur on traveled highways and roads, the vehicles are often towed from the scene shortly after the accident. Broken glass, shattered chrome, and bent metal are swept up or otherwise removed. Even skid marks and other tire tracks may become indistinguishable from others in just a few days. Eyewitnesses may go about their business and forget the accident—and what they saw or heard. Time and the weather may remove or hide all other traces of the accident. After that has happened, it may be too late to investigate the accident scene to develop evidence that would be admissible in court and that would substantiate your version and refute the other party's version.

Report the accident to the appropriate law-enforcement authorities as soon as possible. Call them to the scene of the accident and provide assistance so that the officer who makes the official police report will be fully informed of your version of what happened. You will also have to fill out standard accident report forms for the local police and the state motor vehicle registry. Do not complete those reports in a hasty, haphazard manner. They may become one of the most important records of your version of the accident. Be sure you recount the accident correctly and completely while it is fresh in your memory. Make sure you keep copies of any report you provide to law-enforcement agencies or others. Your insurance company should also be notified immediately and any reports required should be completed. You may jeopardize your insurance coverage if you report the accident late or not at all.

If you are able to do so or if someone will do it for you, investigate and photograph the scene of the accident as soon as possible after it occurs. Even if police arrive and make their own report, do your own photographing and investigative work. Keep a complete record of your notes and observations. If you do not have paper and pen, ask a bystander or police officer for them. If you do not have a camera available, ask a bystander or people in nearby homes or apartments if you could use one of theirs or if they would take a few pictures for you. If a newspaper or other photographer appears, be sure to get his or her name and affiliation. Do the same if the police take photos. No written or oral account of what happened will be as convincing or as powerful as well-taken photographs. Photographs bring home to everyone who sees them—especially a jury—what the road conditions and weather conditions were, where the vehicles ended up, how badly each vehicle was damaged and where, where broken glass and severed metal was located, where street lines, street lights, traffic signals, and other markings were located in relation to each vehicle, and other critical factors. Photographs can also be used to substantiate your claim for property damage to your motor vehicle as well as property damage claims by homeowners, businesses, or others whose property was damaged by the vehicles.

Make written notes of your observations regarding the position of the vehicles, weather conditions, street conditions, amount of traffic, the direction and speed of each vehicle before impact and at impact, any pertinent information regarding lighting conditions, street lights and traffic signals, lines in the road, road signs, the location of curbs and sidewalks, where broken glass or severed chrome or metal from each vehicle was located, the location and nature of any damage to each vehicle, the nature and extent of injuries to each person, the names and addresses of all persons involved, the licenses of all vehicles, the names and addresses of all witnesses, the names of the police officers at the scene, the names of newspaper or other media people, ambulance and emergency personnel, and others. The more accurate and thorough your records, the more convincing will be your account of the accident and your testimony in court.

It is important to realize that much of this information cannot be gathered in a reliable manner even a few hours or a day after the accident. It must be collected as soon as possible. If your injuries prevent you from doing so, contact someone you know as soon as possible and have them go to the scene of the accident with pen, paper, and camera. If the accident is serious, contact a professional investigator—an attorney will recommend one—to do a professional investigation. A professional investigation can make a big difference in how convincingly you and your lawyer present your case. If the accident occurs away from your home town or city, contact one of the national automobile clubs. They maintain lists of professional accident investigators. Have them recommend a reputable investigator and a reputable attorney.

As time passes after the accident—as weeks, months, and even years go by—your recollection of what happened will fade. Your memory may become confused and contradictory. You may wonder whether you are remembering or misremembering the accident. This is why you should make every effort to assemble an accurate, complete, and preservable record of what happened. Write everything down. Take as many photographs as possible. If, months or years later, you find yourself in a courtroom and you are unable to recall the accident vividly, the jurors may think you aren't telling the complete truth or that it wasn't a serious accident. Lapses of memory, confusion, contradictions, an "it-happened-so-long-ago" attitude may undermine your case. By contrast, if you have complete notes and realistic photographs to prod your memory, especially just before you take the witness stand, your testimony will be lucid, complete, and consistent. You will sound sure of yourself and will convey that what happened was serious and that you deserve to be believed by the jury.

Keep an accurate and complete record of your injury and its progress as well as a record of all costs and expenses related to your injuries.

Just as you should assemble an accurate and complete account of the accident—including photographs—you should also maintain a diary or record of your injuries, including their nature, extent, history, and prognosis, and take photographs of every stage during your recovery. Keep a complete record of the types of injuries, all medical and related treatment and care, medication, the use of traction, casts, physical therapy, prosthetic devices, and rehabilitation services. Also note and photograph all visible manifestations of the injuries—scars or disfigurement, loss or impairment of any bodily function, discoloration or other visible signs. Also make a photographic record of the history and progress of your injuries—if you are hospitalized, have photographs taken of you in the hospital bed. If you are in traction or must use a cast, take photographs. Take a photograph of your injuries once each week to have a regular, visual history of your recovery. As with your account of the accident, your testimony months or years later may suffer from a confused or faded memory. Through the use of your written record or diary and realistic photographs, your case will be much more convincing—especially to a jury.

Pain and suffering are often a major part of a personal injury lawsuit. Your ability to convince a judge or jury of the nature, extent, and severity of your pain and suffering will be considerably enhanced by recounting passages from your diary or record and by showing the judge or jury photographs of your injuries, of yourself in the hospital, in traction, in a cast, undergoing physical therapy. Of particular importance are photographs of visible scars, swellings, discoloration, or disfigurement which might heal or otherwise disappear before you go to court. Photographs of that nature will bring home to the judge and jury the pain and suffering you endured.

Also keep an accurate record of all losses and expenses associated with the accident and your injuries. Add up medical bills. Calculate lost wages and the cost of all accident-related expenses such as renting a replacement vehicle, damage to personal property, counseling or psychiatric services necessitated by the shock or trauma of the accident, and all other related items.

The more thorough you record the accident and your losses and expenses, the more complete and convincing your case will be.

Determine the fault and no-fault proceedings which may be initiated by you or against you and the procedures and timetables involved.

Depending on whether you seek to prove that someone else is liable for the accident and your injuries or whether you must protect yourself from someone else's accusations that you are liable for the accident and their injuries, you must determine what proceedings can be initiated and what procedures and timetables will be involved.

In those states that have no-fault insurance, the basic terms of no-fault are usually fairly simple. It may also be a relatively simple matter to determine whether you or another party are limited to the no-fault recovery or whether the nature and extent of the injuries permit you or the other party to initiate a private lawsuit.

Of course, not all personal injury lawsuits arising out of motor vehicle accidents end up in court with a full-scale trial. In fact, only a small fraction go that far. Most are settled out of court. This is sometimes done because one party is more or less clearly liable and both parties want to avoid the expense, delays, and risks of a trial. At the outset, however, you will want to know what no-fault benefits you can collect immediately (if your state has a no-fault plan) and what legal procedures must be followed to obtain further compensation. You will also want to know how much you will receive under no-fault and how much you can expect from a lawsuit and how long it may take to receive compensation. If it will be many months or even years before your lawsuit gets into court or is settled out of court, you must make arrangements to receive whatever private and public assistance you are entitled to. If you have private health, accident, or hospitalization insurance, your claims must be processed. If you are entitled to unemployment compensation, Medicare or Medicaid, welfare, or other public assistance, your application for benefits must be processed. In this regard, it is important to hire an attorney who is experienced in these types of cases. An experienced attorney can coordinate your claims for private insurance and your applications for public assistance and press for resolution of any lawsuit. If you have been injured, you will need to know as much as possible about how to provide for yourself and your family financially and otherwise after the accident and until you are fully recovered. An experienced attorney can provide practical assistance as well as sound legal advice.

DEALING WITH LAWYERS

In addition to the general points about lawyers in Chapter 1, keep in mind the following points about dealing with lawyers on a motor vehicle personal injury case.

There are so many motor vehicle accidents in every community that most communities have several or many lawyers who handle motor vehicle accident cases on a more or less regular basis. By asking each attorney you contact about his or her experience and background in this area, you will increase your chances of avoiding inexperienced attorneys and finding a qualified lawyer.

When you discuss fees with a lawyer, you are talking about money. If you were injured, you are talking about the money that may be won on your case—out of which the lawyer will take his or her fee. Be candid. Your case means money, both to you and to your lawyer. To receive compensation for your injuries and losses, you must sue another party and hopefully win enough money to pay your bills and related expenses and compensate yourself for pain and suffering. If you are being sued for someone else's injuries, your objective will be to disprove or minimize your liability. In that situation, you must pay a lawyer money in order to hopefully avoid paying a lot more money to someone else if you are found liable for the accident and their injuries.

If you hire an attorney because you are being sued in connection with a motor vehicle accident, the lawyer may quote a flat fee or an hourly fee. A flat fee is a specific amount of money for which the attorney agrees to handle all necessary and customary aspects of your case through the first trial. If your case is more or less routine, the attorney may gauge how much time and effort will be required and set a flat fee accordingly. Have the attorney explain what services the flat fee covers. For example, a flat fee to represent the defendant in a personal injury case normally means the attorney will handle the case through trial. If you lose your case at trial but have valid grounds for an appeal, the lawyer's fee for the appeal is not covered by the original flat fee. You and the attorney will have to work out an additional fee for the appeal.

The attorney may quote an hourly fee. Hourly fees are discussed in detail in Chapter 1.

If you are hiring an attorney because you want to sue another party, the attorney may quote a contingent percentage fee. The word *contingent* means that the attorney will charge a fee only if your case is successful and you recover an amount of money. The *percentage* means that the attorney will take, as his or her fee, a percentage of the money recovered whether it is won in court via a jury judgment, or won out of court via a settlement. Typical contingent percentage fees for motor vehicle personal injury cases are from 25 to 40 and as much as 50 percent. Most lawyers charge that percentage "off the top." That is, the lawyer's percentage is taken out of the gross settlement or money judgment. You are left with the remainder—minus unpaid bills and reimbursements. For example, if you have unpaid medical bills, they will have to be paid out of the money you win. If you must reimburse private insurance providers or public assistance agencies, those sums will be paid out of the money you recover. If there are other expenses or bills relating to your case, they will be paid out of the money you recover. The following figures present a graphic example of the difference between the gross amount of the settlement or money judgment and the net amount you actually receive:

	$10,000	Gross settlement or money judgment
minus	3,333	Lawyer's one-third fee
	6,667	
minus	750	To pay outstanding medical bills
	5,917	
minus	2,700	To reimburse out-of-work payments (from private insurance, unemployment compensation, or other plan)
	3,217	
minus	450	To pay investigator, photographer, stenographer and other expenses
	$ 2,767	Net to you

As the above figures suggest, many people are overly impressed with the gross amount of the settlement or money judgment. After the lawyer takes his or her fee, after outstanding medical bills not covered by insurance are paid, after you reimburse out-of-work payments or similar items, and after you pay the bills for the accident investigator, photographer, stenographer, and others, there may be disappointingly little left for you.

Be sure you know not only the total amount of the settlement or expected jury award but also how much of that money will go to others and how much will be left for you.

A major problem with the contingent percentage fees charged by lawyers on personal injury cases, such as motor vehicle accident cases, is that the amount of money the attorney receives as his or her fee is unrelated to the amount of time and effort the attorney puts into the case. Suppose an attorney handles your case through trial and you receive a jury award of $20,000. If the attorney charges a one-third fee, he or she will take $6,666. You will be left with $13,334 (out of which many bills and reimbursable items may have to be paid). If the attorney put 40 hours into your case, he or she is, in effect, receiving a fee of $164 an hour! If the attorney puts less than 40 hours into the case, the hourly rate is even higher!

Contingent percentage fees are even more exorbitant if the case is settled out of court. Suppose you and your attorney agree to settle out of court for $17,000 rather than go through the expense, delays, and risks of a trial. If the attorney is charging a one-third fee, he or she will take $5,666. You will be left with $11,334 (out of which unpaid bills and reimbursable items must be paid.) If the attorney put 20 hours into your case, from start to settlement, he or she is receiving a fee of $283 an hour! If the attorney settled the case with less than 20 hours of work, the hourly rate would surpass $300 an hour!

You can reduce the chances of paying such exorbitant fees by shopping around among lawyers and negotiating over the fee. Shopping around and negotiating can be an effective way of getting the attorney to agree to a lower flat fee or lower hourly fee but it works particularly well with percentage fees. For example, suppose after contacting two or three or four lawyers you learn that the "going rate" charged by lawyers in your community for representing a person injured in a motor vehicle accident is one-third (whether the case goes to trial or is settled out of court and regardless of how much or how little time and effort is required). Counter that simplistic and exorbitant rate with the following flexible schedule:

If your case goes to trial:

30 percent of the first $10,000

25 percent of any amount between $10,000 and $20,000

20 percent of any amount between $20,000 and $50,000

15 percent of any amount over $50,000.

If your case is settled out of court:

25 percent of the first $10,000

20 percent of any amount between $10,000 and $20,000

15 percent of any amount between $20,000 and $50,000

10 percent of any amount over $50,000.

The percentages listed above, in addition to being fairer than flat-rate percentage fees, will lead to considerable savings on attorney's fees. In the example noted earlier, the attorney charged a one-third fee on a $20,000 jury award. The lawyer's fee was $6,666. The client would keep the $13,334 balance (out of which numerous bills might have to be paid). If that client had insisted that the lawyer accept the fairer fee schedule set out above for cases that go to trial, the attorney's fee would have been $5,500 (instead of $6,664). The client would have kept the $1,114 difference! In the second example above, the case settled out of court for $17,000, the attorney, charging a one-third fee, received a fee of $5,666 while the client received a balance of $11,334 (out of which many bills might have been paid). If that client had insisted that the lawyer use the fee schedule listed above for cases settled out of court, the lawyer's fee would have been $3,900 (instead of $5,666). The client would have kept the $1,766 difference!

Of course, if your case is worth considerably more than a $20,000 money judgment or a $17,000 out-of-court settlement, using the flexible schedule of percentages recommended above would lead to even greater savings.

One of the most important advantages you have in negotiating for a lower percentage fee is that the lawyer will have an incentive to do a good job on your case even though you succeed in getting him or her to agree to a lower percentage fee. Suppose the lawyer quotes a one-third fee—regardless of the amount of money won on your case, regardless of whether it goes to trial or is settled out of court, and regardless of how much (or how little) time and effort it requires of the attorney. You, however, succeed in getting the attorney to agree to the schedule of percentages listed above. If the lawyer agrees, he or she still has every incentive to do as well as possible on your case because his or her fee will be a percentage of what he or she gets for you—although a lower percentage than he or she would have liked.

The higher the lawyer's percentage, the lower your percentage. Conversely, the lower the lawyer's percentage, the higher your percentage.

If your case is relatively uncomplicated, emphasize that when negotiating with the lawyer over the fee. Motor vehicle personal injury cases center on three major factors: First, do you have injuries that can be shown to have been caused by the accident and for which you can calculate a reasonable compensation figure ("damages")? Second, can you prove that the other party was at fault or at least more clearly at fault than you ("liability")? Third, is there insurance available to cover the other party ("collectability")?

If you have detailed reports of the nature, extent, history, and prognosis of your injuries and you can calculate a money figure (for example, $5,000 or $25,000) based on medical bills, lost wages, and other known quantities, then the damages aspect of your case is relatively uncomplicated. (*Damages* is the legal term for the money figure which represents compensation for your injuries and losses.) If you can prove that the other party was clearly at fault, perhaps through impartial witnesses or skid marks or the fact that you were hit from the rear, then the liability aspect of your case is relatively uncomplicated. Finally, if the other party has insurance to cover the amount of money you win in court or agree to in an out-of-court settlement, then the collectability aspect of your case is uncomplicated.

If all three aspects of your case—damages, liability, and collectability—are uncomplicated, then you are in an excellent position to reject a high percentage fee, such as one-third or 40 percent, when it is quoted by a lawyer. Negotiate for a lower percentage fee such as the schedule set forth earlier in this section. If you wish to rely on a more simple counteroffer, offer the attorney one-fourth (25 percent) if the case goes to trial and one-fifth (20 percent) if the case is settled out of court.

An attorney may deserve a large fee if he or she must investigate evidence of the other party's fault and combat evidence that suggests that you may have been at fault. By contrast, where fault is clearly on the other side, the attorney's work is relatively easy. Similarly, if the nature, extent, history, and prognosis of your injuries are readily available in medical reports, your bills and lost wages can be easily calculated, and the other party has ample insurance, your attorney will not have to do as much work as he or she would if your injuries were questionable or if the other party lacked adequate insurance.

Far too many people unwittingly agree to pay their attorney a high fee, such as one-third or 40 percent, on uncomplicated, straightforward automobile personal injury cases that do not require much time or effort on the attorney's part. This is particularly true when the case is settled out of court. An out-of-court settlement obviously requires less time and effort on the attorney's part than a full-scale trial.

When is the attorney's fee due? Since a contingent percentage fee comes out of the money you win, it is payable when that money is recovered. If you win a jury award or if your case is settled out of court, the lawyer will deduct his or her fee out of the check when it arrives. If you agree to a flat fee or an hourly fee, work out an arrangement to pay the fee in installments. It may be many months or even years before your case is resolved. If that is true, arrange to pay the lawyer in monthly installments or on some other periodic schedule. An installment arrangement makes the fee more affordable. Also, it gives the attorney an incentive to keep working on your case—if he or she neglects your case or does something of which you don't approve, you can withhold further installments until he or she gets working on your case again or corrects his or her conduct.

14 Consumer Rights

WHAT DOES A CONSUMER RIGHTS CASE INVOLVE?

A *consumer* is an individual who purchases goods or services primarily for personal, family, or household use. This distinguishes a consumer from someone who purchases goods or services in the course of business, commercial, or professional dealings. Whether you purchase goods from a retail outlet, from a wholesaler, or directly from the manufacturer, if the goods are to be used for your personal, family, or household needs, you are a consumer. Similarly, if you purchase services, whether from an unskilled or skilled worker or from a professional, if the services are for personal, family, or household purposes, you are a consumer.

A consumer may have numerous rights and remedies to pursue if the goods or services are defective or deficient or if the business, worker, or professional engages in unlawful practices.

Much has been written and said about the largely bygone era of *caveat emptor*. Those Latin words mean, "Let the buyer beware." In other words, a person who purchases goods or services has only him- or herself to blame if the goods turn out to be defective or the services deficient or shoddy. Considerable disparaging commentary has been directed at the caveat emptor rule of law as it was developed by the courts of England in past centuries and carried over into American law. Little mention is made of the fact that, in societies where goods and services are not of a highly technological nature and where businesses, workers, and professionals and their customers live in a small, word-of-mouth community, caveat emptor was largely a reflection of a general attitude held by many purchasers as well as sellers. For example, in an agrarian and semiskilled trade society, the average "consumer" was likely to be as knowledgeable about goods, wares, and services as the average merchant, supplier, or worker. Since the consumer stood on an equal footing with the seller, it was an accepted practice that a purchaser should examine, test, and otherwise inspect goods, wares, and services before purchasing them. If the goods or wares turned out to be defective or deficient or if a worker for hire did shoddy work, the reputation—and therefore the business—of the goods maker, merchant, or worker would suffer. In addition, the purchaser might seek a self-help remedy such as convincing or intimidating the goods maker, merchant, or worker to replace or correct the defective goods or services or refund the purchase money. Certainly there were other means of "getting even" with shoddy practices by sellers. The court-developed rule of caveat emptor meant only that courts and other dispute resolution tribunals of the day did not recognize a basis for a lawsuit if a consumer purchased goods or services which he or she knew or should have known were defective or deficient. Thus, the consumer could not go to court to have legal measures taken against the seller. The consumer was left to his or her own devices. Of course, as few commentators note, contract law, warranty and guaranty law, usury laws, fraud and deceit law, and other fields of law which provided a foundation for consumer protection developed at the same time as the doctrine of caveat emptor.

In contemporary American law, the rule of caveat emptor has been largely reversed and replaced by a wide range of grounds on which a consumer may bring legal action against a business, worker, or professional for defective or deficient goods or services or for unfair, deceptive, or otherwise unlawful practices. Rather than leaving the consumer to self-help remedies and a limited number of grounds for a lawsuit (such as breach of contract and fraud and deceit law), modern legislatures have enacted statutes and modern courts have announced rules of law which create and continue to expand the grounds on which a consumer may avail him- or herself of the power and sanctions of the law and government tribunals (the courts and administrative agencies) to remedy many, but by no means all, consumer abuses.

The proliferation of consumer rights laws which make the seller of goods and services accountable in court or before an administrative agency for their products, services, and practices is necessary in a society where purchasers—consumers—are not on an equal footing with sellers. The technology and specialized knowledge that go into modern-day products and services make it impossible for the average or even the sophisticated consumer to ensure that the product is safe and free from defects or that the service is competent and reliable before purchasing. In addition, the national and international scale and complexity of the American economy makes it impossible for the word-of-mouth controls of a small, self-contained community to be effective in safeguarding consumers from workers, businesses, and professionals who bilk their customers or engage in unfair practices.

Two important but sometimes overlooked aspects of modern consumer protection are professional licensing and product liability laws. Although licensing of professions and occupations such as doctors, lawyers, beauticians, electricians, and real estate brokers may contribute to monopolization of those fields, a major attribute of licensing, when coupled with minimum competency testing and trade policing, is to ensure, to some degree, that competent, law-abiding people engage in the particular occupation or profession.

Licensing of numerous occupations and professions is important to consumers of the services and products sold by the members of those occupations and professions. An aggrieved consumer may be able to rectify a consumer abuse by calling upon the supervisory and enforcement powers of the board or commission charged with licensing and therefore regulating, to some extent, the practitioners of that profession or the members of that occupation. For example, consumer abuses by insurance salespersons, funeral parlor directors, pharmacists, lawyers, veterinarians, stockbrokers, and others can be brought before the licensing board for that occupation or profession. Often, a member of a licensed profession or occupation will be more concerned about a complaint filed with the licensing board than about a lawsuit. In a lawsuit, a court may order the worker or professional to pay a money judgment if the consumer prevails. By contrast, a serious and substantiated complaint filed with the licensing board could jeopardize that person's license to engage in his or her chosen profession or occupation.

Product liability law also has considerable consumer protection attributes. Product liability means that the manufacturer or designer of a given product must ultimately bear responsibility if the product, in the course of its normal and expected use by a consumer, causes injury or loss through a defect or unsafe condition which the consumer could not reasonably have foreseen—but which the manufacturer or designer could have foreseen. Product liability makes it the manufacturer's or designer's responsibility to test a product before putting it on the market. If tests reveal or should have revealed dangers or unsafe conditions under normal or expected use, the manufacturer or designer may have to redesign the product, or install safety devices, or provide understandable and effective warning labels or instructional material. Naturally, safety tests, redesign efforts, safety devices, improvements, and warning labels all cost money. But that money is simply added to the cost of the product on the market. In this manner, all purchasers pay a share of the cost of the protective measures that went into that product. Likewise, all consumers and users of that product receive the benefit of those protective measures. Product liability law has led to insurance coverage which manufacturers and designers can obtain to pay claims made by consumers who were injured or damaged by the product. The cost of that insurance is added to the market price of the product. Once again, the consumer pays for his or her own protection. Product liability law has expanded considerably in recent decades. It is no coincidence that the use of product safety standards, testing, redesign improvements, safety devices, and warning labels increased markedly during the same period.

Two other developments in recent decades have considerably reduced the deleterious aspects of the caveat emptor rule of law by establishing public controls on certain businesses and industries. These two developments are the rise of public utilities and the proliferation of public regulatory agencies.

When energy, communications, transportation, and other necessary products and services were controlled by unregulated private enterprise, the rule of caveat emptor was often compounded by the abusive practices characteristic of monopolies. If there is only one fuel dealer in your community, only one telegraph company, only one telephone company, only one transportation company, and so on, and those enterprises are not responsible to public officials, you must accept what they offer for the price charged or go without essential services and products. In contemporary American society, numerous energy, communications, transportation, and other service and product enterprises are managed as public utilities or public corporations. They are only semiprivate, which means they are also semipublic; their policies, prices, products, and services are closely supervised and controlled by boards of public officials. Those public officials are responsible to the elected public officials who appoint them, to the public generally, and to the consumers of the products and services of the given utility or public corporation.

In addition, many enterprises that are not public utilities or public corporations operate under government regulations which, according to some of their spokespersons, make them feel and act like public utilities or public corporations. Although "deregulation" is occurring in some areas, regulation by government boards, commissions, and bureaus has been present for many years in such areas as commercial communications, interstate transportation, food and drug marketing, credit services, banking, and insurance.

Other government regulatory bodies have wide-ranging authority to investigate and set standards for product and service quality and safety. These include the Federal Trade Commission and so-called mini-FTCs established by a number of states. Federal, state, and local regulatory agencies and consumer protection offices provide information and assistance to consumers and act as watchdogs against consumer abuses. Many private, nonprofit consumer protection or consumer advocate groups also assist in protecting consumers and advancing the interests of consumers.

The development of consumer protection standards in such traditional fields of law as contracts, fraud and deceit, warranty and guaranty, and usury; the development of new areas of law specifically addressed to consumer rights and consumer protection; the development of professional and occupational licensing and trade policing; the development of product liability law; the rise of public utilities and public corporations and the proliferation of government regulatory agencies and public and private consumer protection offices—all have contributed to the demise of caveat emptor and the rise of consumer rights.

Consumer rights are standards established by law which enable a consumer who has been victimized by unlawful practices to bring legal action against the offending business, worker, or professional.

Of course, bringing appropriate legal action against a business, worker, or professional requires knowing what your consumer rights are and how to remedy the situation if those rights have been violated. In many instances, initiating formal legal action is not necessary. The business, worker, or professional may be amenable to a private resolution of the matter. Perhaps the manufacturer, seller, worker, or professional will repair or replace the defective goods or provide substitute or corrective services. Perhaps a money refund would be an adequate and fair resolution. These and similar resolutions occur every day. They exemplify remedies and recourse undertaken by the consumer and worked out directly between the consumer and the business, worker, or professional. Such private resolutions may have been commonplace during the days of caveat emptor as well. Today, most businesses, workers, and professionals realize the numerous avenues consumers can follow to rectify violations of their rights. With that in mind, businesses, workers, and professionals are, in many instances, willing to work out a private resolution of a dispute with an aggrieved consumer.

This chapter, however, discusses situations in which the consumer must initiate formal legal or administrative action against a business, worker, or professional to determine whether there has been a violation of the consumer's rights and, if so, what remedies and other recourse the consumer can pursue to rectify the consumer abuse. These are situations in which the consumer will need legal advice and assistance to some or a large extent. No doubt, there are numerous consumer protection laws. Many of those laws, however, are complex and difficult to understand and apply. Many require that detailed procedures be followed by the consumer to preserve and protect his or her rights. Many provide specific remedies (corrective measures or money judgments). Some require that the consumer take steps to minimize his or her losses or to allow the business, worker, or professional to correct the situation privately. Other consumer protection laws provide specific standards of proof which the aggrieved consumer must meet before the court or administrative agency will find against the business, worker, or professional. Because of the number, complexity, and intricacy of consumer protection laws, it is important to consult an attorney or someone else who is knowledgeable and competent to provide legal information when your consumer problem cannot be resolved to your satisfaction after you have made direct efforts to work the matter out with the business, worker, or professional. If you must pursue legal avenues, you will need legal advice and assistance.

It is equally important to realize that although you may need legal advice and assistance, it doesn't necessarily follow that you must go to a private attorney and pay a substantial fee. The section of this chapter entitled "Dealing with Lawyers" discusses numerous public and private agencies and groups which provide valuable and competent legal information and help for consumers at no cost. That section also notes that there are many laws which provide that if you hire your own lawyer and win your case, the court or administrative agency that hears your case can order the offending business, worker, or professional to reimburse you for your attorney's fee. Finally, that section discusses class action lawsuits, a device by which you can join with other aggrieved consumers to share legal expenses initially and, if you win your case, have the court order the malfactor business, worker, or professional to reimburse you for your attorney's fees.

In pursuing and protecting your consumer rights it is important to keep in mind that every time you stand up for your consumer rights, you are standing up for everyone's consumer rights.

WHY DO YOU NEED TO CONSULT A LAWYER OR OTHER COMPETENT LEGAL ADVISOR?

The proliferation of complex consumer protection laws makes it difficult for consumers to know what their rights are, when their rights have been violated, and what they must do to correct the situation. In effect, although largely unintentionally, the consumer rights movement has made consumers highly dependent on accurate and reliable legal information and assistance.

A knowledge of consumer law is essential to correctly handle consumer abuses. Do not undertake self-help tactics unless you know your rights and obligations. Some self-help tactics may ruin your chances of getting what you want. Or those self-help tactics may violate the rights of the business, worker, or professional who you believe has wronged you. Unwittingly, you may make yourself liable to the business or person you want to take legal action against. For example, suppose you purchase a new or used car from a dealer. To finance the car, you take out a car loan with a loan company that handles car loans for that dealership but which is not legally affiliated with the dealer. The car turns out to be a "lemon." After numerous trips to the dealer for repairs, after being stuck on the road several times, after getting fed up with driving a defective and possibly dangerous automobile, you get so upset you return the car to the dealer demanding your money back and stop paying the car loan. Several days later, you seek legal advice from a local or state consumer protection agency or from an attorney. The advice you receive is that you may be able to sue the dealer for breach of warranty or misrepresentation, depending on what you can prove the dealer led you to believe about the car. What legal action, if any, you can bring against the dealer would also depend on the court decisions and statutes in your state that govern warranty law and the law of misrepresentation (fraud and deceit). On the other hand, if the dealer continues to offer to try to fix the problems you complain about, that may be the only obligation the dealer has under the law. Or if the dealer offers to provide you another car of the same make, model, and year, you may have to take it—or stick with the lemon. Again, what the dealer is legally obligated to do may be very different from what you think he should have to do. You may not be able to sue the dealer and require him to take back the lemon and return your purchase money in full. Also, you may not be able to collect the money it cost to rent a replacement car while the lemon was being fixed. Nor can you sue for the aggravation the faulty car caused you. What's more, you have no right to stop payment on the car loan. In fact, if you do not make up the missed payments and get back to paying on time, the loan company will probably file suit against you for the balance of the loan plus nonpayment penalties, interest, collection costs, and other charges.

Taking steps you may feel are justified and demanding measures you feel are appropriate and fair can get you into legal trouble. In many areas of law, what you would like to do and have others ordered to do is very different from what the law allows you to do or can order others to do. That is often the case with consumer protection laws. There are laws that protect consumers, but those laws only protect against certain abuses—by no means do they protect against all consumer abuses. Also, consumer protection laws are usually detailed and have mandatory procedures; that means you must follow specific procedures to obtain specific remedies. You must get accurate information about your consumer rights and available remedies and act accordingly. Engaging in self-help tactics and imposing your own will or demands on people may get you into serious and costly trouble.

It is necessary to seek and abide by sound legal advice so that you will make sure you get what you are legally entitled to without getting yourself into legal trouble. One important point is to find out who is legally responsible for the consumer abuse. Determining who is liable for the consumer abuse may be easy or it may be a matter of some complexity. For example, suppose you purchase an extension ladder so that you can paint your house. After several hours of painting near the roof, the metal ladder jack (the metal coupling which allows one section of ladder to be extended beyond the other) cracks and you plunge to the ground seriously injuring your legs and back. Who is legally liable? To begin with, you bought the extension ladder from a local hardware store. They are responsible for having sold you a ladder that proved to be defective under normal use. You can sue them for that. But they will respond by admitting that they sold you that ladder (if your records or their records establish that fact) but claim that they alone should not have to compensate you for injuries because they relied on the materials distributor from whom they purchased the ladder. Thus, they will turn around and join the materials supplier in the lawsuit you initiated. The materials supplier will turn around and bring in the manufacturer who sold them the ladder. The manufacturer will look to the engineer or other person who designed the ladder jack in a faulty manner. If the manufacturer's own designer is responsible for that ladder jack, the manufacturer is stuck. If an outsider designed the ladder jack, they will add that person or company to the lawsuit.

Now that you know whom you must sue (to start the chain reaction of liability suits), what must you prove to the court before the court will find in your favor and order the defendants to pay you money to compensate you for your injuries? You must prove that the ladder jack was designed or manufactured in such a manner that it was unsafe for normal use and that you did not contribute to its faulty condition. Expert engineers and metallurgists can be hired to examine the ladder jack, perform metal stress tests, and render expert opinions on whether the fault was in the design or in the method of manufacture. You must also show that you didn't contribute to or cause the faulty condition—for example, by putting too much weight on the ladder, by extending it beyond the recommended point, or by allowing rust or other corrosion to weaken the ladder jack.

Legal advice and assistance is necessary to understand what consumer rights, if any, were violated, what procedures you must follow to seek compensation and corrective measures, what amounts of compensation and types of corrective measures you can pursue under the law, what is required to prove your case, whom you must bring legal action against and how to make sure you get everything you are legally entitled to.

As a consumer, you want to make sure you are compensated for the losses you incurred as the result of a given consumer abuse. But what can be done to prevent other consumers from falling prey to the same defective product or deficient services or shoddy practices? Admittedly, the lemon you bought from the car dealer may prove to be 1 car in 50. With the defective ladder jack, however, it may be that every ladder with a jack of that design or manufacture is defective. Every person who uses such a ladder runs the risk of serious injury or even death. Having learned that their product is defective, that it has led to a substantial lawsuit and may cause many other injuries and lawsuits, the manufacturer of the ladder jack, in light of contemporary product liability laws, may notify distributors, wholesalers, and retailers to take ladders with their jack off the market. In addition, recall orders can be sent to all known purchasers of ladders with that type ladder jack informing them that the product is not safe and that the manufacturer will refund the purchase price or provide a substitute ladder at no cost. Moreover, an advertising campaign may have to be conducted to warn purchasers who cannot be located by checking sales information. If the manufacturer does not take those steps out of a desire to prevent further accidents and injuries or out of fear of further lawsuits, a court or administrative agency may order the manufacturer to do so and impose severe penalties if the manufacturer fails to comply. Similarly, if a given consumer abuse is a companywide practice, a consumer lawsuit against that practice may cause the company to stop the practice. If the company doesn't stop, other lawsuits or intervention from government or private consumer protection groups may force the company to cease the consumer abuse.

What if a consumer abuse consists of shoddy, unfair, or otherwise illegal practices by an individual businessperson, worker, or professional? For instance, what if the owner of a small auto repair shop charges you grossly exorbitant prices for replacement parts and labor? What if you pay a home insulation company $2,500 to insulate your home only to find that the insulation material they used is highly flammable and causes breathing problems for you and your family—side effects which they did not caution you about beforehand? What if you hire a lawyer to represent you on a consumer abuse case but the lawyer fails to follow the required procedures and your case is lost through the lawyer's neglect or fault?

Where the consumer abuse is an individual incident perpetrated by an individual businessperson, worker, or professional (as opposed to a defective mass-produced product or a companywide illegal practice), you may be able to sue on such grounds as breach of contract, breach of warranty or guaranty, or fraud or deceit. In addition, there may be specific laws or legal standards which the businessperson, worker, or professional has violated which enable you to bring legal action to rectify the situation. For example, you may be able to file charges against the auto repair shop for violating federal or state price-gouging regulations or for violating state law by failing to provide an estimate of the repair costs before doing the repair work. There may be violations of other statutes or regulations which govern auto repair shops. An examination of the laws applicable to auto repair shops must be made. The home insulation company that installed highly flammable insulating material that causes breathing problems may have violated state or local building code regulations or federal, state, or local regulations governing home insulation materials and promotional and sales practices by home insulation companies. The laws that govern home insulation companies must be examined.

In addition to filing a lawsuit against the auto repair shop or the home insulation company, you can file a formal complaint with a state or local consumer protection agency or state attorney general's office, or the auto repair licensing board or state agency that supervises home insulation companies. The local or state better business bureau, chamber of commerce, private consumer protection groups, and others may also be able to take action against the offending business, worker, or professional once you file a complaint. There may be many government agencies and private groups that would advocate your rights once you explain the situation and file a formal complaint.

What about the lawyer who lost your case through neglect or some other fault on his or her part? What action can a client/consumer take against a lawyer who damages the client's case or otherwise violates the client's consumer rights? The client can sue the lawyer for malpractice. An attorney may be held liable for malpractice if he or she fails to exercise the knowledge, skill, and ability ordinarily possessed and exercised by lawyers, or if the lawyer fails to handle a client's case with reasonable competence, diligence, and care, or if the lawyer fails to act honestly and in good faith in all dealings with the client. If the client's case was lost through the lawyer's neglect, incompetence, or other fault, the client can sue the lawyer for an amount of money which represents what the client would have gained had the lawyer not damaged the client's case. Given the reliance and trust clients must be able to place in their attorneys, and given the client's dependence on the lawyer for accurate information, sound advice, and diligent work in the client's best interest, it is particularly important for consumers to be aware of their consumer rights with regard to lawyers. Malpractice is a broad legal concept which allows a client to sue his or her lawyer for almost any damage done by the lawyer to the client's property or the client's claims, rights, or interests. In addition to suing for malpractice, every state has a bar association grievance committee—some states also have a lawyer review board—which hears complaints filed against lawyers by clients. The bar association grievance committee or the state lawyer review board may initiate an investigation and in some cases may present the matter to the state's highest court for possible disciplinary action against the lawyer (such as a reprimand, censure, suspension from the practice of law for a limited time, or disbarment from the practice of law). Every client of every lawyer should be fully informed of his or her rights as a client, how to deal effectively with lawyers, how to avoid problems with lawyers, and what to do if problems develop. To obtain that information, consult my *Lawyers: A Client's Manual*, also published by Prentice-Hall.

If the consumer abuse was perpetrated by someone in a business, occupation, or profession that is supervised by a government regulatory agency, you may be able to rectify the situation by filing a complaint with the appropriate regulatory agency. This is particularly true for public utilities and public corporations and those businesses, industries, occupations, and professions that have special regulatory agencies with watchdog authority over them. The federal Food and Drug Administration, a state insurance commission, and a local licensing commission are examples of government regulatory agencies which provide information and assistance to consumers who have been victimized by a business, occupation, or profession regulated by each.

As the victim of a consumer abuse, you may have a number of courses of actions available to rectify the situation: There may be one or more grounds for a civil lawsuit; if the consumer abuse involves a violation of criminal law, you can file criminal charges; there may be a government agency which regulates the business, trade, or profession in question and which will assist you; there may be federal, state, or local consumer protection agencies or offices that will take up your case or handle your complaint; there may be private consumer protection or consumer advocate groups willing to help you; your federal, state, or local elected officials may be able to intercede on your behalf; the particular business, trade, or profession may have its own self-regulatory body which may be interested in doing something about a member that breaks the law and gives the entire group a bad name; media representatives, particularly local newspaper, radio, and television consumer affairs personnel and investigators may be interested in exposing the particular consumer abuse. Having read this paragraph, you may be surprised how many courses of action and sources of consumer assistance there are where once you thought there might be little or nothing you could do and no one who could help.

Some courses of action can be taken in conjunction with others; some can be taken only to the exclusion of others; some may be more expensive than others; some may promise quicker results; others may offer better results; all will require a knowledge of the laws and procedures governing the particular consumer abuse. You will need to consult an attorney who has experience and training in consumer law or someone else who is familiar with consumer law who can provide competent legal advice and assistance. Failure to seek such legal advice and assistance may cause you to lose your case or not obtain all the relief you are entitled to. Also, you may unwittingly get yourself into legal trouble by violating laws or procedures of which you are not aware. The best way to remedy the consumer abuse and increase the chances that it will not be perpetrated on other consumers is to seek competent legal advice and assistance.

HOW TO THINK ABOUT LEGAL AND RELATED ASPECTS

The following sections discuss important points to think about with regard to your consumer rights case.

Determine what consumer rights were violated and how you can prove it.

Not all consumer abuses are against the law. Sharp practices by a business, worker, or professional may seem unfair to you. They may be unfair. But unless a law is violated, the law will provide no recourse. Of course, you can file complaints against the business, worker, or professional. Also, you may be able to work out an acceptable resolution if you make it clear to the business, worker, or professional that the unfair practice they perpetrated on you could hurt their reputation and their business unless they make good with you. Nonetheless, if a practice is unfair, but not illegal, you are largely on your own. The courts of law, regulatory agencies, and government consumer protection offices may be powerless to help you if the practice, although abusive and unjust, does not constitute a violation of a given law.

Many consumer abuses, however, do involve a violation of the law. As noted, there are many laws which govern the quality of products and services and the consumer practices of businesses, workers, and professionals. In fact, the number and complexity of those laws may make it difficult for a consumer to understand what legal right has been violated and what legal recourse and remedies the consumer can seek.

Generally, consumer rights violations fall into one or more of the following categories:

Breach of Contract If a business, worker, or professional fails to live up to the terms and conditions of their contractual agreement with you, you can sue them in court. Although most contracts are in writing, many contractual agreements are enforceable by a court even though the terms were not put in writing. Of course, if the terms of the agreement between yourself and a business, worker, or professional were not put in writing, it may be difficult for you to prove that a violation occurred. Whenever possible, put the terms and conditions of an understanding or agreement in writing. If a businessperson, worker, or professional verbally agrees to specific terms, put those terms on paper and have the other party sign it.

Breach of Warranty A *warranty* is an assurance on the part of a business, worker, or professional regarding some aspect of a product or service on which you may rely. If the assurance on which you relied turns out to be false or mistaken, you can sue the business, worker, or professional for breach of warranty. For example, if an auto dealer warranties that the engine in a given used car is good for another 10,000 miles but the engine breaks down after only 1,000 miles, the dealer can be required to make good on his assurance that the engine would be good for 10,000 miles. Many warranties, especially for mass-produced products, are printed and attached to or packaged with the product.

Warranties can be oral. (However, there is a danger that the businessperson, worker, or professional may later on deny having made the warranty statement.) If someone makes a verbal warranty, have them put it in writing and sign it. People who intend to stand by their word will put their word in writing.

The law imputes certain warranties—called implied warranties—into almost every commercial transaction involving products sold by businesspersons. Generally, the law requires that the product be fit for the general purpose it is to serve. Moreover, if you inform the seller that you intend to use a product for a specific purpose and ask the seller to recommend or supply a given product in light of that specific purpose, that product must be fit for the particular purpose for which the seller knew you intended to use it. If a product is not fit for the general purpose it was made to serve or if the product is not fit for the particular purpose of which the seller was aware, you can sue the seller for the loss you incur because of the defective or deficient product.

Breach of Guaranty Many people use the word *guaranty* interchangeably with the word *warranty*. However, they are different and create different legal rights and obligations. As noted, a warranty is an assurance made by a seller regarding a product or service on which you have the right to rely. If the product or service does not live up to that assurance, you can sue for breach of warranty. A guaranty, by contrast, is an agreement or promise by one person that he or she will answer for the debt, default, or miscarriage of another person. For example, the owner of a watch repair shop or roofing company may guaranty the quality and effectiveness of the work performed by his or her employees. That means that if the employee assigned to repair your watch does a poor job or if the employees assigned by the roofing company to repair or replace your roof do shoddy work, the owner must make good on his or her guaranty and see that additional work is done to correct the situation. If the owner does not do so, you can sue for an amount of money which will enable you to have the watch or roof put in the condition the watch repair shop owner or the roofing company owner said it would be in. Essentially, a guaranty is an assurance, on which you have the right to rely, made by one person that he or she will stand behind the work of another person. Unlike warranties, many businesses, workers, and professionals make statements which constitute a guaranty but do so orally: "They'll do a good job. I guaranty it." If someone says that or makes a similar guaranty, have them put it in writing, and sign it.

Fraud and Deceit A *fraud* occurs when a person makes a representation which he or she knows or should know is untrue, he or she makes that (mis)representation with the intention that you will rely on it, and you do rely on it and you incur a loss or damage because of your reliance on that person's knowing (mis)representation. The representation must be such that you would not have entered into the agreement or made the purchase had it not been for that representation. For example, suppose an antique dealer tells you that a certain table is a rare and valuable antique. In reality, the dealer knows that it is an excellent imitation and not a real antique. Nonetheless, the dealer convinces you that it is an antique. Relying on that (mis)representation, you purchase the table for a price that is substantially higher than you would have paid if you had known it was only an imitation. In fact, you wouldn't have bought the table if you had known it was only an imitation. Later, you learn of the fraud that was perpetrated on you. (For example, you learn the name of the person who sold that table to the antique dealer and that person is willing to testify that he or she sold the table for a low price and informed the dealer that it was only an imitation antique.) You can sue the dealer for fraud. You can sue to have the dealer take back the table and return your purchase money or you can sue to keep the table but have the dealer pay you the difference between the table's real market value and the exorbitant price you paid for it.

Deceit is, in most jurisdictions, synonymous with *fraud*. As another example of fraud or deceit, suppose you purchase a home. The owners told you the plumbing is less than two years old and there are no serious plumbing problems. After purchasing and moving into the house, however, you discover that numerous pipes are cracked or corroded and that severe water damage has occurred inside several walls where those pipes are located. A plumbing company estimates it will cost $2,500 to replace the cracked and corroded pipes and another $2,500 to replace the walls, wiring, insulation, and other material damaged by the leaking water. Whether you call it fraud or deceit, you would not have bought that house at that price if it hadn't been for the owners' (mis)representation regarding the condition of the plumbing. You can sue the owners. You can sue for the cost of putting the house in the condition it would have been in had the plumbing been in the condition the owners said it was in. Or you can sue for the difference between what the house was really worth and what you paid for it. In some cases, you might even be successful in getting the court to order the sellers to take back the house and return your purchase money.

Unfair Business Practices or Violation of Special Consumer Protection Laws The federal government and each state have statutes, court decisions, and regulatory agency rulings which make it unlawful for businesses, workers, or professionals to engage in certain practices. For example, the federal government has established truth-in-lending laws, fair credit laws, and antitrust laws, to name just a few, which set forth numerous consumer protection standards. The states have additional consumer protection laws as well. For example, loan companies cannot charge interest in excess of state usury laws. Some state laws require businesses, workers, and professionals to follow specific procedures in the conduct of their business. For instance, in many states auto repair shops must give you an estimate, in writing, of the cost of the repair job before they may do any work. Also, they must keep parts which they took from your car so that you can inspect those parts to make sure they were in need of replacement. Other consumer protection laws require businesses, workers, and professionals to inform you of some of your consumer rights at the time you do business with them. Several states have "cooling-off" laws which require door-to-door salespeople to advise you that even after you sign a contract to purchase their goods or services, you have three days (or some other period of time) in which to cancel the order with no obligation.

Every year, new unfair business practice laws and special consumer protection laws are promulgated. One or more such laws may outlaw the consumer abuse you encountered and may provide specific courses of action you can take to redress the wrong.

Violation of Licensing Standards or Regulations Many businesses, occupations, and professions are licensed. The members of a licensed occupation, business, or profession must conform to standards of conduct and business regulations established by state law or promulgated by the licensing authorities. If the consumer abuse perpetrated on you constitutes a violation of a licensing standard or regulation, you may be able to have corrective measures taken by filing a complaint with the licensing authorities. This can be done in addition to pursuing other courses of action, such as filing a lawsuit. For example, if a licensed funeral parlor director does shoddy work or acts in a reprehensible manner, a complaint filed with the state board of registration of funeral parlor directors may cause that funeral parlor director to make amends for his or her work or conduct. If your stockbroker or real estate broker engages in wrongful conduct or practices, corrective measures may be forthcoming once you notify the appropriate licensing authorities. Similarly, if your lawyer neglects your case, does shoddy work, or engages in offensive conduct, you can (and should) file formal complaints with the local or state bar association's grievance committee and with the state lawyer review board (if your state has one). After all, the last thing that a licensed businessperson, worker, or professional wants is to have a serious consumer abuse brought to the attention of the licensing authorities.

judgment or award you can seek in court or before an administrative tribunal to compensate for your losses. Remedies also include the various measures a court or administrative tribunal can order the other party to take to correct the situation—for example, an order to cease the practice, take the product off the market, issue recall orders, refund the purchaser's money, conduct more tests, or take other measures.

There may be a number of different approaches you can pursue and different results you can aim for. There may be more than one type of lawsuit you can file against the business, worker, or professional. In addition, it may be advisable to file a formal complaint with the appropriate licensing authorities or regulatory agencies. A number of civil and administrative remedies may be practical and worth pursuing.

Don't overlook the possibility of filing a criminal complaint. Some consumer abuses involve such criminal violations as embezzlement, larceny, forgery, perjury, extortion, and even assault and battery. Criminal violations should be brought to the attention of the appropriate law-enforcement agencies.

Before embarking on a given course, make sure you have an understanding of the procedures involved, particularly the time and money those procedures will entail. Although the time and costs—particularly the attorney's fee—may seem prohibitive, be aware that many consumer abuses, once proven, entitle you to have your attorney's fee and other costs and expenses reimbursed by the offending business, worker, or professional. Or you may be able to obtain free legal advice and assistance from a government consumer protection agency or a private consumer advocate group. Moreover, there may be procedures, such as a class action lawsuit, that make it economically feasible for you and others to pursue expensive legal proceedings you would not otherwise be able to afford. These matters—reimbursement of attorneys' fees, free legal assistance, and class action lawsuits—are discussed further in the next section.

Think out a plan of action. Take into consideration the nature of the consumer abuse, the available remedies, and what each avenue of recourse will involve and cost.

In most situations, it is advisable, initially, to seek a private resolution of the matter by directly confronting the worker, business, or professional. Sellers of products and services are often willing to iron out consumer complaints through an informal arrangement. They may not want to lose you—and the people you know—as customers or otherwise impair their reputation. Of course, if the abusive practice is illegal, they may want to avoid being brought to court or having that practice brought to the attention of other authorities. On the other hand, some sellers hope that by agreeing to a private settlement they can keep that consumer quiet while they continue to engage in the illegal practice with other consumers.

At some point, you may have to decide whether your objective is to seek redress for yourself—and not be concerned about whether others may fall victim to the same practice—or whether you should take other steps to insure that the consumer abuse is stopped once and for all.

Some cautions should be reiterated. First, although you feel you have been abused or victimized by a consumer abuse, that does not necessarily mean that the worker, business, or professional violated the law or that they can be required to rectify the situation in the manner you think is appropriate. Many abusive and "unfair" practices exist and are legal. Do not initiate serious and expensive legal action unless you are reasonably sure you have a good case and are on sound legal ground.

Next, decide what you want to accomplish, and then fashion your strategy after that objective. If your objective can be achieved by private talks with the business, worker, or professional, pursue them. If the talks fail or if the seller denies any wrongdoing and refuses to talk, examine the various remaining approaches available and identify those that have the best chance for achieving what you want. For instance, you may have one or more grounds for a successful lawsuit, but it may take many months or a year or more to get into court. Other tactics, such as filing a formal complaint with a licensing authority or a regulatory agency, may be a better and quicker way of attaining your objective. If you hire a capable consumer lawyer or if your case is handled by a government consumer protection agency or a private consumer advocate group, the objectives you can attain may be expanded and your chances of success markedly increased.

DEALING WITH LAWYERS

In addition to the general points about lawyers in Chapter 1, keep in mind the following points about dealing with lawyers on a consumer rights case.

There are many competent, experienced lawyers who handle consumer rights cases. There are also many competent, experienced people who work for public agencies or private groups who may be able to provide you with useful legal assistance. Both sources should be checked thoroughly.

Before hiring an attorney, find out if there are public consumer protection agencies or private consumer advocate groups which provide consumer rights information and assistance. In some cases, they may be willing to represent you in your dealings with the business, worker, or professional. Many state governments have consumer protection or consumer affairs departments. In some states, the attorney general's office has a consumer affairs division. The federal government has numerous agencies involved in consumer matters. In addition to federal, state, and local consumer affairs offices, there may be private groups or organizations in your community or state that will provide you with information and legal assistance. By contacting these agencies and groups, you can learn what each has to offer and then select the most appropriate agency or group. The telephone directory, the public library, and your local, state, and federal elected officials and their staffs can put you in contact with consumer affairs agencies and offices in your community and state.

Of course, in many situations it is advisable or necessary to hire an attorney. Most public and private consumer affairs offices will provide information and some legal assistance, but they may not have the authority or the resources to represent you, as an attorney can, if you must file a lawsuit, pursue a complaint, or take other legal action.

Nonetheless, it is usually worthwhile to consult public and private consumer affairs offices before hiring an attorney. They may be able to solve your problem at no cost. Even if you do need to hire a lawyer, they may be able to recommend a good lawyer whose work they respect.

If you are going to hire a lawyer to handle your consumer rights case, shop around for a lawyer with experience in consumer protection cases. Consumer law is complex and constantly changing. Although many attorneys handle consumer rights cases, some of those who do are not up to date on current laws and procedures. Others are simply bad lawyers. As explained in Chapter 1, before hiring an attorney, ask several attorneys what special training or experience each has had in consumer rights cases. Ask each attorney how many consumer cases he or she has handled and how recently. How many cases like yours has he or she handled and how recently? How successfully?

In addition to getting the names of lawyers from public and private consumer affairs groups, you can call the local bar association and any lawyer referral service they operate. Be sure to ask specifically for lawyers with experience in consumer rights cases. Also, talk to friends and acquaintances who have hired attorneys on consumer cases. Ask them what they thought of how their attorney handled their case and treated them.

After getting the names of several lawyers, explain your case to each one over the phone or at an office conference, and then select the attorney you feel is the best from among those you consulted.

As noted, you may be able to obtain valuable legal information and assistance from a public or private consumer rights group for free. When you contact such a group or agency, have them explain what services they can and cannot perform. A few consumer agencies and groups will represent a consumer largely as a private attorney would—but at no cost. This may be done where your case represents a widespread or particularly serious consumer abuse. Along with your case, the agency or group may bring other similarly victimized consumers into the lawsuit or other legal action. Also, by taking your case, they may be able to stop that consumer abuse on the local, state, or national level.

If you want to or must hire an attorney, shop around for a good price. Be sure, at the outset, to have the attorney investigate any available procedures by which the other party—the business, worker, or professional—can be ordered to reimburse you for your attorney's fee if you win the case. There are numerous state and federal laws which provide that if a consumer wins a case, the court or administrative agency, under certain conditions, has the discretionary authority to order the offending business, worker, or professional to pay the consumer's attorney's fee. After all, the guilty business, worker, or professional should be required to reimburse you for the cost of taking them to court or initiating other legal action.

If you were victimized by a consumer abuse that is common to many consumers, have the attorney investigate the advisability of initiating a class action lawsuit against the business, worker, or professional. A *class action lawsuit* is one in which one or several people represent not only themselves but many others who are the victims of the same illegal practice perpetrated by the same parties. For example, you may want to sue a company for a defective product or an illegal practice but it may be impractical for you to do so by yourself. The cost of an attorney and other expenses may be far in excess of the loss you suffered. Or suppose you can afford to file suit by yourself but you believe that hundreds or thousands of other people have been victimized by the same consumer abuse. If you file a class action lawsuit, you may be authorized by the court to represent all the people who purchased the defective product or who were victimized by the illegal practice. For example, if a new prescription drug causes serious and harmful side effects, you may be able to sue on behalf of yourself and other people who suffered harmful side effects. Once your group has been certified by the court as a "class," you may be able to have the court order the drug manufacturer to provide you with the names and addresses of all known purchasers of that drug. Through that and other means, you can notify others who were similarly victimized and ask them if they wish to join your common lawsuit. Thus, a class action lawsuit allows a small but representative group to sue on behalf of all the people who were similarly victimized by the same defendant(s). If your group or class wins the lawsuit, the court may order the offending business, worker, or professional to reimburse you for your attorney's fees.

In many instances, free legal assistance from a government agency or private group may not be available. Also, a class action lawsuit may not be possible. You will have to hire your own lawyer and pay that lawyer's fee yourself—although, if you win your case, you may get the court or administrative tribunal to order the losing party to reimburse you for your attorney's fee. You will normally encounter one of two types of lawyer's fees: the flat fee or the hourly fee.

A flat fee is a specific amount of money for which the lawyer agrees to provide the customary and necessary legal services to properly handle your consumer rights case. Once the lawyer has listened to the facts of your case and made a preliminary investigation, he or she may be able to gauge how much time and effort your case should take. With that in mind, the attorney will quote a flat fee that will cover his or her services. Before agreeing to a flat fee, make sure you understand what services the fee covers. Normally, the flat fee will cover out-of-court negotiations with the business, worker, or professional, pretrial preparations, and the trial of the case in the first trial court. Any appeal is not covered by the initial flat fee and must be paid for separately. Also, if the flat fee is to cover taking the business, worker, or professional to court, but later it is determined that you should also try filing a complaint with a licensing authority or with a government regulatory agency, an additional fee for that additional work must be agreed upon. In some cases, it may not be worth going to court if filing a complaint elsewhere will accomplish your goal. Or it may be best to do both—pay the attorney one flat fee to prepare for trial and pay a separate flat fee to pursue other administrative remedies. In any case, be sure you understand what you will be getting for the flat fee and how much any additional work that may become advisable will cost.

In some cases, the attorney may charge an hourly fee. (See Chapter 1 for details on hourly fees.)

In addition to seeking an affordable installment payment schedule, you should negotiate for a lower fee if the fee quoted by the lawyer is too high or strikes you as unreasonable. Negotiating for a lower fee is discussed in detail in Chapter 1. Of particular importance on consumer cases is that you should not agree to pay the same fee if the case is settled out of court as you would pay if the case goes to trial. Obviously, an attorney must do considerable work to prepare for and conduct a courtroom trial. That type of work is difficult and demanding and deserves handsome remuneration when done well. But if the lawyer settles your case out of court after some discussions with the business, worker, or professional or their lawyer, there is no reason the lawyer should get the same fee as he or she would have gotten had the case gone to trial. Suppose the lawyer quotes a flat fee of $2,500 to handle your case through trial. Ask the lawyer what chances there may be of settling the matter out of court. The lawyer should reply that he or she will pursue all reasonable means of achieving an acceptable out-of-court settlement. You should then say, "All right, if you must do all the work necessary to prepare for and conduct a trial, then I assume your services will be worth $2,500. But if we can get a satisfactory out-of-court settlement, I will not agree to pay you more than $1,500. After all, an out-of-court settlement requires much less work than a trial."

It is very important, at the outset of your case, to make it clear to the lawyer that you want him or her to investigate any available procedures by which the business, worker, or professional can be ordered to reimburse you for part or all of your attorney's fee if you win the case. There are, as noted, many federal and state laws which authorize the judge or the administrative hearing officer to order an offending business, worker, or professional to reimburse the wronged consumer for his or her attorney's fee if the consumer wins the case. In fact, some laws authorize the judge or administrative hearing officer to order the offending business, worker, or professional to pay the consumer two or three times the damages awarded to the consumer where the conduct of the business, worker, or professional was particularly offensive or grossly illegal. For example, suppose you prove that a used car dealer sold you a car on which the odometer had been set back 30,000 miles. If you sue that used car dealer and prove that the difference between what you paid for the car and what the car was really worth (had you known the true mileage) was $1,000, the judge may be able to order the used car dealer to pay you $2,000 or even $3,000 in damages instead of just $1,000. The laws which authorize judges and administrative hearing officers to award "double damages" or "triple damages" are designed to penalize businesses, workers, and professionals for particularly abusive practices.

Even if you settle your case out of court, be sure your lawyer tries his or her best to get the business, worker, or professional to agree to pay part or all of your attorney's fee. After all, if they did something wrong, they should pay for it, and that includes not only the losses you incurred but also the costs—particularly the attorney's fee—of bringing that business, worker, or professional to justice.

If you know about and can locate other consumers who were victimized in the same way by the same business, worker, or professional, you may be able to lower the attorney's fee by having one attorney represent all of you and dividing the attorney's fee among a number of people. Here again, as in every consumer rights case, make sure the attorney makes every effort to get the business, worker, or professional to reimburse you for your attorney's fee.

15
Unlawful Discrimination

WHAT DOES AN UNLAWFUL DISCRIMINATION CASE INVOLVE?

What is discrimination? When is discrimination illegal? Suppose you recently graduated from a top-notch law school with a commendable academic record. You apply to a number of well-known law firms. You tell a classmate about the two law firms you most want to land a job with. Your classmate, whose qualifications are similar to yours, retorts that you don't have a chance of getting a job with either firm. She has a chance with one. You ask what she means. She replies that one law firm normally hires only Jewish men, but this year they are looking for a woman (who must be Jewish). The other law firm hires only white Protestant or Irish Catholic men. No exceptions. You are a 23-year-old male of Greek ancestry and Greek Orthodox religion. That is why you don't have a chance with either law firm. A close look at the backgrounds of the members of the first law firm reveals that all 12 are Jewish males. The second law firm has 6 white Protestant males and 4 Irish Catholic males. Subsequently, you receive letters of rejection from both law firms. Your classmate receives an offer from the all-male, all-Jewish law firm that is looking for a Jewish female this year.

Have you been discriminated against? Certainly. Is that discrimination unlawful? In a number of states, the surprising answer is no.

Some states have statutes which prohibit employers—including private law firms—from discriminating in hiring on the basis of race, sex, national origin, religion, and other factors. Many states, however, do not have such wide-ranging laws against discrimination in employment. Or the antidiscrimination laws they do have do not apply to private law firms. There are federal laws which prohibit discrimination in hiring, but some apply only to employers who have 15 or more employees. Others do not apply to private law firms.

It may be difficult to believe that in some states it is legal for a law firm to discriminate against you on the basis of race, sex, national origin, or religion. In other states it is illegal for a law firm to discriminate on those grounds but not illegal to discriminate on such grounds as marital status, dependents, illegitimacy, sexual preference, and other factors. Also, even in those states where discrimination is unlawful, it is commonly practiced by most lawyers and law firms nonetheless.

Suppose you want to sue both law firms for discriminating against you. You bring your case to a private attorney. But that attorney tells you he will not handle your case. He tells you point-blank he will not take your case because he doesn't want to sue two prestigious law firms whose members are his colleagues, some his personal acquaintances and friends. Every lawyer and law firm discriminates and he isn't going to try to stop it by representing you.

Have you been discriminated against? Certainly. Is that discrimination unlawful? Again, the answer is a surprising no. There is no law or government regulation which prevents a private attorney from rejecting clients on the basis of the nature of their case (even if the attorney is qualified to handle that type of case). More shocking is the fact that in many states there is no law or government regulation which prohibits a private attorney or law firm from rejecting a client on the basis of the client's race, sex, national origin, religion, sexual preference, and so forth.

Despite the rejection letters from those two law firms, you receive an offer from another law firm and accept it. Your first assignment is to do legal research on a number of cases involving clients who believe they were discriminated against illegally. A 45-year-old man was not hired by an interstate trucking company because, in their words, he was "too old" to do long-haul trucking. A young couple with two small children were denied an apartment because the landlord doesn't rent to people with small children. A 21-year-old woman who applied for a position as a police officer in a small town was turned down—no reason given. She wants to know if she can sue to find out whether she was turned down because of sex discrimination. A black woman has had trespass charges filed against her because she refused to leave the premises of a private, all-white, all-male social club. She wants that club declared illegal. A group of Spanish-surnamed people believe their streets, seweres, street lights, and other municipal services have been allowed to deteriorate because of discrimination on the part of city officials. Can they sue the city? Finally, a female high school athletic instructor was fired by the school committee because she publicly stated she is a lesbian. Can she successfully sue the school committee for reinstatement?

Each of your six clients has been discriminated against. But which ones have been discriminated against illegally? That is, which ones have been discriminated against in a manner which the law prohibits and for which the law provides remedies?

The 45-year-old man who wasn't hired as a truck driver because he was "too old" has a sound basis for a lawsuit under the federal Age Discrimination in Employment Act which prohibits, among other things, age discrimination in hiring by employers who have more than 15 employees.

If your state has a statute or court decision which prohibits landlords from refusing to rent to people solely because they have small children, the young couple who were denied an apartment on that basis can sue the landlord. If, on the other hand, your state doesn't have a statute or court decision prohibiting that practice and federal housing laws don't apply, the landlord was within his or her rights in discriminating against that couple.

The woman who applied for a position as police officer can file a lawsuit alleging discrimination and demanding that police and town officials explain why they did not hire her. The fact that she is a woman and was not hired suggests that sex discrimination may have been the motive. However, if other women were hired, she would have a tough case to prove. If, on the other hand, that police department has hired few or no women despite numerous qualified female applicants, she would have a stronger case.

The black woman who entered the premises of the all-white, all-male private social club probably can be found liable for trespass if she did not have their permission to be there. Generally, private social groups can discriminate all they want. (Of course, if she would like to establish an all-black, all-female private social club and prohibit all other persons from attending, she can.)

The Spanish-surnamed group have a difficult case. Much depends on the applicable federal and state statutes and court decisions and what proof of discrimination is required. For example, to prove some types of discrimination you need only show that the impact of the practice is disproportionately detrimental to an identifiable minority group which the law (legislators, judges, administrative agencies) is solicitous to protect. In other situations, it may not be enough to show only that the practice harms a given minority more than others; you may have to prove, if possible, that the government officials who implemented the practice did so with the intention of discriminating against your group. Under the first standard of proof, the Spanish-surnamed group will have a difficult case. After all, city officials may be able to show that the municipal services received in the Spanish neighborhoods are, on the whole, no worse than in some white neighborhoods. Under the second standard of proof, a successful lawsuit is even more unlikely. It may be impossible to prove that city officials intentionally set about to lower or at least ignore the quality of municipal services in Spanish neighborhoods as opposed to other neighborhoods.

The female athletic instructor's case may require considerable legal research. In most states the legal rights of homosexuals are unclear. Some states and communities have statutes or ordinances which protect homosexuals from some forms of discrimination. Some courts have interpreted state or federal laws to protect homosexuals from certain types of discrimination. Other states and communities do not have such statutes or ordinances or court decisions. As with every case of discrimination, it is not enough to show that you were discriminated against; it is also a question whether there is a law which makes that type of discrimination illegal.

The foregoing illustrations reveal the variable, complex, and often uncertain nature of contemporary discrimination law.

To properly understand and assess your discrimination case, you must examine the following:

- How were you discriminated against? That is, what harm or privation did you suffer? (Were you not hired? Denied equal pay? Denied access to integrated public schools? Fired? etc.)
- Who discriminated against you? Of considerable importance is whether it was a government official or employee or a private party. If a private party, was it a business or commercial enterprise (employer, landlord, bank, credit service, etc.) or a private individual or group (private social club, quarrel between two individuals, etc.)?
- Can you prove that discrimination occurred? Can you establish that your group characteristic was the deciding factor and not an individual attribute relating to your qualifications or ability (or lack of qualifications or ability)?
- If you can prove that a group factor was the basis for the discrimination, is there a law prohibiting that type of discrimination? In some states, a private law firm can legally refuse to hire a person because of that person's religion. By contrast, a government agency could not do so. Only some forms of discrimination have been outlawed.

- What remedies or corrective measures are available? What the law provides may not be what you want done. On the other hand, there may be a number of different remedies available; the advantages and disadvantages of each must be assessed and an overall strategy devised.
- Is your primary concern to remedy this particular incident of discrimination against yourself or do you want to put a stop to a large-scale discriminatory practice and, hopefully, prevent all others from being similarly discriminated against? This will effect who you must sue and what remedies you must seek.

The most common bases of unlawful discrimination are the following:

Race Historically, blacks, Hispanics, Orientals, American Indians, and other noncaucasian races in the United States have encountered severe discrimination and privation on the basis of race. Some modern judicial and legislative efforts to remedy race discrimination have utilized preferences or "affirmative action" programs which favor minority races. Many whites have challenged these efforts arguing that they constitute "reverse discrimination."

Sex Sex-based discrimination has been pervasive in American society and was built into American law, although it has not been all of one kind. Some discriminatory laws were intended (patronizingly) to favor women (e.g., laws requiring husbands to support their wives). Also, some laws discriminated against men (e.g., providing certain government benefits to widows but not widowers, drafting men but not women for military service).

Religion/Creed Laws prohibiting discrimination on the basis of religion are popularly understood to outlaw hiring, firing, and so on on the basis of the religion or creed a person espouses. Such laws are less well understood and considerably less effective at protecting people who do not espouse any religion or creed. The First Amendment to the U. S. Constitution requires a separation of church and state; thus, the acts and policies of government officials are supposed to be untainted by religious discrimination. Other federal and state laws prohibit religious discrimination in the same areas of the private sector (i.e., in hiring, firing, etc.).

National Origin/Ancestry Although all citizens of the United States are entitled to "equal" rights under the law, ethnic and nationality discrimination continues to be a pervasive factor in American society. Of course, ethnic and nationality discrimination often overlap with race discrimination and religious discrimination.

Mental/Physical Handicap It is largely in recent years that legislatures and courts have begun to respond to the needs—and rights—of mentally and physically handicapped persons by outlawing physical barriers, establishing the right to equal opportunity in employment and education, ensuring access to public facilities, and so forth. By necessity, mentally or physically handicapped persons must have laws which discriminate in their favor if those laws are to effectively compensate for the physical and attitudinal discrimination handicapped persons encounter.

Sexual Preference Considerable controversy has arisen in recent years regarding whether the legal rights of homosexuals should be any different than those of heterosexuals. Unlike other bases for discrimination, much of the controversy centers on whether homosexuality should be considered a healthy or acceptable sexual preference or alternative. Whether the law should protect homosexuals from discrimination depends on what one thinks about homosexuality as well as what one thinks about discrimination.

Marital Status This basis includes many forms of discrimination. Should a landlord have the right to evict a tenant if the tenant is living with a person of the opposite sex but they are not married? Are there legitimate reasons—which the law should allow—for hiring married people in preference to unmarried people or vice versa? Discrimination on the basis of marital status occurs frequently in tax laws and government programs such as Social Security and welfare. Marital status discrimination often overlaps with sex discrimination.

Dependents Should whether a person has children or other dependents be a legally permissible basis for refusing to rent to them? For refusing to hire them? For taxing their income differently?

Illegitimacy Throughout history, illegitimate children have suffered for the supposed transgressions of their parents. Some laws have been struck down by the courts as discriminatory against the illegitimate (e.g., denying welfare or other public benefits to persons who have illegitimate children). Should all laws which disfavor the illegitimate be prohibited? Should illegitimacy be outlawed as a basis for discrimination on the part of private citizens as well as on the part of the government?

Poverty/Indigency Needless to say, poor people cannot assert and protect their rights as well as wealthy people. But how much of this disparity should the government eliminate by law? If it takes money to combat this disparity, whose money should be used? Under current law, an indigent person has a right to an attorney, paid for with taxpayers' money, to assist in his or her defense against criminal charges. Should the right of indigents to a lawyer be extended to civil lawsuits? Should wealthy people be taxed more heavily so that poor people can send their children to schools that have the same per-student expenditures as schools attended by the children of the wealthy? One cannot discriminate against the poor without discriminating more so against the children of the poor. What rights do the children of the poor have? Are there ways of legally distinguishing involuntary poverty from voluntary poverty and outlawing discrimination against the former but not the latter?

Age Should government and private employers be allowed to refuse to hire a person because of that person's age? Should discrimination favorable to the aged (e.g., tax breaks, senior citizen's rates) be promoted? Should mandatory retirement age laws be allowed? What rights should minors have with regard to government, their parents, public schools, criminal laws, and so on?

All forms of discrimination have one thing in common: an individual is treated better or worse solely on the basis of a group characteristic. Suppose all males between the ages of 18 and 32 are subject to a military draft. This constitutes double discrimination. An individual is subject to the draft or not depending on whether the person is male or female—without regard to individual ability, circumstances, or qualifications. Within the class of males, only those between the ages of 18 and 32 are subject to the draft, despite the fact that many males below and above those arbitrary age limits can serve as well as those within the age limits. It is the fact that a judgment is based solely on a group characteristic that makes for discrimination. It is not what *you* are but what your *group* is perceived to be that lays the basis for such prejudgment, better known as prejudice.

Most forms of discrimination penalize or reward a person for possessing a characteristic over which he or she has no control; these indelible attributes include sex, age, national origin or ancestry, some types of mental or physical handicap, illegitimacy, and some types of involuntary poverty. Other bases for discrimination center on factors over which the person has some choice; these include marital status, religion or creed, dependents, sexual preference, and voluntary poverty. Still, all forms of discrimination have a common element—they penalize or reward not on the basis of individual attributes (such as ability, qualifications, experience, or lack thereof) but solely on the basis of a group characteristic.

As noted, not all discrimination is illegal. In some situations, the law can attempt to eradicate discrimination—for example, by outlawing unequal pay for equal work. In other situations, however, the law must choose which form of discrimination to prohibit—and which to allow. For example, if the law permits a landlord to refuse to rent to couples who have small children, couples who have small children will be discriminated against. However, if a law is passed making it illegal for landlords to practice that type of discrimination, then tenants who want to rent an apartment in a building where there are no small children will be discriminated against.

For a particular discriminatory practice to be illegal, it must contravene a specific law. The most far-reaching antidiscrimination law is the "Equal Protection" clause of the Fourteenth Amendment to the U. S. Constitution. Under that amendment, neither the federal government nor the states (or any subdivision of a state, such as a city, town, or county) can deprive any person of the equal protection of the laws. Although historically the Fourteenth Amendment was enacted (in 1868) primarily to eradicate the second-class citizenship of emancipated slaves and other blacks, the language of the amendment is not limited to race discrimination: No "person" shall be denied "the equal protection of the laws," by the federal or state governments or those acting on behalf of the federal or state governments.

Like many antidiscrimination laws, the Fourteenth Amendment only prohibits discrimination by the government (federal or state). Private individuals acting independently of any government authority are not governed by the Fourteenth Amendment. There are, however, many federal and state statutes and court decisions which prohibit numerous forms of discrimination in the private sector (e.g., employment, housing, transportation, service industries). Also, businesses and organizations, whether profit or nonprofit, which receive government money or administer government programs are usually subject to the same antidiscrimination laws that apply to the government.

In contrast to general antidiscrimination laws such as the Fourteenth Amendment to the federal Constitution, there are numerous federal and state statutes which prohibit specific types of discrimination. For example, the federal Age Discrimination in Employment Act prohibits discrimination on the basis of age—but only with regard to certain employers and only with regard to persons between the ages of 40 and 65.

Despite all the laws which prohibit various discriminatory practices by government officials and employees and despite all the laws which prohibit various discriminatory practices by businesses, organizations, and individuals in the private sector, there remain large areas of private activity not reached by antidiscrimination laws—at least not yet. The example at the beginning of this chapter of law firms that discriminate in hiring on the basis of religion, sex, and national origin illustrates the point. What could be more deplorable than law firms which hire and fire employees and accept or reject clients on the basis of the crudest forms of discrimination!

One of the great bastions of blatant discrimination in contemporary America is the legal profession. Ironically, lawyers and law firms remain exempt from many of the antidiscrimination laws they require others to abide by.

But the realm of "freedom to discriminate" neither begins nor ends with lawyers. Unless a specific law prohibits you from discriminating, you are, quite simply, free to do so. Most family, social, and interpersonal dealings are not subject to antidiscrimination laws. Private clubs and groups, for the most part, may discriminate at will. Many small businesses, professions, and private organizations (such as private schools) are not covered by antidiscrimination laws. Antidiscrimination laws exist—but only go so far.

There is also the problem of the not-yet-settled areas. Is it unlawful sex discrimination if a restaurant owner fires a woman employee because she does not shave her legs as most American women do? Is it race discrimination if an insurance agency rejects a black applicant because her "black English" is difficult for nonblacks to understand? Is it age discrimination if state law entitles parents to take money earned by their minor offspring? Isn't it discrimination to entitle or deny an individual any benefit or protection solely on the basis of a group characteristic? If so, what forms of discrimination should the law prohibit and, in doing so, enable persons to initiate lawsuits and seek injunctions, money damages, and other relief?

In addition to constitutional provisions and state statutes which outlaw various types of discrimination, there are thousands of federal and state court decisions interpreting and applying those constitutional and statutory antidiscrimination laws. Moreover, within the federal and state governments are numerous administrative agencies primarily or partially charged with combatting specific types of discrimination. The Equal Employment Opportunity Commission of the federal Department of Labor was established to combat discrimination in public and private employment. Many states have antidiscrimination agencies either within the office of the state attorney general or as independent agencies. These antidiscrimination agencies, along with the courts, are the forums in which disputes over the legality of allegedly discriminatory practices are fought.

In addition to government antidiscrimination agencies and the courts, there are numerous private groups and organizations which strive to combat discrimination. The American Civil Liberties

Union (ACLU) is perhaps the most famous. Organizations such as the National Association for the Advancement of Colored People (NAACP) and the National Organization for Women (NOW) provide antidiscrimination assistance to persons of a given group. Finally, corrective legal measures can also be pursued by hiring a private attorney. How readers can obtain information and assistance from government antidiscrimination agencies, private groups, and lawyers is discussed in detail in the section of this chapter entitled "Dealing with Lawyers."

An illegal discrimination case requires proving that discrimination occurred and that the type of discrimination perpetrated is illegal.

Proving that discrimination occurred may require examining the practice of the business, government official or agency, private group, or individual over a period of time. For example, if a 75-member police department has hired 10 blacks in the past three years and hired 3 blacks other than you this year, it may be difficult for you to establish that you were rejected because you were black and not for some other, valid reason. By contrast, if you can show, using company records and testimony from male and female employees, that a given company has paid female employees less than male employees doing the same job and has done so for many years, you have what is needed to prove that discrimination occurred.

In some cases, it is enough to prove a discriminatory impact. Once that is shown, the other party must show that the result did not come about because of discriminatory decisions. For example, in many public school desegregation cases the courts have looked at patterns of student assignments, teacher assignments, enrollments, availability of special programs, and other data to determine whether there are a disproportionate number of all or mostly white schools and a distinct and separate group of all or mostly black schools with less experienced teachers, fewer and lower-quality special programs, and so forth. These patterns, in themselves, suggest a design on the part of school authorities to create and perpetuate a racially segregated school system in which nonwhites are second-class students. Showing a racially discriminatory impact is enough; school officials must then show that these patterns were not racially motivated and do not foster the ills associated with racial segregation. Of course, the facts speak for themselves in these cases.

In other discrimination cases, however, you may have to go beyond showing a racially discriminatory impact. You may have to prove that the other party acted out of a discriminatory motive. For example, if the city fire department has 8 percent nonwhites but the general nonwhite population in the city is 21 percent, that might suggest that the fire department has been racially motivated in its hiring practices. But if fire department officials produce records that reveal that only 10 percent of the people who apply for positions on the fire department are nonwhite and that one out of five of them fails the written or physical exam, it would seem that the racially discriminatory impact (only 8 percent nonwhites on a fire department in a city where the general nonwhite population is 21 percent) does not, in and of itself, create a clear presumption that racial discrimination was the cause of that impact. To be successful in suing the fire department to increase the number of nonwhites on the department, the court or administrative agency hearing the case may require that you show that fire department officials had a discriminatory motive. For example, you may have to show that the written exams were unfairly difficult for nonwhites or that the physical exams were administered in a biased manner. The point is that in some instances of discrimination the facts can be proven readily and the facts, themselves, suggest discrimination. In other cases, however, the facts do not suggest discrimination or the facts can be rebutted with other facts and you must go behind the facts to the actual attitudes and motives of the officials or persons involved and prove that their decisions consciously centered on perpetrating discriminatory practices.

It is important to realize what you must prove to establish a case of unlawful discrimination and how you must prove it. Will you need testimony from experts? The party who discriminated against you? Others? Will you need records? If so, covering what period of time and what practices? Will you need statistical analyses? How can you obtain the testimony, records, and analyses you need? It may be that someone discriminated against you. But can you prove it in court or before the appropriate administrative agency?

In addition to proving that discrimination occurred, you must show that a specific law prohibits that type of discrimination as practiced by that person, organization, or group. For example, in many states the state and local building codes require that all buildings and facilities open to the public be so designed and built that they provide reasonably convenient access to persons who must use wheelchairs. Private residences, including apartment buildings, however, are usually exempt from those requirements. If you must use a wheelchair, you may find that the restaurant you go to must provide ramps and other conveniences but the apartment building where you live is not legally required to have such ramps. It depends on the wording of the wheelchair access law and what buildings it covers.

If you can prove you were the victim of unlawful discrimination, what can be done to rectify the situation? This may be a difficult issue to resolve. If you are a woman who has been paid less than a male employee would have been paid for the work you have done for the past five years, you would at least seek the amount of money you would have received had you been paid equal pay for those five years. But what if you were also denied promotions on the basis of sex? How can you prove what promotions you would have received had you not been discriminated against?

If a landlord refuses to rent to you because you and your live-in paramour are not married but you find another apartment you like better and take it, what damages—losses—have you suffered? What can you sue for?

If a citywide public school system has been intentionally operated in a manner which segregates nonwhite students from white students, what would you ask the court to do to rectify the situation? What if the court orders school officials to assign students according to a rigid racial balance formula and use busing to meet that formula but thousands of white students are taken out of the public school system by their parents and placed in private schools that are not subject to antidiscrimination laws?

To successfully pursue a discrimination case, you must prove you were discriminated against and that the type of discrimination perpetrated is illegal; you must also devise and request remedies and corrective measures which compensate you for your losses and which put you, as much as possible, in the position you would have been in had you not been discriminated against. Penalties such as a substantial money fine may be appropriate if the person or group which discriminated against you did so in a particularly flagrant or egregious manner.

You must also consider the extent of the discrimination and the extent of the remedy necessary to correct it. If you were denied a job because of your age, what about other people turned down by that employer for that reason? What can be done to locate them and get them to join you in suing that company so that as many people as possible who were discriminated against will receive some amount of compensation and so that the extent of that discriminatory practice will be revealed and appropriate measures taken against that company to make sure it does not continue that discriminatory practice?

At the least, you want the discriminatory practice stopped. Courts can issue injunctions (orders to cease a given practice, either temporarily or permanently). But what must be done to stop that practice and prevent it from recurring? The nature and extent of the discriminatory practice must be fully understood before you can devise an appropriate program for correcting the situation.

What if the law goes against you? For example, suppose you are a white male and want desperately to get into an advanced training program offered by your company for employees who did not have good public education opportunities. Regrettably, you learn that you will not be selected for the special training program. You also find out that your chances of getting into the program were severely reduced because of the 200 applicants, 160 were white males, 20 were females, and 20 were nonwhite males. With only 70 openings for the training program, company officials decided to let in every female who met the qualifications and every nonwhite male who met the qualifications, while white males were chosen at random—by lot—for the remaining openings. Thus, all females who qualified got in. All nonwhite males who qualified got in. But even though you qualified, you had to take your chance with 159 other white males in drawing lots for only 30 openings.

Were you discriminated against? Certainly. But what if your lawyer tells you that not only is that form of discrimination legal, but it is encouraged by the court! What do you do?

If you have been discriminated against and find that form of discrimination by that official or person is illegal, you can sue. But what do you do if you have been discriminated against and find that that type of discrimination by that official or person is not illegal? You can try to change that practice privately or try to change the law and make that discriminatory practice illegal. In the case of the affirmative action special training program, you and other employees may be successful at getting the company to revise its selection process so that it will be less unfair to white males. Or you may try to get the state legislature or Congress to enact a statute outlawing that type of practice. If there are indications that some courts (state or federal) may be inclined to declare that that type of practice is "reverse discrimination" and ought not be permitted under laws already on the books, it might be worthwhile to file a lawsuit in the appropriate court and seek a favorable ruling.

As can be seen, some antidiscrimination laws are clear and not likely to change. Others are vague and subject to conflicting interpretations and change. New antidiscrimination laws are enacted every year. Present ones are reinterpreted by the courts and administrative agencies in different ways each year.

WHY DO YOU NEED TO CONSULT A LAWYER OR OTHER COMPETENT LEGAL ADVISOR?

To properly understand the legality or illegality of the discriminatory practice that was perpetrated against you and what you can and cannot do about it legally, you must seek the advice and assistance of a competent legal advisor.

You may feel you were discriminated against. You may think

the discrimination perpetrated against you is illegal. You may want specific action taken against a given person, group, or organization. However, whether you were discriminated against, whether that discrimination is unlawful, and what can be done about it legally are questions which require the advice of a lawyer or some other competent legal advisor.

Some discrimination laws are clear; many are complex. Much depends on whether the discrimination was perpetrated by a government official or employee or by a private individual, business, or group. Some forms of discrimination are unlawful; other forms, though reprehensible, are legal. In addition, discrimination laws change. Every year new statutes, new court decisions, and new administrative agency rulings are announced regarding the legality of various types of discrimination in thousands of specific circumstances. Some antidiscrimination laws are federal and therefore are fairly uniform throughout the country (in interpretation if not enforcement). On the other hand, considerable variation exists with regard to the antidiscrimination laws of individual states. For example, some states have equal rights amendments to the state constitution which prohibit discrimination on the basis of sex. Many other states, however, have not adopted an equal rights amendment. This creates considerable difference in the way women can be treated legally in different states.

The states vary widely not only in the number and type of antidiscrimination laws but also in level of enforcement. Some states have special commissions established to assist the victims of discrimination; in other states victims of discrimination are left largely to their own resources.

The differences between federal antidiscrimination laws and state antidiscrimination laws and the variations among the states contribute to the confusion, misunderstandings, and myths which characterize popular notions of what constitutes discrimination and what types of discrimination are illegal. Competent legal advice is essential to properly understand what laws govern the discriminatory practice you encountered.

If the discrimination perpetrated against you is unlawful, you must find out about the legal standards and procedures that must be met and followed so that a complaint is filed with the proper authorities, your case is proven in the required manner, and effective legal remedies are taken. For example, some discrimination cases must be filed in a federal court, others in state court, still others before a federal administrative agency, and others before a state administrative agency. Rules relating to procedure, evidence, statutes of limitation, jurisdiction, recoveries, and other matters vary considerably.

You must also find out what you can expect the authorities to do if you successfully prove your case. In some cases, you may be entitled to money to compensate you for your losses and any privations or degradation you suffered. But how do you know what amount of money to sue for? What about corrective measures? What can the court or administrative agency do to stop the discriminatory practice and prevent it in the future? The answers vary depending on the type of discrimination, the type of privation and losses you suffered, the specific provisions of the antidiscrimination law that was violated, and the authority and remedial powers of the court or administrative agency which hears your case. Given the variety and complexity of discrimination laws, given the differences in the legal forums (state and federal courts and administrative agencies) which may have jurisdiction over your case, and given the range of money damages and corrective measures you may be able to pursue, you will need advice and assistance from an experienced legal advisor.

That legal advisor should be someone who is familiar with discrimination laws and who has first-hand experience in handling discrimination cases in and out of court. It is important to make sure that the legal advisor you consult has some expertise in discrimination law and practice. Most attorneys know something about discrimination law. Many of those lawyers, however, take discrimination cases only on an occasional basis and do not have a thorough, up-to-date knowledge of discrimination law. Look for an attorney with considerable knowledge and regular experience in this area.

Also keep in mind that there are many sources of legal advice and assistance on discrimination matters in addition to private attorneys. Numerous federal and state antidiscrimination agencies provide free legal information and some legal assistance to victims of unlawful discrimination. The U. S. Attorney General's office has a Civil Rights Division charged with enforcing federal antidiscrimination laws. Many departments of the federal government have bureaus or commissions charged with enforcing particular antidiscrimination laws, such as the Equal Employment Opportunity Commission in the Department of Labor. Similarly, most state attorneys general have antidiscrimination divisions to enforce state antidiscrimination laws. Also, many states have a number of antidiscrimination agencies which deal with specific areas of discrimination.

There are also many private, nonprofit groups and organizations which advocate the rights of victims of discrimination, provide information and some free legal assistance. The ACLU, NAACP, and NOW are examples of private, nonprofit groups that combat unlawful discrimination.

Only some government antidiscrimination agencies and private antidiscrimination groups have the authority and resources to represent individuals and bring lawsuits on their behalf in the courts or before administrative agencies. Many government antidiscrimination agencies and private antidiscrimination groups can provide information and make official complaints or inquiries but cannot represent you the way a lawyer can. In these instances, you will have to hire your own lawyer to pursue the matter in court or before an administrative agency and seek money damages and other corrective measures. Nonetheless, you can get valuable information and assistance, usually at no cost, from government antidiscrimination agencies and private antidiscrimination groups. They may be able to resolve your problem or show you how to resolve it yourself. If they cannot perform the necessary legal work and you must hire your own private attorney, these agencies and private groups can help you find a good attorney. They may also be willing to explain how your case should be handled and how to deal with attorneys. Even if you hire an attorney to handle your case, considerable free assistance can be obtained by keeping in contact with these government antidiscrimination agencies and private antidiscrimination groups. They can assist you and your attorney with their knowledge, experience, resources, and contacts—free of charge.

Finally, you should be aware that there are a number of laws which authorize the judge or administrative hearing officer who hears your case to order the other party (the person or group that discriminated against you) to reimburse you for part or all of your attorney's fee if you win your case. Those laws are designed to encourage people to take legal action against the perpetrators of unlawful discrimination. Make sure your lawyer or legal advisor determines whether such a law applies to your case. You should not have to bear substantial attorneys' fees if the law authorizes the judge or administrative hearing officer to order the other party to reimburse you for part or all of those fees. Of course, as noted, this is only done if you win your case.

To successfully prove your case, win the money you deserve, and obtain appropriate corrective measures, you will need legal advice and assistance from an experienced lawyer or other qualified legal advisor.

HOW TO THINK ABOUT LEGAL AND RELATED ASPECTS

The following sections review important points to consider with regard to an unlawful discrimination case.

Determine the nature of the discrimination and what person, group, or organization is responsible for it.

On what basis—that is, on the basis of what group characteristic—were you discriminated against? Sex? Race? Religion or creed? National origin or ancestry? Sexual preference? Physical or mental handicap? Marital status? Dependents? Illegitimacy? Poverty? Age? Some other basis?

Determining the nature of the discrimination that was perpetrated against you is essential to determining how to prove that that discrimination was unlawful. Also, identifying the group characteristic that was the basis for the discrimination is necessary to find out whether other people who have that group characteristic were discriminated against and whether some or all of them want to join you in taking legal action.

It may be difficult to determine whether you were discriminated against on the basis of an unlawful factor. If an employer who didn't hire you doesn't give you a reason or gives you a false reason, or if the landlord who doesn't rent to you doesn't give you a reason or gives you an obviously fabricated excuse, it may be difficult to determine whether that employer's or landlord's decision manifested unlawful discrimination or a legally permissible choice.

To properly assess whether you were discriminated against illegally, consult an experienced legal advisor.

Also, determine who is responsible for the discrimination—what person, group, or institution can be held legally accountable. When dealing with a landlord or small business, it may be easy to identify who discriminated against you. When dealing with a large company or a government agency, it may be difficult to identify the responsible party. In those situations, it is important to ascertain whether the discrimination was the practice of one individual or whether it is the official or unofficial policy of the company or government agency. Your legal course of action may vary considerably depending on whether you must combat an individual practicing unlawful discrimination on a small scale or whether you must confront a big business or government agency which has an official or unofficial policy of perpetrating discrimination on a large scale. The resources, legal and otherwise, of the party that discriminated against you will affect the resources you will need to successfully contest that discriminatory practice.

Determine whether the discrimination is unlawful under federal or state law.

Again, you will need competent legal advice. There are many antidiscrimination laws. Changes and developments occur in this area every year. It is essential to seek advice from a lawyer or other competent legal advisor who has an up-to-date knowledge of discrimination law. Whether the discrimination perpetrated against you is unlawful must be determined. What can be done about it legally must also be determined.

If it is clear or likely that you were discriminated against in an unlawful manner, you must investigate what legal courses of action are available and which course of action is best given your circumstances and objectives. Much will depend on whether the discrimination is a violation of federal law, state law, or both. Which court or administrative agency hears your case will depend on whether there is a violation of federal or state law. The corrective measures and monetary compensation you can seek will vary depending on whether there is a violation of federal or state law. The scale on which you can combat the discrimination will depend on whether it is a violation of state or federal law. For instance, if you want to combat a discriminatory practice perpetrated by a local business in violation of state law, it may be economical and appropriate to sue in state court. On the other hand, if you want to combat the discriminatory practices of a nationwide business or organization and that discrimination is a violation of federal law, you must sue in federal court. In some instances, the discriminatory practice may be a violation of both federal and state law; considerable thought must then be given to which court to sue in and under which laws.

If you are told by your lawyer or other legal advisor that the discrimination perpetrated against you is not illegal, that does not necessarily end the matter. After all, it was legal to segregate black students from white students in public schools prior to 1954. Other forms of discrimination were not outlawed until the 1960s or 1970s. New antidiscrimination laws are established every year. If you believe the discrimination practiced against you should be illegal, but it isn't at present, find out what action can be taken. Contact lawyers and government and private legal assistance groups with regard to filing legislation on the state or federal level or bringing a lawsuit to overturn previous court decisions. The discriminatory practices that are illegal today would not be outlawed were it not for the efforts of persons who advanced legislation and filed lawsuits to break new ground in earlier years.

Find out if other people were similarly discriminated against. If so, determine whether they will join your legal action or whether they have initiated legal action you can join.

If other people were or are being similarly discriminated against, you can substantially increase your chances of having corrective measures taken if you contact those people and get them to join you in combatting that discrimination. Or you may find that some of them have initiated legal action you can join.

Generally speaking, the more people you find who were discriminated against in the same manner and by the same person or group, the easier it will be to prove your case. The more of you there are, the more formidable your efforts will be. The cost of legal services can be shared, making it considerably more affordable for each. The practical and legal leverage of a large group is greater than that of an individual. Faced with a legal battle brought by a large number of people all claiming to have been illegally discriminated against in the same manner, the person, group, or institution which perpetrated the discrimination may be more willing to accede to more of your demands than if only a small group or individual were complaining.

It is also important to contact other people who may have been similarly discriminated against to determine the extent of the discrimination. Unless you know the extent of the discrimination (in numbers of people and length of time), you may fail to seek appropriate corrective measures. For example, a large company that discriminates against women in one department may be discriminating against women in many other departments. If the women in each department unite, they can increase their numbers, resources, and "power" generally. They can then work together to eliminate discrimination against women wherever it exists in that company rather than limiting themselves to fighting individual battles with the company within each department.

Determine how to prove your discrimination charges.

You may feel you were discriminated against. Proving it is another matter. If the other party is willing to admit that they unlawfully discriminated against you, your job is easy. But that is highly unlikely. The burden is on you to prove there was discrimination and that it was unlawful. If there has been a pattern of discrimination, perhaps other people similarly discriminated against will come forward to support your cause and testify. In some circumstances, statistics, records, or documents will substantiate your charges. Or other means may be available to substantiate your charges. Make sure you review with a lawyer or other legal advisor the proofs you have that discrimination occurred or what you need to prove your charges. You may need access to the company's records or to a government agency's files. The crucial point is to make sure your evidence is admissible before the court or administrative agency that will hear your case and that that evidence is convincing.

As noted earlier, in some cases you must show discriminatory results. This can be done by pointing out undeniable facts or presenting statistics which clearly suggest discrimination. In other cases, however, you may have to prove that the other party consciously intended to discriminate against you and that the impact or results of the other party's actions could not have been the result of a permissible, discrimination-free decision.

Sometimes a decision that appears to be discriminatory to you may be based on legitimate factors. Even if discrimination was part of the basis for the decision, it may be difficult to prove that an unlawful discriminatory factor was the controlling factor in the decision. For example, if you are not hired solely because the company doesn't hire persons over 45, you may have legitimate grounds for a lawsuit based on age discrimination in employment. But if your qualifications were questionable and other applicants had better qualifications, can you prove your age was the deciding factor? Or that some other unlawful discriminatory element was the deciding factor?

Do not overlook the possibility that there may be more than one ground for filing discrimination charges. You may have been discriminated against on the basis of more than one impermissible factor. For instance, suppose a public school committee fires a black woman teacher who is a self-avowed lesbian and a vocal member of the Jehovah's Witnesses faith. The school committee claims she was fired because she ignored required course materials and created a poor learning environment for students. The woman may claim she was fired in part because she is a woman, in part because she is a black, in part because she is homosexual, and in part because of her religion. She has four grounds for charges of unlawful discrimination any one of which, if proven in court, could entitle her to be reinstated as a teacher.

The laws which make a given type of discrimination unlawful may specify what type of evidence is admissible and what amount of evidence is necessary to prove your charges. You should consult a competent legal advisor to determine what you must do to prove your charges in the required manner.

Find out what courses of action can be taken, what each would involve, and the corrective measures and money compensation you can seek.

There will be, in most cases, a number of alternatives to consider. First, it may be possible to approach the person or group that discriminated against you in an informal manner and attempt to work out a mutually acceptable agreement to compensate you for and correct the discrimination. For example, if a company, government agency, or private institution discriminated against you, there may be an official or an internal review committee which will receive your complaint, allow you a hearing, and institute corrective measures if they find in your favor. This may be the most convenient and least expensive way to get the problem corrected.

Even if formal legal action is necessary, it may be worthwhile to pursue avenues short of filing a lawsuit, at least at first. There may be a government agency with which you can file a complaint and request a hearing. At the hearing, you and the person or group that allegedly discriminated against you will be given an opportunity to present your version of what happened and why it happened. There may be opportunities during this process for both of you to work out a mutually acceptable settlement. Or, under pressure from the government agency if it is inclined to find in your favor, the other person or group may agree to compensation and corrective measures recommended by the government agency.

If private entreaties and settlement talks fail, if review within the company, agency, or institution fails, if you file a complaint with a government agency and a hearing is held but appropriate corrective measures are not taken, it may then be advisable to file a lawsuit in court or file a complaint with a government agency that has authority to order the person or group that discriminated against you to take corrective measures and compensate you for your losses and the violation of your rights.

Deciding whether to file a lawsuit or a formal complaint with a government agency may involve a number of important considerations. For example, you may be able to sue in state court or in federal court. What your case will cost, what you must prove, and what you can accomplish may depend on which court you file your lawsuit in. Similarly, there may be a number of state and federal administrative agencies that have authority to hear your discrimination charges. What it will cost, the procedures you must follow, what you can accomplish, and your likelihood of success may vary depending on which government agency you bring the matter to.

Find out as much as you can about the alternative legal courses of action you can take and what each would involve. How long will each course take? How much will it cost? Where must you go for hearings and other formal proceedings? Should you hire your own attorney to represent you or can you obtain legal assistance from a government agency or private antidiscrimination group? What compensation can you seek for your losses and the violation of your rights? What corrective measures can the court or administrative agency require of the other party? Can that court or administrative agency order the other party to reimburse you for part or all of your attorney's fee if you win your case? If the other party is found liable by the court or administrative agency but they want to fight the matter further by taking an appeal, where will that appeal be heard and what will it cost and involve? How long will the whole process take? What else will be involved? You will need the assistance of a lawyer or other competent legal advisor to properly answer these important questions.

Perhaps the two most important factors are cost and likely remedies.

How far and how successfully you can fight a case of unlawful discrimination may depend to a large extent on how much you can afford. If you are fortunate, you may get a government antidiscrimination agency or a private antidiscrimination group to provide legal and related assistance at no cost. But if you cannot get free legal assistance and must hire an attorney, what you can accomplish may depend on what you can afford. (You may find a lawyer who will take your case for a low fee if that is all you can afford. Also, in many instances, if you win your case the court or administrative agency may have authority to order the losing party to reimburse you for part or all of your attorney's fee. These and other fee-related matters are discussed in more detail under "Dealing with Lawyers" later on in this chapter.)

The available remedies should be scrutinized. By "remedies" is meant corrective measures to stop the discriminatory practice and money compensation to cover your losses and compensate you for the violation of your rights. For example, if a building does not have proper facilities and design elements for access for handicapped persons, corrective measures would include railings, ramps, lowered fire extinguishers, and so forth. With regard to money compensation, suppose you were fired, unlawfully, from a state college teaching position because you espouse atheism. You would be entitled to an amount of money equivalent to the pay and benefits you would have received had you not been fired improperly. Also, an additional sum should be paid to you as compensation for having had your rights violated.

If you can establish that the person or group that discriminated against you did so in a flagrant, malicious, or egregious manner, you may seek punitive or exemplary damages (in addition to compensatory damages). Exemplary or punitive damages is an amount of money which the culpable person must pay to you as a penalty for violating your rights in a particularly reprehensible manner.

In part, the type and amount of corrective measures and money compensation will depend on whether you are trying to redress acts of discrimination perpetrated only against yourself or whether you are one of a group. The more victims of discrimination in the group and the more widespread and damaging the discrimination, the more extensive and substantial the corrective measures and money compensation should be. If you are suing because you were underpaid for two years because you are a physically handicapped person but did equal work nonetheless, that is one amount of money. If, on the other hand, you find 100 other physically handicapped persons who have been underpaid by the same company despite the fact that all of you did work equal to that of nonhandicapped persons, you will be suing for a much more substantial amount of money and for corrective measures that must be imposed on a wide scale. For instance, you may request that the court or administrative agency continually monitor the company that engaged in that discrimination. You may even try to identify those persons within the company who are responsible for perpetrating that discriminatory practice and have them personally assessed with special fines or money damages (as well as making the company pay compensatory damages out of company money).

The courts and administrative agencies that hear and decide discrimination cases have varied powers to deal with unlawful discrimination once it is proven. Be as inventive as the situation requires in devising corrective measures that will end the discriminatory practices and prevent them in the future. Be as thorough as possible in determining the losses you incurred as a result of that discrimination and calculating an amount of money that will compensate you, as much as money can, for your losses and the violation of your rights. Often discrimination will abate only in proportion to the diligence, ability, and perseverance with which it is opposed and the amount of financial and related penalties it costs the person, group, or organization that perpetrated that discrimination.

Given the available courses of action, devise a plan in keeping with your concerns and objectives.

A word of warning: The lawyer or other legal advisor who assists you on your discrimination case may agree that you have been discriminated against in an unlawful manner. It may be a more or less routine task to determine how to prove that discrimination occurred and what procedures must be followed to present your case effectively to the proper court or administrative agency. But with regard to what is to be accomplished—what remedies to aim for and what money compensation to seek—there may be serious differences between what your lawyer or legal advisor wants and what you want or think is right. If a government antidiscrimination agency or a private antidiscrimination group provides legal assistance, they may try to get you to seek the corrective measures and compensation they feel is appropriate. Similarly, if you hire a private attorney, that attorney may decide what corrective measures and money compensation he or she thinks is appropriate without consulting you on that matter and obtaining your approval.

Never lose sight of the fact that you are the one who will have to live with the results of the legal action you pursue. Your lawyer or other legal advisor should explain the alternative courses of action, what different corrective measures can be sought, and what amounts of compensation can be requested and justified—but it is up to you to decide which course to follow, which corrective measures to aim for, and what amount of compensation to seek.

You are the victim of unlawful discrimination. Your rights were violated. True, since you were discriminated against on the basis of a group characteristic, all members of that group (all women, all blacks, all Jews, all homosexuals, etc.) have to some extent been stigmatized and victimized. But it is the effect that discrimination has on you and your life that is of primary concern to you. If you feel you should view this incident as a member of the stigmatized group, as a representative of it, do so and devise a plan of action commensurate with that view. If, on the other hand, all you want is to have the situation remedied with respect to yourself and within the confines of your own life and dealings, make that clear. Do not become someone else's cause. Do not become the unwilling and perhaps unwitting foil for what others think should be done. There may be times during your case when your attorney or the government antidiscrimination ageny or private antidiscrimination group may want to take positions or seek legal actions because of how they feel and what they want to achieve and regardless of how you feel and what you want. If this happens, remind them that it is your case, your rights that were violated, and your life that will be affected by the results obtained. Do not allow others—your lawyer or any other legal advisor—to convert your discrimination case into a cause or vehicle for goals or objectives with which you do not agree.

DEALING WITH LAWYERS

In addition to the general points about lawyers in Chapter 1, keep in mind the following advice about dealing with lawyers in an unlawful discrimination case.

Before you contact private attorneys (who charge substantial fees for their advice and services), contact government anti-discrimination agencies and private antidiscrimination groups (such as the ACLU, NAACP, NOW, and others) that provide free legal information and some free legal services to victims of discrimination. Your federal, state, and local elected officials and their staffs can help you get in contact with the appropriate government agencies and private groups. The telephone company or government information services may be helpful in putting you in contact with the appropriate government agency or private groups. For example, if you feel you have been the victim of unlawful discrimination because of a physical handicap, your state department of public health or human services may have a commission or official who will provide you with free information and assistance and how to deal with that situation. The local office of the federal Department of Human Services may be similarly helpful. Or there may be a private group concerned about the rights of physically handicapped persons that will provide you with free information and assistance and, if need be, help you pursue legal recourse and recommend reputable lawyers. The point is that you should investigate government and private sources of free legal information and assistance before you pay money for an attorney.

Additional information and assistance can be garnered by contacting local media representatives who specialize in discrimination. For example, your local newspaper may have a reporter who covers sex or race discrimination incidents. Or a local radio or TV station may have a special program on the rights of mentally and physically handicapped persons. Media people can often provide a wealth of information at no charge.

Also, contact representatives of the appropriate group, such as civil rights leaders, the head of the local gay rights organization, or the spokesperson for the local or state women's rights group. Other community leaders who have shown an interest in discrimination cases may be helpful. All these people are potential sources of useful, effective, and free advice and assistance.

Be sure, when you contact someone at a government antidiscrimination agency or a private antidiscrimination group or anyone else who is not a licensed, practicing attorney, that you inquire about that person's training and qualifications in discrimination cases. Many agencies and groups have lawyers on their staffs or as consultants or advisors. These lawyers can often provide you with expert legal advice for no cost. Moreover, some of the nonlawyers who work for these agencies and groups have acquired considerable expertise in discrimination law; their advice may be qualified and dependable. Nonetheless, some of the people who work for government agencies and private groups have little practical experience or formal training in discrimination law. Before relying on legal advice and information from a nonlawyer, ask the person what legal training and experience he or she has had. It may be advisable to double-check the information you get with an attorney.

After contacting government antidiscrimination agencies and private antidiscrimination groups and exhausting the information and assistance they provide, it may be necessary or advisable to hire a private attorney to pursue legal action which those agencies and groups cannot provide. Get the names of reputable lawyers from the persons you have talked with at those agencies and groups. They may also be able to provide useful information on what questions to ask the lawyers you contact, how to make sure the lawyer you hire knows what he or she is doing, and how to get a second opinion if you have doubts about your lawyer's handling of your case.

As noted in Chapter 1, before hiring a private attorney, contact three or more lawyers. Ask each how much training and experience he or she has had in discrimination cases. How many discrimination cases has he or she handled and how recently? How many cases like yours has he or she handled and how recently?

To get the names of lawyers to contact, ask the officials and employees of government antidiscrimination agencies and private antidiscrimination groups; ask your federal, state, and local elected officials and their staffs; ask news media representatives, civil rights and community leaders, and others. The local bar association may operate a lawyer referral service which lists lawyers by the fields in which they practice. Ask for the names of lawyers who handle unlawful discrimination cases. Finally, if you know or have heard of someone who was represented by a lawyer on an unlawful discrimination case recently, ask that person what he or she thought of his or her lawyer.

If your case cannot be handled for free by a government antidiscrimination agency or a private antidiscrimination group and you must hire a private attorney, contact three or more attorneys and ask each what fee he or she would charge and how and when it is to be paid.

Be sure to have the lawyer investigate whether, if you win your case, you can have the judge or administrative hearing officer who hears your case order the other party to reimburse you for part or all of your attorney's fee. Fee reimbursement laws encourage people who were victimized by unlawful discriminatory practices to sue and place the burden of part or all of your attorney's fee on the culpable party—where it belongs.

Of course, your attorney will normally insist that you pay his or her fee. If, later on, you win your case and the judge or hearing officer orders the other party to reimburse you for part or all of your attorney's fee, that money will go to you if you have already paid your lawyer. If fee reimbursement laws do not apply to your case or if the judge or hearing officer does not order the other party to reimburse you, you will be responsible for your attorney's fee whether you win or lose your case. Whatever the outcome with regard to the fee, you should know some basic information about attorneys' fees before agreeing to a fee.

The most common fees charged by lawyers on discrimination cases are the flat fee and the hourly fee.

The flat fee is a specific amount of money for which the attorney agrees to perform the necessary and customary work required to properly handle your case through the first court trial or administrative agency hearing. For example, if you want to sue an employer for refusing to hire you on the basis of sex, race, or sexual preference and you have a fairly clearcut case, the lawyer may quote a flat fee of $1,000 or $2,500 or more to file a lawsuit and have the court order the company to hire you and compensate you for the losses you incurred and for the violation of your rights. If your case is more complicated or involves more money, more widespread discrimination, or more people, the lawyer's fee will be higher. Suppose you are 1 of 30 Chicanos who have been paid wages below the legal minimum wage for two years. The company, according to your best estimates, owes your group about $100,000 in back pay. With that number of people, amount of money, and such widespread discrimination involved, the attorney may anticipate a bitter legal battle with the company. The attorney may quote a flat fee of $10,000 to represent your group, initiate a lawsuit, do the appropriate legal research and out-of-court negotiations, and, if a settlement cannot be reached, prepare for and conduct a trial that could last several days or weeks.

Whether the lawyer quotes a flat fee of $1,000 or $10,000, do not hire the lawyer until he or she explains in detail what services the quoted fee covers. Also, be sure to contact two or more other attorneys and compare the fees quoted and services covered.

Recall that a flat fee normally covers the lawyer's time and work only through the first court trial or administrative hearing. If the court or administrative agency rules against you and you want to appeal or if it rules in your favor but the other party appeals, the original flat fee does not cover an appeal. You must work out an additional fee for the time and work required of the lawyer for an appeal. Also, if the lawyer based his or her original flat fee on certain conditions or understandings but unanticipated complications arise, the attorney may have to confront you with a request for an additional fee before he or she will do work in addition to that which was anticipated at the time the original flat fee was estimated. For these reasons, make sure, before you agree to a flat fee, that you know what services that fee covers and what developments might necessitate an additional fee. Instruct the lawyer to notify you as soon as he or she learns that additional work warranting an additional fee may have to be done on your case.

The other type of fee commonly charged by lawyers on discrimination cases is the hourly fee. (See Chapter 1 for a detailed discussion of hourly fees.)

If your case is expected to take several weeks or months or a year or more, work out an installment payment schedule. (See Chapter 1 for details.)

Chapter 1 also discusses ways to save money on lawyers' fees. In addition to the money-saving advice in that chapter, you should also be aware that if your case is a clear example of unlawful discrimination and there is ample proof of that fact, your case will not require as much work on the attorney's part as would be the case if your charges were difficult to prove. Also, if the type of discrimination perpetrated against you is unquestionably illegal, the attorney will not have as much of a problem proving and winning your case as would be the case if you were alleging a new or unusual basis of discrimination. The more clear-cut the discrimination and the more unquestionably illegal it is, the easier the lawyer's job. On such cases, you should not pay the high fee some lawyers may quote. By pointing out how clear-cut and easy to prove your case is, you may be successful at getting the attorney to lower the fee. If he or she doesn't, try other lawyers.

Of course, if you cannot afford the fee quoted, do not be reluctant to point that out and ask for a lower fee.

You may be able to persuade the lawyer to lower the fee if you explain your limited financial resources and the justness of your case. Some lawyers will lend a sympathetic ear if you cannot afford a high fee. Also, some lawyers are more altruistic than others when representing victims of discrimination. In some cases, this is because the lawyer is a member of the group that is stigmatized by that type of discrimination. If you are black, a black lawyer may be more concerned about your case of racial discrimination and may take your case for a lower fee than other lawyers have quoted. The same may occur if you are a woman and you hire a woman attorney to represent you on a sex discrimination case—and so on.

Finally, remember that lawyers are not in the business of turning away business. If you consult a lawyer on a discrimination case, that lawyer may try to convince you to hire him or her so that he or she can charge you a substantial fee—but without telling you that there are government antidiscrimination agencies or private antidiscrimination groups that might handle your case for free. The best way to avoid paying a lawyer a large fee for legal services you can get for free is to investigate the available sources of free legal services first; then, if necessary, hire an attorney to do what those agencies and groups cannot do.

16 Landlord-Tenant Disputes

WHAT DO LANDLORD-TENANT DISPUTES INVOLVE?

The most common disputes between landlords and tenants center on the following:

- rent and what is included in the rent (utilities, taxes, etc.)
- security deposit
- condition of the premises, including who is responsible for repairs and upkeep
- uses the tenant may or may not make of the rented premises
- uses the tenant may or may not make of areas or facilities not part of the rental unit (hallways, common rooms, common lawns, or storage areas)
- the manner in which the tenant vacates the rental unit and the tenant's reasons for doing so
- the manner in which the landlord seeks to evict the tenant and the landlord's reasons for doing so
- subleasing
- insurance or other compensation for losses or damage to the rental unit or the tenant's property

Note: This chapter discusses the legal aspects of disputes between landlords and tenants regarding residential property. It does not deal with the different problems and procedures involved with commercial rental property.

- premises security (from the landlord, from other tenants, from vandals or intruders)
- one tenant's problems with other tenants and what, if anything, the landlord can or should do about it
- personal injuries sustained by the tenant or a guest while on the rented premises or on common areas.

Whatever the nature of your landlord-tenant dispute, it is important to realize that there is a considerable body of law which governs the rights and obligations of landlords and tenants. There are numerous statutes, ordinances, court decisions, codes, and administrative regulations which govern the relations, rights, and duties of landlords and tenants. Unfortunately, many landlords and tenants are either ignorant of these laws or they are misinformed about what the law allows or requires. For example, many landlords and most tenants may be ignorant of a state statute which governs security deposits. That statute may specify how much of a security deposit the landlord can demand; it may require that the landlord keep the security deposit in a separate bank account and pay accrued interest to the tenant; it may state when the security deposit must be returned to the tenant; what amounts the landlord can deduct from the deposit to compensate for damage to the rented premises or unpaid rent, and the penalties the landlord will incur if he or she violates the statute. If either or both the landlord or tenant are ignorant of that security deposit statute, or if either or both are misinformed about what it requires and allows, serious disputes may develop unnecessarily.

Because the laws which govern landlord-tenant relations are so comprehensive and detailed, it is important to make sure you know what your legal rights and obligations are, whether you are a landlord or a tenant.

Understanding what a landlord-tenant dispute involves, legally, requires an understanding of the various sources of law that may govern landlord-tenant relations. Naturally, if there is a written lease, the lease *may* be an important source of legally binding agreements and understandings between landlord and tenant on a given disputed matter. However, a lease, as a contract between private parties, cannot contravene federal, state, or local laws. Therefore, simply because a given agreement or clause appears in a written lease does not necessarily mean it is legally binding on the landlord or tenant. Neither the landlord nor the tenant can avoid, by means of a lease, paramount obligations or rights established by law. For example, suppose the landlord inserts in the lease a clause absolving him or her from liability for personal injuries suffered by a tenant or a tenant's guest while in or on the rented premises or common areas. That clause, in many states, is illegal. The courts will not enforce it. Unfortunately, many tenants may believe they are bound by such a clause if they see it in the lease.

Many written leases contain illegal or unenforceable clauses. Many leases utterly fail to reflect all the legal rights of the tenant or all the legal obligations of the landlord. Usually, this is because leases are drafted by landlords or attorneys who represent landlords. Also, many standard lease forms are seriously out of date and do not reflect recent changes in landlord-tenant law—many of those changes being favorable to tenants.

Almost every tenant and landlord would be surprised and probably shocked if he or she took the written lease to an attorney who specializes in landlord-tenant law and asked that attorney to examine the lease and comment on whether it accurately reflects current landlord-tenant laws. In many cases, the attorney would find numerous clauses that violate the rights of the tenant or misstate the obligations of the landlord. Many leases simply omit any reference to many of the tenant's rights. In addition, most written leases say nothing about the tenant's rights and remedies if the landlord violates a given clause. On the other hand, the lease may expressly grant the landlord rights and remedies not permitted by law. For example, many leases state that the landlord may evict the tenant if the tenant violates any clause in any manner, no matter how serious or minor the infraction. A clause to that effect is commonplace in written leases despite the fact that it is misleading; generally, courts will not allow a landlord to evict a tenant unless the tenant violates an important lease provision or law and does so in a serious manner. Most courts will not allow a landlord to evict a tenant if the lease violation is minor or if the landlord is using the violation as a pretext for harassing the tenant or discriminating against the tenant or getting the present tenant out in order to raise the rent for the next tenant.

Keep in mind that although the lease *may* govern the rights and obligations of landlord and tenant, it is not necessarily true that a given clause is valid or that it will be enforced by the courts simply because it is in the lease. If you question the legality of a clause, consult a lawyer or other legal advisor. You may find that your rights and obligations are quite different from what is stated in the written lease.

Whether you have a written lease or not, state statutes, local ordinances, and court decisions govern landlord-tenant relations. For example, a state statute may specify the procedures a tenant or landlord must follow in order to properly terminate the tenancy. A city or town ordinance may impose rent control. State and local health codes govern the condition in which the building and apartment must be kept. In addition, there may be court decisions which outlaw discrimination by landlords in renting or which authorize the tenant to pay reduced rent if necessary repairs are not made in a timely manner. Other laws may govern the landlord's right to check a prospective tenant's credit rating and background before renting. Still other laws govern the liability of tenants and landlords for personal injuries suffered by a tenant or a tenant's guest while in or upon the rented premises.

Even where there is a written lease or oral understanding between the landlord and tenant, a statute or court decision may dictate how that clause or agreement must be interpreted. These laws can add to, reduce, or otherwise alter the rights and obligations of the landlord or tenant. For example, some landlords insert into the lease a clause which provides that if the tenant sues the landlord and loses the lawsuit, the tenant must reimburse the landlord for his or her attorney's fee. Although most courts have upheld this clause, many courts have gone further and have read into the lease a reciprocity requirement: if a clause states that the tenant must reimburse the landlord for attorneys' fees if the tenant sues the landlord but loses, the court will require that if the landlord sues the tenant but loses, the landlord must reimburse the tenant for his or her lawyer's fees.

In numerous ways court decisions and statutes modify written leases and oral agreements between landlords and tenants in an attempt to protect tenants from exploitation by landlords and to protect landlords from troublesome tenants. Some court decisions and statutes, however, reflect an extreme special-interest orientation on the side of either landlords or tenants. Regardless of the rationale for a given statute or court decision, it is important to keep in mind that the laws which govern landlord-tenant relations are comprehensive; if you act without first determining what your rights and obligations are, you may unwittingly forfeit your rights or unintentionally violate legal obligations for which you can be held liable in court.

Statutes, codes, and court decisions govern landlord-tenant relations whether or not there is a lease provision or oral agreement on the matter in dispute. For example, in almost every state there is a "warranty of habitability" which is an implied part of every landlord-tenant agreement—whether or not there is a written lease or oral agreement and whether or not the landlord or tenant mentions or fails to mention that warranty. The "warranty of habitability" means that the landlord is responsible for making sure that the rented premises are reasonably fit for human habitation. If the premises become unfit and fall below reasonable standards for decent living quarters (for example, through insect infestation or lack of heat or running water), the tenant can stop paying rent and sue the landlord for having violated the implied warranty of habitability. Of critical importance is the fact that the warranty of habitability is an implied part of every tenancy; it is an obligation which the landlord cannot deny or avoid or induce or coerce the tenant to forego.

In addition to statutes, ordinances, codes, court decisions, and administrative regulations that govern landlord-tenant regulations generally, there are special laws and regulations which govern your tenancy if you live in government-operated or -financed housing. For example, if you live in a government housing project or use welfare income to pay rent, there are special laws which govern your rights and obligations as a tenant and the rights and obligations of your landlord (whether the rental property is owned by a government agency or a private individual or business.)

Still other laws come into operation in particular situations. For example, if the tenant fails to pay the rent, debtor-creditor laws may dictate the procedure the landlord must follow to collect the unpaid rent. If a guest of the tenant is injured while in or on the rented premises, personal injury law and property law determine whether the tenant is liable to the injured guest, or whether the landlord is liable, or whether no one is. If the landlord spies on the tenant or steals the tenant's property, civil laws governing invasion of privacy and harassment and criminal laws governing theft will determine what steps the tenant may take against the landlord.

Determining what your rights and obligations are as a tenant or landlord entails finding what steps can be taken to protect your rights and what steps the other party can take to protect his or her rights and require you to fulfill your legal duties. In many instances, landlord and tenant disputes are resolved between the landlord and tenant on an informal, personal basis. Regrettably, however, many such informal resolutions of disputes are achieved without the landlord or tenant knowing what his or her legal rights and obligations are. A tenant may concede to an unjustifiable demand by a landlord because the tenant isn't aware that he or she had the right to do otherwise. Conversely, a tenant may damage the premises or violate valid agreements in the lease and intimidate the landlord into not taking legal action by threatening to do worse things or to cost the landlord a fortune in legal expenses if the landlord tries to evict the tenant.

For both present and future purposes, it is best for both the landlord and tenant to consult a lawyer or other legal advisor; usually, that is the only way both landlord and tenant can learn about each one's and each other's legally enforceable rights and obligations.

If legal action must be taken, there may be different forums in which the dispute can be heard. Many states and localities have special housing courts which adjudicate disputes involving residential rental property. In other states and communities, you must file your lawsuit in the regular trial court. If the dispute involves only money and the amount is small enough, you may be able to use the local small claims court. If you live in government-operated or -financed housing or otherwise come under government housing laws, there may be a review board or other administrative agency to which you must bring your dispute instead of, or at least before, going to court. More and more landlords and tenants utilize private mediation. There may be a mediation program sponsored by the local court or a government agency or private organization. You and the other party will be given an opportunity to present your respective sides of the dispute to one or more mediators. After hearing both sides, the mediators decide who is right and wrong and issue a decision which you and the other person must agree, in advance, to abide by. Mediation is growing in popularity because it usually involves less time than court proceedings, is less formal and less expensive, and doesn't require that you be represented by an attorney.

WHY DO YOU NEED TO CONSULT A LAWYER OR OTHER LEGAL ADVISOR?

By consulting an attorney or other legal advisor if you are having or anticipate a dispute with a landlord or tenant, you can become informed about your rights and obligations and how to handle the matter in the proper legal manner. You should find out not only what you can do and how to do it legally but also what the law prohibits you from doing and what actions might result in financial or other liability or even criminal charges. Unfortunately, in all too many landlord-tenant disputes, the landlord or tenant gets into serious and costly legal trouble by taking actions which they thought, mistakenly, they had the right to take. For instance, some landlords think, mistakenly, that if the tenant falls two or three months behind in the rent, the landlord can empty the tenant's apartment into a hallway or onto the sidewalk, change the locks on the doors, and thereby force the tenant to move. Other landlords believe, incorrectly, they have the right to enter the tenant's apartment at any time of the day or night to inspect for damage or to show the apartment to a prospective tenant without giving the present tenant any advance notice. Landlords who do such things may find themselves on the losing end of a lawsuit filed by a tenant who thinks, correctly, that his or her rights have been violated and who engages a lawyer or other legal representative to take legal action against that landlord.

Some tenants, on the other hand, mistakenly think they can deduct from the rent amounts they spend on any type of repairs if the landlord didn't have the repairs done immediately. There are laws in most states which allow a tenant to deduct repair costs from the rent—but only if it is the landlord's obligation to make the repairs and only after the landlord has been properly notified of the nature of the needed repairs and has had at least 24 or 48 or 72 hours (depending on the law) to make the repairs. If the tenant does not comply with these and other specific procedures required by law, the tenant may forfeit the right to deduct the repair costs from the rent. Similarly, many tenants believe, incorrectly, they can sublet their apartment to others without first consulting the landlord. In most standard leases, however, there is a clause which prohibits the tenant from subletting unless the landlord approves of the person who is to sublet the apartment and also approves the terms of the sublease. A tenant who violated that clause may find the landlord evicting the sublessee (subtenant) and suing the tenant for rent—for which the tenant may be held liable even though he or she isn't using the apartment.

Clearly, it is advisable to consult a lawyer or other legal advisor as soon as a serious dispute arises or when you realize that a serious dispute is about to develop.

Of course, it is a good practice to consult a lawyer before you sign a lease or agree to rent without a written lease, whether you are the landlord or the prospective tenant. If you already rent, bring your lease to a lawyer or legal advisor. If you don't have a written lease, explain the oral agreements you have made with your landlord or tenant. You can avoid many costly disputes by finding out about your rights and liabilities as a landlord or tenant, taking steps to avoid violating the other person's rights and making sure you live up to your legal obligations.

Needless to say, one of the reasons tenants and landlords alike avoid consulting a lawyer or other legal advisor is cost. Each may fear that the lawyer's fee will be too high compared to the costs involved in the dispute. There are, however, many sources of free or low-cost legal information and services. For tenants, many communities have tenants' associations or tenants' rights groups which provide free legal information. For landlords, there may be a local landlord's association or real estate board that will provide free legal information. If you are a tenant living on welfare or on other government support programs, you may be entitled to free legal assistance from the local Legal Services office. If you are poor and can't afford a private attorney, you may be eligible for free legal advice and assistance from the local Legal Aid office. Whether you are a tenant or landlord, the local bar association may be able to provide you with the names of lawyers who will answer some of your questions for free or for only a nominal fee if it doesn't take much of the attorney's time to do so. When contacting an attorney, explain the dispute or problem and ask the attorney at the outset, "Could you give me some legal information and advice on this and, if so, how much will it cost?" You may find an attorney who is willing to answer your questions for free or for a small fee. Even if the attorney replies that it will take time and research to answer your questions, it may well be worth $100 or $200 or more to get a professional answer you can rely on.

Another source of free legal information is the clerk's office at the local housing court or other court in your community which hears landlord-tenant cases. Many clerks and assistant clerks will answer some of your questions over the telephone or in person for free. If they cannot answer your question or if you need an attorney, they may be able to recommend an attorney or other legal advisor who will answer your questions for a modest fee.

If you contact a lawyer or other legal advisor about a particular problem or dispute, during the course of your conversation you may be able to get answers to questions on other areas of landlord-tenant law. In fact, you may gain a wealth of information that will hold you in good stead whenever you rent an apartment, whether you are a landlord or a tenant.

You may be able to get some legal advice and assistance for free. Some answers or legal services may cost money, but if you find out what the cost will be, you may realize that you can afford it or, more likely, that you can't afford not to know the correct answers to important legal questions.

HOW TO THINK ABOUT LEGAL AND RELATED ASPECTS

The following sections review important points to keep in mind when deciding how to handle your landlord-tenant dispute.

Determine the exact nature of the dispute, your position and reasons, and the other person's position and reasons.

Whether you are a landlord or a tenant, think about what caused the dispute. What are you complaining about? Why? What do you think the other person should do about it? If it is the other person who feels wronged by something you did or didn't do, try to understand exactly what he or she is complaining about, why, and what he or she wants you to do about it. If a tenant is two months behind in the rent, what the landlord is upset about is clear. What the landlord wants the tenant to do is also clear. On the other hand, suppose, in the middle of a cold winter, the pipes freeze and break and your apartment is without heat. You must move to a hotel for four days while the landlord hires repairpersons to fix the pipes. The landlord offers to let you deduct four days' rent from your next rent bill. You want to do that plus deduct the cost of the hotel room. In addition, you had a $200 plant that died because of the cold apartment. You feel the landlord should either reimburse you for the fair market value of that plant or let you deduct that amount as well from the rent. The fact that the apartment was unheated for four days is not in dispute. The dispute centers on what expenses and losses suffered by the tenant because of that situation should be chargeable to the landlord in the form of deductions from the rent.

Of course, determining the exact nature of the dispute involves determining who is responsible for the problem. If the tenant complains because his or her apartment was burglarized, the tenant may feel it is the landlord's fault that the security of the building was not adequate. The landlord may feel that any measures he could have taken would not have prevented the burglary and that the tenant is at fault for not putting stronger locks on her apartment—which is her responsibility. Needless to say, the burglar is the truly culpable party. But the burglar, unless apprehended and successfully sued by the tenant, is not available to make up for the tenant's losses. In that situation, the tenant must determine if the landlord's actions or failure to take certain measures makes the landlord legally liable. The landlord, predictably, will deny responsibility for the actions of the burglar and will seek to absolve himself of legal liability.

Another instance in which other parties are involved occurs when one tenant is disturbed or harassed by another tenant. Perhaps a tenant plays a stereo loudly late at night or is a peeping Tom or is known to use and sell drugs in his or her apartment. The offended tenant wants the landlord to intercede. If the landlord does but the offending tenant's behavior continues, what then? If the landlord doesn't intercede, then what? Both landlord and offended tenant should consult a lawyer or other legal advisor to find out what their legal rights and obligations are.

Many disputes arise because the landlord and tenant did not

discuss a given matter before renting the property; now that a problem has developed, the landlord and tenant have different and conflicting ideas about who is responsible and what should be done. This may happen when the tenant brings a pet into the apartment only to learn at that time that the landlord does not allow dogs or cats in the building. The tenant argues that he or she should not be prevented from having a pet because the landlord didn't say anything about that when the tenant agreed to rent. The landlord argues that it has always been his policy to prohibit pets and that since the tenant rented the apartment without asking whether or not pets were allowed it is not the landlord's fault that the tenant learns of this at this late date.

Many apartments and other rental premises are rented with surprisingly little in the way of express agreements between landlord and tenant as to how various situations that might arise will be handled. That is why it is advisable to consult a lawyer or other legal advisor at the time you rent. Given the lawyer's or legal advisor's experience with landlord-tenant disputes, he or she may be able to anticipate potential problem areas and work out agreements beforehand that will avoid or at least minimize disputes.

In many situations the tenant does not understand the landlord's position and vice versa. When you determine the exact nature of the dispute, try to talk about it with the tenant or landlord. Make your position and reasons clear but also try to understand the other person's position and reasons. You may find enough common ground on which to base a compromise or settlement that will resolve the dispute while avoiding ill will and costly legal action.

Find out about the rights and obligations of the tenant.

Whether you are the tenant or landlord, consult a lawyer or other legal advisor and determine what rights and obligations the tenant has under the lease and applicable laws. In some cases, the tenant's rights and obligations may be clear. For example, if the tenant wants to sublet the apartment for six months to someone who is unknown to the landlord and who has no credit or character references, the lease or state law may provide that the tenant does not have the right to sublet without the landlord's permission. Or suppose the tenant's apartment is cold during the winter. The tenant contacts a local tenants' association and learns that state law requires that residential rental property must be heated to at least 65°F during the daytime and 58°F during the nighttime from November 1 to March 1. The tenant's legal right to have the apartment heated to that temperature is clear.

In other situations, however, the rights and obligations of the tenant may be unclear. That is, the law on the subject may be unsettled. Suppose a tenant who moved into the apartment alone now has a live-in roommate of the opposite sex? In some states, the courts have held that it is illegal for a landlord to evict or harass a tenant simply because the tenant has such a live-in arrangement. In other states, however, the courts have not answered that question of law and it may be permissible for the landlord to evict the tenant—at least until a court clearly decides that the landlord does not have the right to do so.

It is important to find out what rights and obligations the tenant has under the law. In many situations the tenant may have the right to do what he or she is doing despite the landlord's objections. In other circumstances, the tenant may be clearly in the wrong. Then there are those situations in which the law is unsettled or unclear; it may require a lawsuit to resolve the legal issues. In any case, if you are the landlord and especially if you are the tenant, it is important to find out what a tenant's rights and obligations are under the circumstances. If you don't consult a lawyer or other legal advisor, you may get yourself in trouble by relying on misinformation or by acting out of ignorance.

Find out about the landlord's rights and obligations.

If you are the tenant and especially if you are the landlord, consult a lawyer or other legal advisor and find out what legal rights a landlord has under the circumstances and what legal obligations a landlord can be required to fulfill. The landlord's rights and obligations will depend, like the tenant's, on the written lease (if there is one), any oral agreements between landlord and tenant, and a complex web of statutes, court decisions, codes, and administrative agency regulations. Keep in mind that certain clauses in the lease may not be valid or may not accurately reflect the rights and obligations of the tenant and landlord under current law.

It may be that the landlord's rights and obligations are clear. For example, if the tenant ruined three walls with improperly imbedded nails and screws and it will cost \$300 to replaster those walls, the landlord normally has the right to deduct \$300 from the tenant's security deposit when the tenant leaves or, if there is no security deposit, sue the tenant for \$300. On the other hand, if the tenant has done no damage to the apartment other than normal "wear and tear," the landlord may be required by statute to return the tenant's security deposit in full and with interest set by statute.

In other situations, the rights and obligations of the landlord may not be clear—perhaps because there is no lease, perhaps because although there is a lease it does not address the situation in question, or perhaps because the law is unclear. For example, if the tenant complains about offensive conduct by other tenants, it may be unclear what, if any, authority or obligation the landlord has to make the other tenants desist in their conduct or vacate the building. As a practical matter, the landlord may not want to take sides in a confrontation between tenants. Whether one tenant can require the landlord to do so may have to be resolved through a lawsuit if the law on the subject is unclear—especially if the circumstances are peculiar and have not been addressed in a published court opinion.

If it is clear that the landlord is liable, what losses suffered by the tenant are chargeable to the landlord? Suppose you rent an apartment as of July 1. On that day, however, you learn that the present tenant has not moved out. In fact, the present tenant stays over two months in the apartment—that's how long it takes for the landlord to get into court and have the tenant evicted. You had to stay in a hotel for those two months. Can you sue the landlord for the difference between the rent you would have paid had you moved into the apartment on time and the cost of the hotel room for two months? Can you sue the landlord for the cost of moving into the hotel and the cost of moving from the hotel into the apartment once the former tenant left? After all, both moves were required because the apartment the landlord agreed to rent to you as of July 1 was not available. Of course, the landlord will argue that it isn't his or her fault that the former tenant didn't move out on time. Nor is it his or her fault that it took two months to get the court to order that tenant out. Why don't you sue the former tenant? Because you can't, legally. (Your legally binding agreement was with the landlord, not with the former tenant.) If you sue the landlord, how much money should you sue for (how much money will make up for the losses you incurred as a result of the landlord's inability to fulfill the agreement he or she had made with you)?

To properly assess what you can and should do to resolve a landlord-tenant dispute, you must determine the rights and obligations of the tenant and the rights and obligations of the landlord. Then you can assess the situation from the proper legal viewpoint and, in doing so, make sure you are on sound legal ground and know how to avoid legal pitfalls and liability.

If advisable, pursue avenues to resolve the dispute without formal legal action.

Once you understand your side and the other person's side of the dispute and have learned your rights and obligations and the other person's rights and obligations, consider whether it is possible and advisable to settle the dispute by talking it over and working out a mutually acceptable agreement. If you have had good dealings and relations in the past with that tenant or landlord, it may be a mistake to let one dispute ruin an otherwise harmonious relationship. In addition, working out a mutually acceptable settlement avoids the costs, delays, and problems associated with taking formal legal action.

Of course, agreeing to a mutually acceptable compromise does not mean being coerced or intimidated into accepting less than you think is fair or something other than what you think is right. It may help, during your talks with the other person, to mention that you sought legal advice and that you know you are acting within your rights and have an understanding of the other person's legal obligations as well as your own. Some landlords and tenants try to bluff or bluster their way out of disputes. If you know about your rights and obligations and the other person's rights and obligations, you will be better equipped to resolve the dispute fairly.

If you and the other person do not make much headway by talking things over, consider submitting the dispute to an impartial third person—that is, a mediator. The local court may have mediators to whom you can bring your dispute. Or a mutually respected person might act as mediator.

If you do initiate formal legal action or hire an attorney to sue the other person, keep in mind that a mutually acceptable settlement should not be foreclosed or forgotten simply because you or the other person have filed a lawsuit. An out-of-court settlement will spare both of you the costs, risks, and inconvenience of a trial.

If a lawsuit or other legal action is advisable, find out how to proceed, what it will cost, and what will be involved.

For this you will need the advice and assistance of a lawyer or other competent legal advisor. Find out what steps you can or must take to protect your rights and interests and fulfill your legal obligations. Many tenants and landlords do themselves a disservice or get themselves into serious legal trouble by acting without consulting an attorney or other legal advisor. You may be forfeiting or ignoring your rights. You may be unwittingly exposing yourself to liability. Base your decisions and actions on competent legal advice, not hunches, guesses, or ignorance.

There may be a number of alternative courses of action to consider. The lawyer or legal advisor you consult may suggest that, through him or her, efforts be made to work out a mutually acceptable agreement without or at least before initiating formal legal action. If formal legal action is appropriate or necessary, there may be more than one type of legal action you can take. For instance, you may be able to file a lawsuit in court or file a complaint with an administrative agency; there may be more than one ground on which to file a lawsuit or complaint. Different courses of action will normally involve different costs, timetables, procedures, and possible outcomes. Your lawyer or legal advisor should be able to explain what steps you can take and what amount of money and what corrective measures you can seek.

You may find that what you want done is something the court or administrative agency can order the other person to do. For example, if the landlord refuses, unreasonably, to return your security deposit in full, you have the right to bring the landlord to court and have the court order him to return it in full if he is withholding it unlawfully. If a tenant has violated the lease or the law and the landlord wants him out, the landlord can take the tenant to court and have the court order the tenant to move out of the rented premises if the tenant's actions provide legal justification for an eviction.

On the other hand, you may find that the court or administrative agency does not have authority to order the other party to do what you feel ought to be done. For example, the landlord may want to evict the tenant but the tenant's actions do not constitute lawful grounds for an eviction and the court will not order the tenant to get out. Or the tenant may want to sue the landlord for losses for which the landlord, under the law, is not responsible and therefore cannot be sued (as when a sonic boom causes valuable ceramics to fall to the floor in the tenant's apartment and break—the law does not require that landlords make apartment buildings sonic-boom-proof).

Have your lawyer or legal advisor outline the alternative courses of action that are available and what corrective measures and monetary compensation you can realistically expect. Then devise a plan of action in light of your resources and objectives.

An important consideration will be the cost of formal legal proceedings. Many landlord-tenant disputes involve small amounts of money or other problems that do not warrant a large investment in lawyer's fees and court costs. On the other hand, if you are able to obtain free legal advice and services, cost will not be an inhibiting factor. Of course, if the principle involved is important enough, cost may be secondary. Finally, in some cases you may be able to have the judge or administrative hearing officer order the other person to reimburse you for part or all of your attorney's fee if you win the case (see the next section for more information on fee reimbursement procedures).

In addition to obtaining a realistic estimate of the costs involved in pursuing formal legal action, find out how much time will be required to bring the matter to court or before the administrative agency. Find out when your case will be heard, what you will be called upon to testify to, how much time may elapse before the judge or administrative hearing officer makes a decision, and what steps will have to be taken if the decision goes against you or if the decision goes against the other person but he or she doesn't willingly comply with the decision. Also, if the decision goes against you, what can you do to appeal and seek a reversal? If the decision is in your favor, find out what the other person can do to appeal and seek a reversal.

DEALING WITH LAWYERS

In addition to the general points about lawyers in Chapter 1, keep in mind the following advice about dealing with lawyers on a landlord-tenant dispute.

Before contacting private attorneys (who charge fees for their time and services), find out whether there are government agencies or private groups in your community with experience in landlord-tenant law who provide free or low-cost legal advice and assistance. There may be a local tenants' association or tenants' rights group which offers legal and related information to tenants free of charge. There may be a landlord's association or real estate board that does the same for landlords. If you are entitled to legal assistance from Legal Services (a government legal assistance program for persons on welfare, the recipients of certain other government programs, and the indigent) or Legal Aid (a privately funded program that provides legal assistance to the poor), contact the local Legal Services or Legal Aid office. Your local, state, and federal elected officials may be able to put you in contact with agencies or groups who provide free or low-cost legal information and assistance. You may have some questions answered by calling the clerk's office at the local housing court or other court that hears landlord-tenant cases. If you talk with a person who is not a lawyer, ask about that person's training, experience, and background in landlord-tenant law. Although some of the people at tenants' associations, real estate boards, and elsewhere are experienced and well informed in the law, others are not. Don't rely on information and advice from a nonlawyer unless that person's training and experience warrant it. You may want to double-check with an attorney before relying on information or advice from a nonlawyer.

If it is necessary or appropriate to hire a private attorney, get the names of recommended attorneys from the local tenants' association or landlord's association, Legal Aid or Legal Services, or elected officials or the clerk's office at the local housing court. Also, talk to people who have hired a lawyer on a landlord-tenant case recently. Ask them what they thought of the way their lawyer handled their case and treated them. In addition, the local bar association may operate a lawyer referral service. If so, contact that referral service and ask for names of three or four lawyers who handle landlord-tenant cases.

If yours is a minor dispute with a landlord or tenant, it may only be necessary to contact an attorney and pay a small fee to have the attorney answer your questions. Some attorneys will answer some questions free of charge. On the other hand, if your problem is serious or a substantial amount of money is involved, contact three or four lawyers and explain the matter to each. Before hiring one, ask each about his or her training and experience in landlord-tenant cases. How many landlord-tenant cases has he or she handled and how recently? How many cases like yours has he or she handled and how recently? You can then compare the lawyers you contacted on the basis of their training and experience and the overall impression each presented as to his or her familiarity with landlord-tenant law.

Be sure to ask the lawyer at the outset whether it is possible, if you win your case, to have the other party reimburse you for part or all of your attorney's fee. In some situations the judge or hearing officer who hears your case can so order if you win the case. Have your lawyer investigate any available procedures for seeking such fee reimbursement from the other party.

In other situations, you will be responsible for your attorney's fee. Even if there is a possibility of getting part or all of the attorney's fee reimbursed if you win your case, your attorney will want you to pay the fee initially. (If you win your case and the judge or hearing officer orders the other party to reimburse you for part or all of your attorney's fee, that money will go directly to you since you already paid your lawyer.) Whether you will be responsible in full for the attorney's fee or whether a fee reimbursement procedure can be pursued, you should understand some basics about attorney's fees.

The most common fees charged by lawyers on landlord-tenant cases are the flat fee and the hourly fee.

The flat fee is a specific amount of money for which the attorney agrees to perform the necessary and customary work required to properly handle your case through the first court trial or hearing or through the first administrative agency hearing. For example, if you want to sue your landlord because your apartment was burglarized and $5,000 worth of property was stolen and you believe the landlord was negligent in not providing better security, the lawyer may quote a flat fee of $1,000 (or some other amount) to represent you. That flat fee covers the lawyer's time and effort in talking to the landlord or the landlord's attorney, investigating the facts of the incident, filing a lawsuit, researching the law, drafting papers, and otherwise preparing for and presenting your side of the case at court (if the case is not settled out of court). If you lose but want to appeal or if you win but the landlord appeals, that appeal is a separate and distinct fee. Also, if the lawyer quoted the original flat fee on the basis of certain understandings about what your case would involve but complications subsequently develop which require additional time and work on the lawyer's part, the lawyer will charge an additional fee to cover the unanticipated work. For instance, if you are a landlord and want to evict a tenant, the lawyer may quote a given flat fee to file papers in court, conduct a hearing, and get a judgment against the tenant ordering him or her out of the apartment. If, however, the tenant does not vacate the apartment willingly after the judgment is issued by the court, the lawyer will have to do additional work for which he or she will charge an additional fee. (The lawyer must go back to court, hold another hearing, and have the court issue additional papers to the sheriff authorizing the sheriff to physically remove the tenant.)

Whether the lawyer quotes a flat fee of $200 or $2,000 or $10,000, do not hire a lawyer on a flat fee basis unless the lawyer explains in detail what services the flat fee covers and what developments might arise which would necessitate an additional fee.

The second type of fee commonly charged by lawyers on landlord-tenant cases is the hourly fee. (See Chapter 1 for a detailed discussion of hourly fees.)

Several ways to save money on attorney's fees are discussed in Chapter 1. A point of particular interest on a landlord-tenant case is that if your rights have clearly been violated by the landlord or tenant and it is a relatively simple matter to prove that in court, your case will not require as much work on the attorney's part as would be the case if the law is unclear on the matter or if it is difficult to prove your charges in court. If the lawyer explains that your case involves a fairly clear-cut violation of your rights and there is ample proof on your side, reiterate those points to the attorney if the attorney quotes a fee that strikes you as being very high. If the lawyer won't come down on what you feel is a high fee, try other lawyers.

Of course, if you cannot afford the fee quoted, do not be reluctant to point that out and ask for a lower fee.

Recall that you should investigate sources of free legal assistance *before* hiring a private attorney. If you go to a private attorney first, that attorney may try to get you to hire him or her and pay a substantial fee even though the attorney knows there may be a government agency or private group that could answer your questions and handle your case for free or for considerably less than the attorney wants to charge. Keep in mind that attorneys are not in the business of turning away business. You must take steps to find out how much information and assistance you can obtain for free or at low cost before hiring a private attorney.

Index